W9-CHQ-527

**MAY THE
JOURNEY
OF LIFE
BRING YOU
CLOSER
TO PEACE**

To KAREN and HARVEY,

ENJOY THE RIDE!

Steve Kat

A typical, atypical morning by the holy River Ganges.
(Varanassi)

HOLY COW!

HILARIOUS
MIS-ADVENTURES
IN
INDIA

A Spiritual Passage
Through The Madcap Mayhem
Of India

By

STEWART KATZ

Peace In Our Time Press
Salt Spring Island, British Columbia

© Copyright 2004 Stewart Katz. All rights reserved.
No part of this publication may be reproduced, stored in a retrieval system, or transmitted, in any form or by any means, electronic, mechanical, photocopying, recording, or otherwise, without the written prior permission of the author.

Printed in Victoria, Canada

A cataloguing record for this book that includes the U.S. Library of Congress Classification number, the Library of Congress Call number and the Dewey Decimal cataloguing code is available from the National Library of Canada. The complete cataloguing record can be obtained from the National Library's online database at: www.nlc-bnc.ca/amicus/index-e.html
ISBN: 1-4120-2603-2

Cover design by Mark Hand

Published in assosciation with:
Peace In Our Time Press
105 Ontario Place
Salt Spring Island
British Columbia, Canada
V8K 2L5

holycow@saltspring.com

TRAFFORD

This book was published *on-demand* in cooperation with Trafford Publishing. On-demand publishing is a unique process and service of making a book available for retail sale to the public taking advantage of on-demand manufacturing and Internet marketing. On-demand publishing includes promotions, retail sales, manufacturing, order fulfilment, accounting and collecting royalties on behalf of the author.

Suite 6E, 2333 Government St., Victoria, B.C. V8T 4P4, CANADA
Phone 250-383-6864 Toll-free 1-888-232-4444 (Canada & US)
Fax 250-383-6804 E-mail sales@trafford.com
Web site www.trafford.com
TRAFFORD PUBLISHING IS A DIVISION OF TRAFFORD HOLDINGS LTD.
Trafford Catalogue #04-0431 www.trafford.com/robots/04-0431.html

10 9 8 7 6 5

To Julie and Nathan,
My loves,
You are the abundance in my life

To my mother, Elaine
Whose love has taught me the true meaning of "unconditional"

And
To the many generous, kind-hearted souls of India
May you all be blessed

FOREWORD

The following adventures convey my own experience and journey of personal growth. They are in no way meant to be representative of everyone's relationship with India. My hope though is that in joining me, you will discover yourself resonating with elements of the universal human condition.

These travels occurred between the years 1991-1993, and while I am sure that certain superficial changes have taken place since then - like cybercafes - I am also of the belief that India's essence, then, now, and forever, remains eternal. It is that which I hope to have captured in these journals.

Enjoy. I did.

STEWART KATZ

I

STRANGER
IN
AN
EVEN
STRANGER
LAND

Chapter 1

FLY ME TO THE MOON

My watch stares back at me with blank expression.

It is 4:30 A.M., yet I haven't a clue what time it is.

I am somewhere in the sky, sailing over unknown continents, confined to an airplane now for such an existential eternity that the concept of "time" has effectively been rendered redundant. Out my round porthole window, my reflection looms like a forlorn spirit suspended in purgatory; the night is black and starless, nothing but an endless ocean of darkened clouds. Somewhere it is morning and the sun is creeping above skyscrapers over a world I once knew. Here the night is a vacuum, stale and never-ending, and "time" seems no more able to orient me to where I'm heading than that amorphous sea of clouds.

Everything has happened so quickly. A week ago I was at my desk, feet up, schmoozing on the phone, now I am cramped in an airplane chair breathing artificial air. A week ago, I was a successful Toronto talent agent, saying things like, "Baby, baby!" and "You'll never work in this town again!" Now, I am the one who may never work in that town again. Without warning or notice, I quit the agency, gave up my downtown apartment - rent control no less, I must really be crazy - sought counsel from a suspect travel agent and booked myself a one-way flight to India. It could have been a ticket to the moon for all I cared! Five days to pack, buy traveler's cheques, secure a visa, get my shots, have my sanity questioned, choose a guidebook, say farewell. Then off to the airport! Last night in Toronto, this morning in London, this afternoon in Dubai, this evening in Sri Lanka, and now... to the bathroom. The bladder knows no time save the present.

"Yabladabaldabladabaldablah!" The intercom blasts a jumble of unfamiliar syllables. I wait for the English translation and realize... that *was* the English translation. I glance over at my neighbour, an elderly Indian man.

"What did he say?" I ask.

"Soon we are landing in Madras," he replies in a tone as though his vocal chords were being fed through a reed. He has a long silver beard, his hair is greased back neatly and he wears a white cotton outfit that resembles pyjamas, his un-tucked shirt falling well below his knees.

"Uh, what do you call your outfit?" I ask.

"Salwar Kameez."

Sounds like a sneeze.

"Gezundheit," I say, offering him a tissue.

He just stares.

"Do you have the time?" I ask.

"What time would you like?" he says, accepting the tissue.

"You know, the kind with hours, minutes, early evenings," I say smiling.

"Do not be so attached to time," he says abruptly. "Everything occurs precisely at the instant it is meant to, not a moment before. Time can bring you great suffering if you try to bend it to your will."

"You don't have a watch."

"No," he says, "but I have a tissue!"

I am about to ask him if I can squeeze by - it's getting increasingly harder to bend my bladder to my will - when I notice the airline's three beautiful stewardesses approaching me, wearing saris of burgundy, honey and lime. One offers me hot compresses, the other hot curries. The third is just hot.

"I've never seen a sari before," I say, "or should I say, I'm sorry to say I've never seen a sari... before. Unless, of course, you mean my mother's Great Auntie Sari, who, I'm sorry to say wasn't so great, but she looked great in a pantsuit. Are you girls married?"

They are speechless, obviously overwhelmed by my sophisticated Western charms. I am about to engage them further when they retreat in stunned unison behind a velvet curtain into First Class. I glance over at my neighbour.

"Do not be so attached to stewardesses -" he begins to say, but my bladder pushes me past him into the aisle.

I wait in line for a vacant toilet. My stomach grumbles, a man snores, an infant wails. Finally, I enter the narrow cubicle. Sitting on the toilet, I think. I have never been so completely alone. Where I am going, I am unknown. No one, not a single soul knows me. And where I come from, no one that knows me truly knows where I am going, because I don't really know where I am going. I am utterly, disturbingly solitary, flying forward into a future that I cannot possibly predict. And it's making me sick! A meditation teacher of mine once told me: "Spirituality is a function of how much you surrender." Well, the only thing I'm liable to surrender at this point is my dinner.

I am relieved to find toilet paper in the bathroom, though. I have heard they don't use it in India, but am not quite ready to wipe my bum with my "left hand" just yet. I stash a roll under my shirt and walk quickly back to my seat. I can't sleep. The airplane pillow may look like a giant marshmallow but it feels like a sack of rice. I am restless, not just physically, but metaphysically, I'm dissatisfied. My twenties have been in turmoil ever since the senseless death of my father from cancer. I have bounded from one failed relationship to another. On the outside, I portray an appearance of functioning efficiently, even happily, but on the inside, I am constantly battling a tendency towards fury and despair. My life has amounted to little more than coddling neurotic actors by day and obliterating my senses with intoxicants by night. I need to get away. I need a change, a holiday. But am I just running scared?

I gaze drowsily out the airplane window, when, to my disbelief, for a moment, I think I see my mother's Great Auntie Sari hovering in the midst of a storm-cloud, wearing a plastic, transparent, weather repellent pantsuit. I must be hallucinating! She is calling out to me, "Stewie-koo! Stewie-koo! Vaat are you going to eat in India? Vere are you going to get Montreal Smoked Meat? You'll starve!"

Nothing made my Great Auntie Sari happier than to witness me biting into a bootsize hunk of meat. I was brought up thinking that any problem - emotional or physical - could be treated, cured and dismissed simply by eating steak. She was not shocked when I informed her of my decision to quit my job and travel indefinitely in India. She yawned when I suggested the possible danger I may encounter. But when I told her I would be following a strictly vegetarian diet in the hopes of elevating my spiritual consciousness, she swooned and collapsed onto the kitchen floor, staring up at me through eyes made glossy by years of ingesting copious amounts of chicken fat. Suddenly, she grabbed me tightly by the hand and whispered, "No meat?"

"No," I said.

"Vaat about liver?"

"No, no liver, Auntie Sari."

"Roast Beef?"

"No."

"A taste of veal? A chop of lamb? A slice of tongue? That's not meat, it's just a little meat!"

"No, sorry, Auntie Sari," and with that she passed out.

Now here she is outside my airplane window! I rub my eyes, shake my head, but she's still there, waving a fatty chicken leg at me. It can only be a result of one of three things, I conclude: prolonged lack of sleep, an acid flashback, or a particularly bloated fear of the unknown - I'm not sure which. Well, what is "real" anyway, I think, leaning back and closing my eyes...

I can see myself at eighteen - the time my Great Auntie Sari arranged a blind date for me with a girl she swore was beautiful beyond compare. That night at the door of my date's dwelling, hopes swelling in anticipation of a beauty queen, I found myself instead greeting a teenage carbon copy of my Great Auntie Sari! Not that my Great Auntie Sari was not beautiful beyond compare - au contraire - but a great *judge* of beauty she was definitely not. The mere thought of dating a look-alike of my Great Auntie Sari was so immediately disturbing that I panicked, awkwardly excusing myself from the date as being a pizza delivery boy with the wrong address.

"A delivery boy in a suit?" the look-alike of my Great Auntie Sari inquired.

"Uh...it's gourmet pizza," I said, slinking down the street out of view.

Not the proudest moment of my life. So why am I recalling it now?

Maybe this whole impulsive trip to India is like the biggest blind date of my life, like a grand leap of faith, only this time there'll be no excuses, no retreats, no pizza. An astrologer recently told me to prepare for great changes. My Saturn would be "returning," he said (I didn't even know it was away). But apparently this planetary phenomenon has been secretly conspiring for some time now to shake up my life. Well, I can't imagine feeling any more shaky than I do right now.

I look out the window. The plane is descending from night into morning sky. In the rapidly approaching distance I spy a runway, paved with the promise of new beginnings. It's time to leave the past behind.

Chapter 2

FIRST CONTACT

Arrival's Lounge, Madras Airport.

I stare at the mob gathered beyond the glass "Exit" doors and feel as though I am witnessing the crazed antics of institutional inmates: a hundred men pressing, jostling, grinning, frowning, frothing. Welcome to India, I think.

I have landed in Madras, the capital city of the southern state of Tamil Nadu, at the advice of that Toronto travel agent, who emphatically informed me that this "village" of five million was undoubtedly a more gentle port of entry at which to arrive in India, than say, Bombay, or Delhi, or heaven forbid, Calcutta. Madras, I was assured, was much cleaner, more modern, less crowded and generally more pleasing to the senses than any of India's other major centres.

"The veritable Paris (pronounced 'Paree') of South India!" he said. "Outdoor cafes along lamplit laneways, charming maitre d's, midnight caleche rides. Monsoon will still be months away. The temperature will be balmy and fresh. Who needs the Eiffel Tower or La Champs Elysee?"

Now, I know it's not right to judge a cake by its icing, or a village by its airport as the case may be, but glancing around the Arrival's Lounge, it becomes instantly clear - this ain't exactly Notre Dame Cathedral. The decor is such a dim shade of yellow, I feel as though I've entered a urinal, not a terminal.

My backpack is ridiculously heavy. It's killing me. That travel agent told me that certain supplies were not readily available in India. So here I am with enough shampoo in my pack to wash a thousand hairdos, enough deodorant to quell an army of armpits, and enough books to stock a small library. I can barely proceed two paces without feeling like my groin is going to collapse from the strain. I quickly realize that I am going to have to dump some of my resources at the first opportunity. I'd rather sacrifice flowery pits and literacy than develop a hernia the size of Bombay.

I step hesitantly over to the "Exit" doors and gaze through the smudges at the barricading horde of dark faces.

"What do they want?" I ask nervously of one of my fellow passengers, an Indian man with thick glasses.

"They wish to take you in their taxi," he says.

"All of them?" I gasp.

I then watch as each member of my recently arrived flight dares cross the airport threshold, only to be pounced upon, pushed around, jerked, yanked, wrenched and finally whisked away by god knows whom, to god knows where - but you can be sure at three times the actual fare.

I consider spending my entire travels in the safe confines of the Madras Airport. I search frantically for a nook or cranny where I could camp for the next, say, thirteen months, but every corner appears taken by families apparently already living there.

I stall, allowing every other passenger to depart before me, gaping as the throng outside devours one hapless body after another, waiting until I stand alone - when suddenly, I charge towards the exit, burst through the doors and plunge recklessly into the frenzied mass of flesh. Beat up brochures are instantly forced inches from my face, tattered signs endorsing dingy hotels are dangled before me. The mob begins shrieking, heckling like wild dogs.

"Listen to me, Hare Krishna Hotel, good hotel -"

"No, no, listen to me, Hare Rama Hotel -"

"No, no, no, listen to me, Hare Hare Hotel, best hotel -"

"No, no, no, no, listen to me, Hare Belafonte Hotel -"

"No, no, me, me, listen to me, you come my taxi -"

"No, no, NO! NOOOOOOooooooooooooo!!" One extremely agitated, sweat-drenched Indian taxi driver fights his way to the forefront, faces me dead-on and wails at the top of his lungs, "No, no, NO! NOOOOOO!! Don't listen to HIM! Don't listen to ME!! Don't listen to ANYBODY!!!" he screams before being sucked back into the maelstrom.

Little did I know that was the best advice I would receive my entire travels.

Minutes later, I am in a taxi, a battered, black 1950's sedan straight out of the sitcom Happy Days, speeding along a highway to god knows where, driven by god knows whom.

"Uh, Madras?" I inquire hopefully.

The driver doesn't quite nod, he sort of shimmies his head from side to side. I take that to mean "yes."

The taxi charges through the barren countryside, past distant blurred bodies and tattered, broken shacks. Sweat drenches my clothes. I pine for an escape from the choking heat, the oppressive glare of the sun, the moldy, close air of the taxi. I lean desperately out the window, when suddenly the taxi angles precariously and I am thrown prone to my seat. Lifting myself to look out the back window, I am flabbergasted to see a cow - a cow! - dead centre in the middle of the highway. She is nonchalantly chewing her cud as though completely unaware that our automobile has just barreled mere inches from flattening her bony frame. She stares at me impassively, growing distant, when out of nowhere a massive dump truck, horn blaring, barely avoids turning her left side into ground beef.

"Holy Cow!" I shriek. I twist to face my driver. "What happens if someone actually hits a cow?"

A frown drifts over my driver's otherwise serene expression.

"Very bad, very bad karma," he says. "One time, I see cow hit by crazy rickshaw. Driver run away, but people chase, very angry, throw rocks, soon, very bad, very bad, he dead driver."

"What about his passengers?"

"Oh, they don't run away, so people beat them but not kill. Very lucky," he smiles.

"Hmm... did you ever consider driving slower?"

"Ha, ha, ha!" he laughs and shimmies his head from side to side. I take that to mean "no."

Suddenly, the taxi swerves again, the grim shadow of a monstrous bus cutting perilously close to my head. Instinctively, I curl like a fetus to the floor, trembling there until an eternity of near collisions and crashes later I feel the taxi slow to a crawl. After several uncertain moments, I finally raise myself from the carpet, squinting out onto a sprawling city boulevard so gummed up with traffic as to grind my taxi to a turtle's pace. Ox-cart to the right of me, horse-cart to my left, rickety bicycles, gagging scooters, motor rickshaws, cycle rickshaws, trucks, buses and an odd variety of farm animals wandering the streets, seemingly oblivious to the urban chaos. Taxis toot, bells beep, horses neigh, cows moo, as reality caves upon me, cowering in the taxi, and I realize profoundly how far, how very far I am from anything even vaguely familiar.

Without warning, the taxi veers off into a maze of narrow streets and confining alleys where shanties sprout like weeds - whole communities crammed into makeshift shelters of tin and cardboard with garbage bag roofs and open fires for kitchens. Forlorn souls wander through rubbish. Children squat and defecate where they play. Finally, we arrive at a run-down hotel where I am led sweaty and weak-kneed up a flight of stairs to a sparse, dim room. The door is closed behind me. I am left to collapse on the single saggy cot and black out.

When I awake it is well past dark. To my horror, there is no escaping the fact - I am in India. I survey my drab hotel room. The walls are a sickly green in the faint, stuttering light. A small, ancient desk occupies an obscure corner. Windows hide behind old dusty shutters, a mosquito net above the bed crawls with spiders. I am terrified to go outside, but am now equally afraid to stay in!

I stumble across the room to the "attached bath." Now I'm really frightened. The walls are chipped concrete, the floor black with filth, the ceiling low and imposing. The only window is completely caked with soot. In the middle of the festering floor is a hole. No toilet, nor tub, but a hole. No mirror, no sink, but a hole - and a faucet. A rusty, sickly-looking faucet, below which is an equally battered bucket and a plastic, grimy scooper, and yes... that hole. Demanding my attention, with two wooden boards on either side, each the size of a foot, inviting me to stand and look within, peer within, to go where no man has gone before, to seek out new life forms, to face not my demons but the decomposing demons of so many before me. That hole daring me to cross over - to the dark side.

I decide to hold it in 'til later.

Out on the gloomy street, I notice that many others have also chosen to forgo the black hole, only to poop publicly in shadowy corners or pee openly against the nearest wall. I quickly learn that when walking in India, it is nearly impossible to distinguish between *mudpie* and *cowpie*, so it is best to step lightly and avoid pie in general.

Ahhh, what I would give for a juicy slice of apple pie about now - hunger being the main impetus prompting me to leave my hotel room, the other being the lingering revulsion at finding an outhouse in-house, so to speak.

The night is dense with heat, the air pungent with bitter aroma, the street thick with dark bodies. A cow glances at me snidely, swipes at me with the sharp edge of its horn, barely missing my cheek. Red eyes glare out at me from the shadows. I am suddenly keenly aware of my skin, white and foreign as snow. I pick up my pace, when out of nowhere four ragged waifs grab at my hands. Instinctively, I pull back, but their grips are fast.

"Maaa, maaaa," they drone, eyes betraying a need so insatiable, I am at a loss how to help. "Maaa, maaaa," they bleat, but how can I, one man, pacify their lifetimes of hunger? What have I to give to quell the desperation in their gaunt faces? "Maaa, maaaa," they whimper. Then, despite a feeling of terrible inadequacy, I reach for my wallet, sheepishly dispensing to each outstretched palm a twenty-rupee bill, wondering if I am really making a difference or merely propagating the problem. The children snatch the bright orange money, then turn and dash away, not even bothering to thank me. I have barely replaced my wallet, when suddenly from the shadows a stampede of other children appears, having seen the flash of cash. They descend upon me, thrusting muddy hands in mine, braying insistently, "Maaa, maaaa!" I try to walk away, but they follow close behind, pulling at my pants legs, nipping at my ankles. I try to run, but they charge in front of me, blocking my path. I turn, but there's an ancient, toothless, rake of a woman, clawing a bony hand at my face. Soon, grimy old men, shoeless young mothers and crippled teens, join to back me into a corner, no longer begging but demanding, "Maaaa, maaa-aaaaaaaaaaaa!"

"I AM NOT AN ANIMAL! I AM A HUMAN BEING!" I want to shout, but I fear the vague reference to the film The Elephant Man will be lost on this crowd, so I refrain. I search hysterically for a dignified escape. I turn again, only to find myself - well, I was going to say nose-to-nose, but the man before me has no nose! Nor fingers, only stumps at the wrist, which he waves in my face.

"AAAAAAAAAAHHH!!!" I scream, and abandoning all decorum, bolt through the barrier of bodies, throwing myself into a nearby restaurant.

The restaurant is jammed with patrons who for the most part pay no particular heed to my presence. What a relief to, if not blend in, then at least remain relatively unnoticed. I attempt to acquire the waiter's attention. Several times he dashes by, ignoring my requests for a menu. How do you like that? First, I'm the unsolicited centre of attention, now it's as though I'm entirely invisible! Finally, I grab the waiter's wrist with my left hand. To my surprise, his face immediately seizes, contorting into a look of grim disgust, and it is then I recall what I was told about "left hands" in India. I quickly remove my grip and whisper apologetically, "Uh... me use toilet paper, heh, heh."

The waiter snarls and brings me a menu. On one side is a list of items in a language I don't recognize. On the other side is a list of items in *English* I don't recognize: Aloo Gobi, Aloo Palak, Palak Paneer, Gobi Mutter, Mutter Paneer, Channah Masala. What, no burger and fries? No Montreal Smoked Meat? Oh, I'm supposed to be vegetarian - no eggplant parmesan? No tofu salad sandwich?

I turn the page. Hey, they have bread! Reading down the list: Naan, Paratha, Chapati, Poori... hmm, I wonder if any of these translates into pumpernickel bagel? My stomach is growling now. I don't know what to order. My Great Auntie Sari was right - I might starve to death here! The waiter returns.

"Uh, I'll have..." I really would like to inquire if he could recommend the dish least likely to induce diarrhea, but I fear he is still holding onto my left hand - figuratively speaking, of course, and decide to stab at it myself. "I'll have... uh, Palak Paneer and, uh... Poori! Yeah, Poori. Palak Paneer and Poori." I smile at the waiter. He is deadpan.

"Drink?" he asks.

"Oh, right, uh... I'll just have water - no! No water, I'll have..." (Back to the menu)

"Uh... I'll have... Frooti. Yeah, Frooti. Mango Frooti!"

The waiter hurries off.

After an hour my food has still not arrived.

Twice, I bring this to the attention of my waiter, who each time shimmies his head side to side and is off again. Strangely, the staff all race at a break-neck pace, yet don't actually seem to be doing anything. Finally, after another half hour, the waiter places two tin dishes before me. One carefully balances a massive, puffed-up, deep-fried pancake, slowly oozing oil onto the table. The other contains a greenish-brown slop, reminding me of something from that black hole back at my hotel. My stomach is no longer growling, it is whimpering.

Well, looks can be deceiving, I think, swallowing hard. I search my table for cutlery. It is then I notice that of all the restaurant patrons around me, not one is using a knife, fork or spoon. In fact, there is not a single knife, fork or spoon around. These Indian men, women and children are heartily engaged in feeding themselves solely with the use of their hand - yes, thankfully, their right hand - hungrily shoveling fistfuls of runny food into their mouths. I look down at *my* hands. They are filthy, nails black with dust from the taxi ride, tropical germs now crawling in the creases of my palms. My stomach is no longer whimpering. It is revolting at the thought of these hands in my mouth. I hunt with my eyes for a sink, but can't find one. I try to stop my waiter to ask him for some water to wash with, but he just brushes past me, ignoring my request. I stare down at my food. I am extremely hungry now. Reluctantly, I tear a piece of Poori, dip it deep into the murky Palak and with trepidation, scoop it in one fell swoop onto my trembling tongue. Immediately, I am seized by images of parasitic microbes, gleefully prancing in the hot tub of my saliva, fornicating, multiplying, spreading throughout my body. Finally, the greasy mixture swishes down my throat. The taste is not so bad, but I decline to go as far as to call it "finger-lickin' good."

I eat quickly, hoping that speed will lessen the possibility of my being poisoned, and upon finishing, sit there, wondering what to do now with my sticky, drippy right hand. Just then my waiter appears and noticing my predicament, points behind him to a small white sink in a far corner of the restaurant. Suddenly I don't feel very well, nearly gagging at the realization that I *could* have washed and avoided eating with germ-infested hands. I consider asking the waiter if he could forget the sink and point me in the direction of the nearest vomitorium, but by now he has run off again. I can't wait for the bill. I leave a hundred rupee note under one of the tin dishes, stagger over to the sink to wash my hands and slink from the restaurant back into the night. Outside, the heat strikes me like a brick, the stench knocks me reeling, blaring Hindi music has me clutching at my ears. Beggars swarm, filth assaults, shit offends, and I realize that nothing - no film, no book, no slide show - nothing back home could have prepared me for the affront of the past few hours.

I dash through the streets, reaching my hotel room within minutes, and bolting the lock behind me, dive beneath the covers of my bed. There, with a flashlight, I desperately flip through the pages of my guidebook, happening upon a description of a beach town some two hours south of Madras - BEACH TOWN?

I decide, fitfully dozing off, to escape the next morning on the first available bus to Mahaballipurum. Say that ten times fast!

Chapter 3

BETWEEN A ROCK AND A HARD PLACE

It strikes me as odd that the city planners of Madras would have situated the Central Bus Station outdoors amidst a cesspool, but there is no denying that stench.

It is six-thirty in the morning, the sun already scalding, as I step from yet another nerve-wracking taxi ride and immediately drop ankle-deep in a puddle whose contents I shudder to imagine. Lifting my foot, I survey the chaos of the bus park, realizing that not only have the thousands who have arrived here before me usurped any hopes I may have had of being an early bird, but also that puddle water has penetrated my boot. If I wasn't quite awake before this... I am now.

I attempt to decipher the logic of the bus system. There are no bus stands with signs, no queues, no uniformed drivers, no ticket terminal, just a labyrinth of dilapidated vehicles and a shape-shifting mass of humanity. For each commuter scrounging the grounds, there appear to be a hundred aimless loiterers, seemingly present for the sole purpose of creating greater confusion. Little children scurry by, chirping loudly for attention, selling bags of nuts and other snacks. Dogs with sores sniff their wounds, scratch at fleas, lick their - well, that's probably enough information for now, and oh, yes, there's a cow. Suddenly, a man with the longest nostril hairs I have ever seen appears inches from my face, forcing upon me a steaming hot milky beverage in a tiny, tarnished glass. "Chai-ee, chai-ee!" he whines and when I decline, he spits on my boot - the clean one, of course.

I begin to shove my way through the crowd, embedding myself in the thick of sweaty bodies. Every bus appears identical, jammed with an excess of passengers. It is impossible for me to tell which might be heading to Mahaballipurum. I fight my way from one antiquated, fossilized bus to the next, feeling like an archaeologist scraping through the skeletal remains of a dinosaur graveyard. Just then, a clunker by any standards groans to life, sputtering not ten yards before it is inundated with frantic human bodies. A fierce battle ensues for a space on the bus. People even wrestle for the chance to occupy the roof. I personally don't care at this point where this bus may be heading, just as long as it GETS ME OUT OF HERE! I attack my way towards the door, hoisting myself into the bus using my backpack as leverage, and claim the last available seat. But bodies continue to flood onto the bus long after sanity would deem the cab full and still as the old bus creaks into gear and pulls out. People are packed like cattle, there are crated chickens at my feet, and without warning a dark-skinned man hands me his crying baby, so that *he* may hold on for dear life. Though I am grateful to be sitting, the rock hard seat bruises the bones of my butt with each frequent bump, jolting me so hard and high that my skull periodically collides with the roof. The driver cranks the radio to a mind-numbing decibel, blasting shrill Hindi music through tinny speakers inches from my ears. My brain vibrates with such vigour, the only thing keeping me conscious is the incessant screaming of the child in my lap. We drive like this through barren countryside for hours, making frequent stops in the middle of nowhere to exchange passengers. Strangely, it seems, every time one person gets off, a dozen people get on to take their place, finding space in the bus where I would swear there simply isn't any! I look over at my neighbour, staring at me, smiling.

"Where are we going?" I ask.

He continues to smile, saying nothing.

"Mahaballipurum?" I say, pointing straight ahead.

"Mahaballipurum! Mahaballipurum!" he exclaims, laughing, shimmying his head.

Hmm... I wonder.

"Madras?" I say, pointing straight ahead once again.

"Madras! Madras!" he shouts gleefully.

"Ha, ha!" I laugh, but inside I'm crying. I could be heading to Timbuktu for all I know. Just then, the bus begins to shake violently and stops, dead. Smoke is rising from the hood. I look at my neighbour. He is no longer smiling.

The entire bus empties save myself. I watch as the driver cautiously approaches the hissing hood, inhales deeply, then wrenches it open in one swift motion. Billows of smoke instantly drive him back. He circles, scratches his chin, then decidedly marches over and kicks the front wheel. Just as he thought, the problem has nothing to do with the tire. I'm thinking we might be here a very long time.

Suddenly, there's a ruckus as an irate passenger bursts from nowhere and kicks *the driver*, grappling him to the ground. A third man with wild, wavy hair rushes over, I assume to break up the fight. But instead, he merely steps over the combatants and crawls beneath the bus. After ten minutes the wavy-haired man emerges, filthy but confident, gesturing wildly to the driver to start up the bus. The driver lifts himself groggily from the dust and enters the cab, but to everyone's dismay, the engine doesn't even turn over. A bad sign.

Meanwhile, a crowd has gathered at my window, staring up at me with a strange mix of dread, innocence and irrepressible curiosity. They can't seem to peel their eyes from me, so alien am I in South India. Maybe the attraction isn't the sight of a white man, I think, but one who's gone green from the bus ride. After several minutes of feeling like a zoo specimen, I decide to risk everything and say...

"Hello!"

The crowd jumps back a step all at once, maintaining a tense silence until finally, a beautiful two-year-old girl, eyes glittering playfully, speaks with a precious, wee voice.

"One rupee?" she says.

My heart nearly melts, sensing these are the only words in English she knows. Unfortunately, her five-year-old brother is much more fluent.

"One rupee? One chocolate? One pen?" he calls out, taking his sister's lead.

"One chocolate pen?" she echoes.

I have no spare pen, and would beg myself at this point for a piece of chocolate, but I do have a pin of the flag of Canada, which I pass down gently to the small, waiting hands of the girl. She is delighted, but now everyone wants pins, even the adults, some becoming quite petulant when I motion that my pocket is empty. Luckily, the wavy-haired man diverts their attention. He has emerged once again from under the bus, clothes and face tie-dyed with motor oil. Urgently, he sends one of the other passengers to a nearby hut. Within minutes the messenger returns, handing the wavy-haired man two items - a cloth and a string. The wavy-haired man quickly returns beneath the bus. I may know nothing about mechanics, but a cloth and a string? Frankly, I'm skeptical. The other passengers look on in anticipation. Then the wavy-haired man leaps to his feet, beckoning the driver to once again start his engines. To my surprise, the motor ignites! The crowd cheers! I can't believe it. Merrily, everyone returns to the cattle-car express, which when full, proceeds tentatively down the highway. Somehow, now I care less about where we're heading, as long as we're heading somewhere!

Within the hour though, the bus chokes and dies once again. This time no cloth or string can save us and I am told to exit the bus with everyone else. There we sit, a hundred of us, by the edge of nowhere, waiting. The late afternoon sun sinks slowly into a haze, when suddenly, like a mirage along the flat highway, I spy a cloud of dust. I rise with excitement, my hopes soaring as I study the approach of another bus, only to have my optimism shattered when I realize it's already full to bursting. Still, it slows to a halt rather than pass us by. There is a brief discussion between drivers, after which we, the passengers of the first bus are incredulously invited to enter the second. There is a moment's hesitation as my fellow passengers and I intellectually attempt to fathom the absorption of over a hundred extra bodies into an already brimming bus. But this is India, and I am learning that the logical mind is not always the best measure of what is possible. In a mad dash, we charge the doors of the second bus, squeezing all one hundred of us into the already excessively cramped cabin. I feel like a circus clown being stuffed into the backseat of one of those tiny toy cars.

The bus then tears off without warning, sending me flying into the lap of a startled old woman. I stumble to standing, but am thrown sideways as the bus veers left, then forwards as the bus brakes, then backwards as it resumes speed. Finally, I manage to grab onto a metal bar and steady myself, surfing precariously the fine line of balance, mile after mile, until I notice a sign out the window: MAHABALLIPURUM 5 MILE.

Mahaballipurum? Hey, not only am I on the right bus, but better yet, soon I'll be able to get off. Only then, panic sets in. What if Mahaballipurum turns out to be just like Madras - beggars at my feet, hidden sinks - it's more than I could bear. Suddenly, I feel quite attached to this bus. It may be a living hell, but a familiar hell is still better than the dread unknown. Wait! Another sign out the window: SILVER SANDS RESORT.

Resort?

"STOP!" I scream at the driver. The bus squeals to a halt, nearly catapulting myself and ten others out the front window. I thank the driver, trip out the door and wait by the side of the road as the bus disappears into the horizon.

I take a deep breath. Everything is actually silent. I am alone amongst palm trees. I cross the road and enter the gate to the Silver

Sands Resort, following a tree-lined path to the reception. Nine hours after leaving Madras, I am led to a small, self-contained cabin, where, much like the night before, I black out.

...In a dream, it is the middle of the night. I am lying in bed, immersed in darkness, when I realize I am not alone. I am being circled. I hear a hushed breath, a faint but audible growl. Suddenly a shaft of moonlight reveals two green, piercing eyes. A curious claw like a dagger nudges my shoulder. A presence thickens about me like fur... Tiger. I freeze. My eyes involuntarily shut. My lungs burn but I must not breathe. My pulse pounds ferociously but I mustn't allow my heart to betray me. I wait, senses straining in agony. I long to open my eyes, but the fear I might be seen moving keeps me blind. Waiting, alone in the dark, I think, I may never open my eyes again...

It is the middle of the night. I jolt up in bed, startled, sweating. The room is black. Suddenly, I hear a shuffle from behind. A shiver tightens my spine. I reach in panic for the light and see - a lizard, staring down at me from the ceiling.

"Some tiger," I muse, exhaling deeply, feeling relieved that I was only dreaming. Then, unexpectedly, a swift pain doubles me over. A horrible pressure grips my left side. Another pain and I am down on all fours, perspiration streaming from my pores. Wave after wave of pain kicks me. I vomit uncontrollably, fever soaring. For two hours I battle the storm of pain. For two treacherously long hours, I cry as nausea twists me like a rag to the floor. I crawl about screaming, pleading, until there's a knock on the door. In rushes a young Indian man, the "room boy," obviously alarmed.

"Hello, sir. Is everything to your liking?"

"Help," I gasp.

"Sir?"

"Doctor. Please!"

"Yes sir, yes sir, I will get taxi. You wait, sir. You wait here."

But I can't just wait. The pain is grinding at my side. I just wanna pee, I wanna pee, I gotta pee, oh, please let me pee, please, please, let me pee, but I can't! No matter what I do, I can't pee. I stumble deliriously to the toilet, stand there, but can't pee. I writhe back to bed - I have to pee. To the toilet, to the bed, until all I can do is pray – God, I will gladly offer all future fortunes to the charity of your choice if you would simply usher forth a single drop of pee from my stingy, spasming kidney! WHERE IS THAT TAXI?

"Your taxi is here, sir."

"Help."

The driver and room boy carry me sprawling to the cab, throw my limp body in the back seat and slam the door. The taxi speeds off. Each bump is like a rabbit-punch to my kidney, each swerve edges me closer to implosion. Suddenly the taxi stops. The back door is opened and I topple limply to the ground, vomiting at the unfamiliar bare feet of a woman in a red sari.

Looking up, everything has a dream-like quality: the dark Indian woman in red, the pale blue morning sky, the checkered-skirted driver, the growing assembly of ogling onlookers. I stare up at the lady in red. She leans over me, adjusting her black spectacles.

"Do you speak English?" I manage to utter.

"This lady doctor!" the driver shouts, as though this in some way answers my question.

"Do you know what a kidney stone is?" I beg. I had two attacks the previous year in Toronto, but I never expected it to happen again here.

"Of course, I do," she retorts in a crusty British accent. "I studied medicine at Oxford, don't you know."

"Thank you, God."

"Bring him inside," she instructs the driver, who drags me to a small grass hut and drops me carelessly to the floor. The Lady Doctor appears with two syringes, filling them in turn with the liquid-y contents of two unidentified vials.

"Sit up," she commands, but I haven't the energy to rise and am gruffly assisted. Quickly, she injects the unknown concoctions deep into the flesh of my arm.

"What -" are you doing, I am about to ask, when I become achingly groggy, try desperately to stand, swoon and pass out.

When I awake, I am back in my room. I am in bed, fully clothed and drenched in sweat, but I am breathing... a good sign. My mouth feels like the inside of a vacuum cleaner. My watch indicates 5:30 P.M., Thursday. Strange, last I remember, it was 5:30 A.M. - *Tuesday*!

Have I made a big mistake? Maybe I'm just not cut out for this traveling life. Would it be so disgraceful if I returned home after only a week away? No, I couldn't do it. What would my friends say? What would my Great Auntie Sari say? I know, I'll just go home, not call anyone for six months and read a lot of books on India. They'll never know the difference. But wait. If everything is supposed to happen for a reason, there must be some deeper meaning to all this senseless torment. I can't go home. I can't look back. I must go forward.

Peeling myself from the bed, I cross the room unsteadily, open the door and step outside. Though late in the day, the sun is still bright enough to blind me, but the breeze that swoops across my face feels sweet, almost syrupy. Palm trees sway gently above. There is silence save the crickets. Indeed, I must go forward. Besides, I'm awfully thirsty.

Two days without water and my lips feel as puckered as old prunes.

I search the grounds of the Silver Sands Resort, my thoughts as reckless as a sandstorm, groping about deliriously like Moses lost in the desert. I half-expect Omar Sharif from Lawrence Of Arabia to appear out of nowhere on a camel, but I see no one, just a solitary woman in the distance scrubbing laundry by hand. Typical... when I want to be alone, people climb out of the woodwork to greet me, but as soon as I'm in desperate need of another human being, especially one carrying a cool beverage, there is not a soul to be found. Finally to my relief, I spot an outdoor dining area and entering, lean against one of the tables, head pounding.

"Heddo!" I call out, wanting to say hello, but my tongue is like parchment, my voice crackled like a distorted radio signal. A young man appears with a broom.

"Heddo!"

"Sir?" He glares at me with alarm. I must look a wreck.

"Drink, can I get a drink? This is the restaurant, isn't it? You do speak English, don't you? Let me start again. Heddo - I mean, hello. Drink-me-you-get?"

Good god, I'm speaking like an idiot!

The young man stares at me blankly.

I drop to one knee, about to die of thirst, when inspiration hits. Quickly, I mime raising an invisible glass - no, a Coke - to my lips, imagining each non-existent drop dripping down the back of my throat, fictitious bubbles tickling my nostrils. Ahhh, Coke, even when you're faking it, it's the real thing. I look imploringly at the young man. He appears confused, almost fearful, but then suddenly, his eyes light up.

"Frooti?" he says.

"No! No Frooti!" I exclaim. I'd rather drink sand than recall the tastes of that first meal in Madras. "Do you have water? Bottled water?"

"Bisleri?"

Sounds like Russian vodka. Well, that'll do.

"Sure, can you get me some of that?"

A shimmy of the head and the young man ducks behind a counter, reappearing moments later with a plastic bottle caked in dust and dirt. He presents it to me, grinning with the satisfaction of a job well done. I smile back, trying to conceal my disgust. I wipe the bottle of water off with my shirt and read the label: "Bisleri."

"Thank you," I say.

"Thank you," he replies.

"No, thank *you*," I say.

"No, thank you," he replies.

"Here's ten rupees," I say. "Thank you".

"Thank you," he bows.

"Thank *you*," I bow.

"Thank you," he bows.

We're obviously at a stalemate.

It is then I spy something unmistakably familiar behind him on the counter and forget entirely about who's thanking whom. I begin to salivate uncontrollably, eyes glued to the first and only recognizable token of Western culture I have encountered since landing in India. I am almost dizzy with desire, when the young man, noticing my fixation, reaches behind him and passes me a brightly coloured, shiny plastic bag - there's nothing like instant gratification. I stare at the bag adoringly, heaving a long satiated sigh, "Ahhh...chips."

But not just any chips. We're talking about an actual North American brand name. Imagine, here, in a remote corner of South India, guided to my hands like a gift from the gods, not just chips, but... RUFFLES! I close my eyes and try to guess the flavour. BBQ? Salt & Vinegar? Sour Cream & Onion? I quickly open my eyes and read the label: "Masala." Masala? What kind of flavour is Masala?

"Sir?" the young man's voice shakes me from my reverie.

"Oh yeah, right... I'll take them," I cry out. "Here's ten rupees." He hands me a bag. "Thank you," I say.

"Thank *you*," he replies.

"Now don't start that again."

I scurry down the nearest path, moments later emerging from thick foliage at a picturesque shoreline. The ocean is vast, the horizon expansive, the enormous sky seared with pinks. I had completely forgotten that when I left Madras I was heading towards a *beach*. I stroll along the sands, feel the waves crash against my feet. I settle in a secluded spot by a rock and drink my Bisleri, eat my Ruffles - okay, they do taste like curry, but they sort of remind me of home.

I take a deep breath and head back towards the Silver Sands. By the time I reach the resort, the sky is a deep, dark blue, the heavens an endless sea of stars. I enter the dining area, now a world transformed. Candles flicker on each table, gentle Indian music drones softly. Waiters move about calmly, their angelic children playing quietly. I am the only guest around.

I am introduced to the South Indian "thali" for dinner, kind of a combo plate, with white rice, "sambar" (a spicy gravy), two kinds of curried vegetables, "pappadam" (a peppery-hot, crispy round cracker), "raita" (a cool yogurt with cucumber and onion), and a bitter, chili-pickled slice of beet. My pleasant waiter describes each item proudly as they are placed before me, not as expected on a platter, but on a wide, fan-like banana leaf, freshly picked from a plant in the garden outside. Everything is actually tasty, and I am even escorted by my waiter *before* the meal to a clean white sink where I wash my hands. The memories of the past few days begin to fade. I am lulled into a dream-like state, wondering... which is the real India?

For the next three days, I hide at the Silver Sands, my every need catered to, my body recovering and my spirit mending. On the fourth morning, I approach the check-in desk and inquire as to my tab. I have been conveniently charging everything to my room.

"Four thousand, three hundred and sixty-three rupees," I am told.

"Excuse me," I say, gasping for air.

"Four thousand -"

"There must be some mistake."

"No, sir, look see. One room, one night, this is four hundred rupees. Seven nights, this is two thousand eight hundred rupees."

"Seven nights?" I count on my fingers. "Oh yeah, that includes the two days I was unconscious."

"Meals, dobhi, lassis -"

"Lassies? I didn't see any dogs?"

"Sir?"

"Collies? Dogs?"

"No, sir. Lassis."

"Irish girls?"

"No, sir. Lassi is drink with curd. See here, twenty-one banana lassis."

"Oh, yeah. What's dobhi?"

"Washing your clothes, sir. Three hundred rupees."

"Oh, yeah."

"Twenty-two bags Ruffles, thirty-five bottles Bisleri, twenty percent service charge, government tax... Four thousand, three hundred and sixty three rupees." He smiles. I am stunned. That's one helluva lot of rupees. It's over two hundred Canadian dollars. I can't afford this rate of spending. I might have to leave the resort.

"Sir?"

And plunge myself back within the fangs of India.

"Sir?"

Ride another one of those buses.

"Sir?"

Squat over one of those toilets.

"Sir?"

I should have never left the airport at Madras!

"SIR!"

"What? Oh yeah. I'm afraid I have to leave - you don't know how afraid." I lean casually over the counter. "What's Mahaballipurum really like? You can tell me, I can take it."

"Very nice, sir. Very good."

"Well, would you be a good man, then, and arrange a taxi for me, say in a week - wishful thinking - I mean, in an hour? Oh yeah, do you take traveler's cheques?"

He shimmies. I pay and am off to pack.

Exactly an hour later a driver arrives at my door. Why is it when you're in a hurry, you're made to wait for hours, but as soon as you're reluctant to leave, the impossible occurs and a taxi is actually punctual?

"Sir?"

"Okay, I'm ready," but I stall, taking a very long time to do up my sandals, hoping the driver won't notice they are slip-ons. I'm going to miss this place, I think, looking around the resort for one last time, but after all, I have come to find the "real" India - well, actually I'm not sure why I've come, but that sounds like as New Age a reason as any - and I know, that the "real" India lies somewhere beyond the manicured gardens of the Silver Sands Resort, somewhere out there in the vast unknown, in the villages, in the people, in the…

"SIR!"

"Right, I know. Get in the taxi."

Well, no use delaying the inevitable… unless, of course, it's for one last look at the beach!

"Keep the motor running," I say. "I'll be right back."

Chapter 4

A DAY AT THE CIRCUS

My taxi pulls into Mahaballipurum, depositing me directly in front of the Mamala Bhavan Hotel, a mid-scale, two-storied establishment with tropical courtyard garden, vegetarian restaurant, and balcony views of the street beyond. Attractive qualities, to be sure, but more importantly, it is surrounded by an eight-foot concrete wall and is barricaded at the entrance by a heavy iron gate. In other words, it looks safe. I pay the driver, acquire a room on the second floor - only one hundred rupees per night - and do not leave the hotel grounds for the next two days.

To my surprise, the Mamala Bhavan Hotel seems to have most modern conveniences. The hotel restaurant is excellent. I'm having thali every meal. There is a hot shower in my room and, believe it or not, a sit-down, Western-style toilet. In fact, I'm amazed at how spic and span the bathroom appears. Of course, with the showerhead situated directly in the middle of the bathroom, right between the sink and toilet, it's no wonder cleanliness is maintained. Everything gets a thorough rinsing every time I bathe. From my balcony, I observe the life of the village beyond the hotel gates, ambling slowly under the heavy glare of the sun. Mahaballipurum appears to be a far cry from the rapid pulse of Madras. On the third day, I risk venturing into the "real" India. I pack my guide-book, water bottle, camera, pocketknife, paints, sketchbook, journal and novel into a daypack and leave my room. "Travelin' light," as Billie Holiday used to sing.

I reach the hotel gateway and stop, unable to convince my legs to press on further. I stand at the threshold, quivering there for more than twenty minutes, as terrified as if I were about to leap from a plane. An old gatekeeper watches me indifferently. I think of asking him to give me a shove, but finally, I force myself to step into the street. Almost immediately, I notice that I am again the target of overt stares. "What can possibly be so interesting?" I wonder. Then I realize, of course, I'm the only one wearing pants. All the other men are wrapped in skirts and here I am in pants - white pants, at that. In fact, my entire wardrobe is white. My shoes are white, socks are white, even my hat, shirt and skin are white. What was I thinking? I may as well be parading in a spacesuit. I must look like some mutant Man From Glad. Nothing else around me even comes close to being white. On the contrary, everything and everyone seem covered in dust. I wish now that I had left at home all that shampoo and brought instead a giant canister of pine-scented Pledge. As much as I try to the contrary, I can't help but find the dust disconcerting. But I know that if I am to remain here, I must learn not to focus on India's dustiness. I must choose to embrace her "earthiness," as in: "My, those children's faces are *earthy*," or "That woman, she's so grimy, she must be Mother Earth."

Walking through Mahaballipurum, I notice that all the buildings appear to be in an advanced state of decay, except for one, not surprisingly, the bank. Entire shops occupy spaces no larger than closets. On Beach Road, I encounter an endless row of flimsy souvenir stalls whose vendors solicit me, not to buy their wares, as I expect, but rather to, "Change money? Good price!" It appears the black market is alive and well in India and not altogether discreet. Even children petition me to "Change money!" One particularly slimy man slickly sidles up to me, whispering, "You want grass, hash, change money, change traveler's cheques, heroin?"

"Uh...no," I say, "but, keep in touch." I quickly enter the nearest stall, as much to escape further pestering as to purchase some postcards. The proprietor is a horse-toothed gent fixated on selling me some tacky, leaf-embroidered greeting cards.

"Really, I just want some postcards," I try fending him off, but he is persistent.

"Very nice leaf," he says.

"Yes, I'm sure, but how much for these?" I have selected a handful of postcards, crusty and yellow with age.

"Two rupees for one."

"How much for ten?"

He calculates. "Twenty rupees."

"I'll tell you what. I'll give you twelve rupees for ten. These post-cards look like they've been here since before Mahatma Ghandi."

The salesman ponders my offer. "Okay, okay," he announces. "For you, eighteen rupees." He begins wrapping up the cards.

"Wait, wait, wait," I say. "Thirteen."

"Ha, ha. Okay, okay, for you seventeen rupees, last price."

"Fourteen."

"Ha, ha, ha. No fourteen. Sixteen rupees, best price."

"Fifteen," I say, "and that's my final offer."

The salesman stares at me then finally reveals his horse-teeth in an exaggerated smile. "Okay, okay. Ha, ha. Fifteen rupees," he says. "Only for you, Baba."

I pay him.

"What about leaf-card?" he asks.

"Uh, no thanks anyway," I say, turning to leave the shop, when suddenly, the salesman urgently grabs my arm and begins begging me to relieve him of some of those leaf-cards.

"But I don't want any," I say.

"But you must admit, Baba, they are most beautiful!"

"Oh, they're beautiful alright, but I still don't want any."

"Okay, okay," he laughs, "how much you give for one?"

"I don't want -"

"Okay, okay, for you... eighteen rupees."

"What? Eighteen rupees?" I protest. "That card's only worth ten rupees at the most."

"Ten rupees? Baba, these *handmade* leaf-cards! Okay, okay, for you sixteen rupees."

"No, I don't want any."

"Ha, ha, okay, fourteen rupees."

"No, I don't want any."

"Okay, ten rupees!"

"No, I don't want any." I push my way out of the shop, but the salesman follows me outside, hailing me as I hurry away down Beach Road. "Baba! Okay, okay, eight rupees! No? Okay, FIVE rupees! No? Okay! Change money? GOOOOD PRICE!!!"

But by this time I am well down the street and out of sight.

The beach at Mahaballipurum is beyond over-crowded, an obstacle course of hand-carved canoes, fishing nets, squatting fishermen and Indian vacationers frolicking in the sea. To my surprise, nobody here wears bathing suits. Men seem unabashed to strip to their underwear to go swimming, while women seem overly abashed, wading in the water, fully clothed in ocean-drenched saris.

It's a challenge but I do manage to locate a relatively quiet spot and start to read, but after only half a page I am interrupted by a loud voice.

"WHAT IS YOUR GOOD NAME?" I look up to find myself surrounded by eight ogling teenage boys.

"YOUR GOOD NAME?" another boy repeats.

Hmm... I've been called some *bad* names. "Uh... Stew," I finally reply.

"Sa-too."

"Stew."

"Sa-too."

"Close enough."

"My name, Saju."

"Hello, Sa-joo."

"What country?"

"Canada."

"Oh, Canada."

"So the anthem goes."

"What is your book?"

"The Fountainhead."

"Oh, is it ... SEX?"

"No."

"Ohhh." The boys look very disappointed. "CRIME?"

"No."

"Ohhh." How do I explain to them that Ayn Rand's book, The Fountainhead, is about one man's unyielding determination to be true to the glory of the individual? Actually, how do I explain that to myself?

"You want?" one of the boys offers me some brandy.

"Uh, no thanks."

"This?" another boy holds out a cigarette.

To the disenchantment of all, I decline. Some foreigner I am, I don't drink, I don't smoke, and I don't read crime-filled sex novels.

I must admit, I feel a little vulnerable in the midst of nine tipsy teenagers who in a foreign language are able to talk behind my back to my face. They squeeze too closely around me, laughing boisterously, hands grabbing excitedly at the contents of my bag. I am perspiring now, as much from theft paranoia as from the unrelenting heat. Finally, I rise and collect my belongings, say goodbye, but the boys leap to their feet and follow, encircling me as we walk, introducing me to everyone they know - and believe me, they know everyone.

"You have coin?" one of them asks.

"Excuse me?"

"Coin, from your country?"

"Oh, no, sorry, but I do have some Canada pins." The teenagers are ecstatic. Soon I am strolling the beach with nine junior ambassadors of Canada, proudly displaying their flags.

"What is that?" I ask, pointing to a distant, giant, armadillo-shaped rock, jutting out from the beach on a peninsula of sand.

"This Shore Temple," Saju says.

"Really, a temple -" I say, but before I can finish my thought, in a flash, my companions have disappeared. I turn to see them racing towards another Westerner, a middle-aged white woman with a deep tan. I watch as they gaggle around her, fawning upon her every detail, feeling somewhat jilted, betrayed. They have completely forgotten about me, taken their pins and run. Well, there's one for the record, I think. I've been ditched countless times for a variety of men, but this is the first time I've ever been left for an older woman.

Continuing down the beach, I am drawn almost magnetically to the Shore Temple, desperate to find there some hallowed semblance of serenity. According to my guidebook, the Shore Temple was constructed around 750 A.D., more than *twelve hundred years* before I was born. Arriving before its ancient walls, I feel as though I am actually standing in the presence of history, basking in the vibration of centuries of prayers. I imagine the men who must have built and worshipped in this temple, not just abstract souls, but men of flesh and blood, men just like me - well, I've never built anything in my life, so maybe men with slightly more construction experience.

I wander silently, reverently around the temple, quietly smiling at a boy nonchalantly petting a wild monkey. Isn't that cute, I think, until the monkey screeches, "EEEEE!" nearly giving me a heart attack.

I pass by two begging children, nodding to them a soft hello. They shock me with a scream of "NO MONEY, THEN GO!" I hurry away, lamenting the fact they see me only as Johnny Dollar and not as "Sat-oo,

The Well-Meaning Westerner."

"SHOES OFF!" another boy barks, as I am about to enter the temple. I must admit, I'm beginning to feel a tad unwelcome. Shedding my sandals, I pass through a low door, follow a damp corridor and soon happen upon a small, dark cave - finally, a place to have a moment alone. I enter and squat down, resting my back against the cool, stone wall, noticing two small statues crafted directly into the rock above - a moustached man and his hippy, sensuously carved girlfriend.

"THIS SHIVA!" a voice suddenly explodes like a cannon in the close chamber. I leap up nearly cracking my head on the low ceiling. It's the "monkey boy."

"THIS GOD - THIS, SHIVA!" the monkey boy bellows, pointing at the statue of the moustached man.

"How did *you* get in here?" I say, checking my scalp for contusion.

"THIS GOD, HIS WIFE - PARVATI," he shouts, indicating the carving of the girl.

"Could you tone it down a little bit?" I plead, rubbing my head. "Uh, did you say... gods?"

"Yes, Baba."

"Like in the sky?"

"No, not sky. Here!" He points again at the statues.

"These statues... they're gods?" I ask.

"Very good gods."

"If you say so." I begin to rise.

"You do puja?" the boy interrupts.

"Puja? What's that?" I ask, slightly warily.

The monkey boy begins to mumble under his breath. "This mantra," he whispers. He proceeds to murmur incomprehensibly for several, long moments. Then, just as he notices my patience ebbing, he reaches dramatically into his pockets producing on his fingertips small samples of red and yellow powder. I watch curiously as in turn he dabs each statue between the eyes, then applies a generous smear to my own unsuspecting forehead.

"This puja!" he concludes with a smile.

"Well, thank you, I guess."

"Ten rupees," he says.

"What?"

"Ten rupees," the monkey boy repeats, extending an open hand.

"For what?"

"Puja!"

"But, I thought you were doing it to be nice, to be my friend, to give me a blessing."

"Yes... also for ten rupees. Plus government tax."

"Don't push it," I say, begrudgingly handing him the money.

As I leave the Shore Temple, I do feel blessed... blessed I was only taken for ten rupees.

Chapter 5

TEARS OF A CLOWN

While sightseeing the next day in Mahaballipurum, I can't believe my luck, all of a sudden finding myself standing before "one of the most perfectly sculptured elephants in India" - at least according to my guide-book. I am not half as impressed with the sculpture as I am with this inane piece of trivia. I can see myself years from now at some boring company Christmas cocktail party recounting this tidbit of information after several moments of uncomfortable silence with some bad-breathed executive from accounting who I wish I had never met. Desperately, I can see myself saying, "By the way, did you know that during my youth I saw one of the most perfectly sculptured elephants in India?" - hoping, of course, not to stimulate further conversation on either art or elephants, but rather to convince the accountant that I may be even more tedious than he, at which point he might spare me and go away.

My other favourite landmark in Mahaballipurum is "Krishna's Butterball" - not, as one would suspect, the most perfectly sculptured turkey in India, but rather, a massive egg-shaped boulder perched high on a hilltop, balanced so precariously on its tip, it looks as though it could be dislodged with the force of a feather. I shudder from below at the potential for damage should this monstrous rock ever be coaxed from its perilous post, and marvel, how incredible it is that it should have endured in that erect position these hundreds, if not thousands of years, withstanding not only monsoon winds, but heavily leaning tourists.

For lunch, I return to the Mamala Bhavan Hotel, have thali, and upon finishing, inquire of my waiter as to the whereabouts of the post office. I want to mail my mother one of those 1950's postcards I bought. I am told to wait by the hotel gate, someone will be sent to guide me. After ten minutes, to my surprise, a five-year-old boy appears. He leads me out of the hotel, behind a pummeled building, past a man urinating in public, through a narrow crack in a wall and into a thorny field inhabited by a motley collection of bristly, black, ornery-looking pigs. If this is the shortcut, I'd hate to see the long way.

Finally, we reach the post office. I hand the boy two rupees and step inside. The room is in utter chaos, an indoor scaled down version of the Madras bus station. No queues, no signs in English, just a mass of people converging on indifferent civil servants who seem completely unfazed by the crush of bodies, the shouting, the flailing hands. They remind me of those serene cows on the highway, oblivious to onrushing traffic. I get "in line" but after fifteen minutes of being shoved, bumped and elbowed, I find myself exactly where I started, at the back, cursing under my breath, customers pressing against me until not only can't I breathe, but my postcard is in danger of becoming even more crumpled than it originally was when I bought it.

"Alright, that's enough!" I want to shout. "Get a grip on yourselves people. Line-up, for god's sake." But the swarm squeezes harder, tighter, until finally I realize I have no choice but to abort. Turning around, I begin to claw upstream against the onslaught of stamp-deprived citizens, battling my way back to the front door until I burst from the post office, escaping into daylight with my life.

Well, I hope my mother believes in that old saying "no news is good news," because I think it'll be a miracle before she receives any mail from me.

Sometime later, I pass by a Twenty-Four Hour International Telephone Centre and decide to phone my mother instead. I enter the shop and am immediately greeted by an excessively thin man with a thick moustache, gentle eyes, and three broad smears of white, uh, makeup, across his forehead.

"V.T. Palani," he exclaims, placing his palms together at his heart and bowing.

"Uh, I'm Stew."

"Sa-too."

"Stew."

"Sa-too."

"Close enough."

"How may I be helping you?"

"I'd like to make a phone call to Canada."

"Oh, very good, very good. Please come sit."

I rest myself on a chair by a small desk and proceed to provide Mr. Palani with the particulars of my mother's phone number in Montreal. He writes everything down then asks me to move to a private booth with an old-fashioned phone hanging from the wall.

"I will tell you when to pick up," he calls out.

I wait and wait in the steamy booth, sweating as Palani dials the phone on his desk, hangs up, dials again, hangs up, dials again, hangs up, and so on. After an excruciating hour, I can wait no longer, peeling myself from the vinyl stool and leaving the claustrophobic booth.

"Problem with the phone line?" I ask.

"Oh no, no problem," Palani smiles. "This is India, we must have patience."

I'd find it easier to have patience if I weren't developing a rash on my bum from that stool. "Uh, how long do I need to wait?"

"Today, tomorrow... next day."

It seems the phone system is about as efficient as everything else I have encountered in India. "Do you mind if I ask you a question, slightly off topic? Why do you have white makeup on your forehead?"

"This?" he says. "This from morning puja!"

There's that word puja again. Instinctively, I reach for my wallet, guarding against the quick exit of another ten rupees, but unlike the monkey boy at the Shore Temple, Palani doesn't seem the least bit interested in my money. Instead, he explains that the three white lines across his forehead are ash, remnants of a daily religious ceremony - or "puja" - identifying him as a worshipper of the Hindu god, Shiva. Not to be confused, of course, with someone sporting a big ashen 'V' on his forehead, indicating a devotee of the god, Vishnu. Hmm... sort of like wearing your heart on your sleeve, I suppose, except on your forehead.

"There are many Hindu gods," he tells me. "I worship also Ayappah, son of Shiva."

Then, shouldn't you have a big 'A' on your forehead, I want to ask, but decide to file that question for later.

"Shall I tell you of my yearly pilgrimage to Ayappah's Temple?" Palani asks.

"Sure," I nod.

"Please, sit."

"Uh, I'd rather stand," I say, discreetly scratching at my behind.

As the story goes, after forty-one days of abstinence from sex, smoking and drinking, Palani and his sons head off on an arduous journey by bus and train across the country to the state of Kerala, culminating in a perilous hike at night through a forest of wild animals. Legend has it that if you've been true and worthy, Ayappah will prevent you from being eaten. If not, chances are you may end up a quick meal to some beast with the midnight munchies. Come morning, those who actually survive, drudge their weary bodies, haggard and barefoot to Ayappah's temple, high on a hilltop, delivering offerings of appeasement to their god, never happier to greet a sunrise as on that auspicious morn.

Wow. To my jaded Western ears, Palani's tale seems to describe an archaic, superstitious, even ghastly rite of passage, but to listen to the conviction in Palani's voice as he relates the good fortune reaped from this religious effort, is to understand faith. According to him, it is only through this trust in Ayappah that he was able to open a phone centre, acquire a vehicle, send his son to catering school. (Catering school? Here?) The man exudes gratitude as he excitedly invites me to join he and his sons on this coming year's pilgrimage. I am honoured, but decline, feeling certain that if my spiritual worthiness is the only guarantee of safety through those wild woods, I would be tiger chow long before ever seeing the light of day upon Ayappah's Temple.

I am about to ask Palani if he could try my mother's number again, when some locals interrupt us wishing to place calls. It seems a phone in the home is a luxury most villagers cannot afford. I watch as Palani calmly negotiates a series of potentially frustrating mishaps. For the first customer, the line rings but doesn't get through. For the second customer, the line does get through but to a wrong number. For the third customer, the number is right but the static so severe that the customer can't even hear the person with whom he's conversing. Then all the lines completely break down! If I were Palani, I'd be on the ground kicking and screaming, but he just smiles, a picture of patience.

By now, it is late afternoon and I have all but given up on reaching my mother. I decide to return to the beach for sunset, bidding Palani a reluctant farewell. We shake hands. He bows. I bow. He bows. I bow. He bows - finally, if only to break this cycle, I reach into my bag and present him with a slightly bent, shiny picture postcard of Niagara Falls.

"You see how strongly these waters flow?" I say. "That's Canada."

Palani is visibly overwhelmed. He bows. I bow. He bows, but

there's no way I'm going to start that again. I prepare to make my way past him but before I do, he suddenly stops me, turning serious.

"Satoo," he says. "Be careful. Remember, not every man in India is honest. Go with god's blessing. Repeat in your heart the Holy Om. Ommmm. Ommmm. It will keep you safe."

I thank him, thinking, maybe not every man is honest, but if there is one honest man, I'm looking at him. Wandering away from the shop down the street, it suddenly dawns on me... I've just met my first Indian saint.

Down at the beach it is a glorious sunset. Feeling refreshed, I decide to head back to my hotel for dinner, but before I get far, I am waved over by two tanned tourists at an outdoor beachside bar.

"Shalom! Come sit down. My name is Zohar. Dis is my friend, Motti."

"Uh, hi," I say. "I'm Sa-too, uh, I mean, Stew."

"We can't believe it. Another tourist! We haven't seen another tourist in weeks," Zohar exclaims.

"At least not one under fifty years old," Motti laughs.

"Come, join us." Zohar pulls up a chair. I sit down.

"Where are you from?" Motti asks.

"Canada," I reply.

"Ah, Canada!" Zohar shouts out. "My brother now lives in Canada. We're from -"

"Israel. I know. I've been there before."

"Hey! A smart man."

"Well, your *shalom* did give it away," I smile.

We each order a beer. I impress them with my knowledge of Hebrew, they impress me with tales of the Israeli army. The hours fly by and so do the beers, until suddenly, it strikes me that, to my horror, night has fallen. Darkness has crept in to envelop all but our little outdoor table. The beach appears empty, the road beyond the bar, shadowy and deserted. The long walk back to the Mamala Bhavan Hotel now looms before me fraught with danger. I attempt to stand but stagger drunkenly and return to my chair, finding safety in yet another beer, when suddenly two Indian men appear, skulking towards us from around a corner.

The Israelis greet them, order them drinks, but from the first, I don't trust them. One of them sits too close for my comfort, a small, rodent of a man, with bloodshot eyes and effeminate manner. He strokes my face with the back of his hand.

"You are beautiful," he tells me, giggling like a schoolgirl.

"Don't touch me," I mumble and pull away.

"Oh, but I like to touch," he says, enticing the gruff laughter of the other men.

"I think you have a friend!" Motti jokes, but I don't find it funny. I turn my chair away, but the slimy man shuffles closer, provoking more laughter.

"You like to kiss?" he nudges me, puckering his lips.

"Stop it!" I shout, but he attempts to nibble my ear, lick my cheek.

"PISS OFF!" I yell, rising from my chair. Everyone is laughing. My temples are pounding.

"Come on," Zohar says. "Sit down. Here, you -" he waves at the slimy man "- leave him alone."

Just then a car pulls up and five Indian brutes get out, one of them a giant by Indian standards. It seems to me no accident that they have appeared. They wait by their sedan, obviously eyeing the slimy man, who seems to grow bolder by their presence. He leans towards me.

"I want to rape you," he whispers.

I freeze. Blood rushes from my face. The slimy man grins. The five thugs edge closer. I am about to lose control of my bladder when Motti slowly rises to his feet followed by Zohar.

"Get up," Zohar says to me and I comply despite wobbly knees. "Lucky you are with two soldiers of the Israeli army."

"YOU WANT A FIGHT?" Motti suddenly cries out. "Let me tell you, we have killed bigger men and uglier men than you. You give us trouble and we will tear you apart with our hands!"

The Indians are not intimidated. They continue to close in. There appears no escape, when -

"RUN!" Motti shouts, bolting past the Indians, Zohar a close step behind. My legs though are like molasses, my reflexes muddled.

"Come on!" Motti roars.

Stricken with fear, my legs somehow kick into gear. The Indians take chase. I'm gasping for air. I'm afraid to look behind me. I think I hear a car coming! At the end of Beach Road, the Israelis veer left, but I swerve to my right, propelling myself towards the gate of the Mamala Bhavan Hotel. Yanking frantically at the bars, I am sickened to find - it's locked. My heart nearly stops. I am panting like an animal, desperate to enter the safety of the hotel, deciding without thinking to scale the wall, but halfway up, my foot catches and I'm trapped, dangling like bait to any passing crook. It is then I hear a shuffle from below and shriek, "Don't touch me!" But it is only the old gatekeeper sleeping.

"Help!" I call down. "It's me, the white tourist!"

Thankfully, he awakens and recognizing me, frees me and opens the gate. Now near hysteria, I dash to my room, pacing away half the night, startling at the slightest sound. At 4:30, I fall into a fitful sleep. At 5:30, I am awakened by a crack of noise like a gun going off in my room. I scream, hear a shot, then another. I run to the window expecting gangsters at my door, but it's only children with cap guns playing in the street.

Just another day at the circus, I think.

Chapter 6

LEAVE NO STONE UNTURNED

If to make a mistake is human and to learn from one's mistakes divine, then to repeat one's mistakes over and over again must lie somewhere between deification and just missing the point.

After my near-rape experience, I beat a hasty retreat out of Mahaballipurum, hopping on the first obtainable bus to my next destination, Pondicherry. But not ten miles from that city's limits, I lose my nerve again at the thought of entering an Indian town. Again, I scream at the bus driver to "Stop!" and again am left by the side of the road in the middle of nowhere, only this time there is no Silver Sands Resort to break my fall. Here there is nothing but farmland or forest as far as my eye can see. But there are still people. Even in this isolated locale, curious faces surround me. It's almost impossible to go anywhere in India and be alone. I am learning that while it is dreadfully easy to get lost in India, India itself just won't get lost, even in the most remote countryside. She is relentlessly demanding. She has a firm grip on my reality. She is becoming a state of mind. She is a smell that permeates my body, a salty mixture of curry and sweat. She is a taste that won't go away, no matter how many Frooti's I drink - or maybe she's the taste of Frooti. She is endless people loitering in my peripheral vision, cows on every street corner munching on mounds of garbage, a five-hour bus ride with a hairy man's armpit mere inches from my nostrils. But thankfully, she is also a land of miracles, and it is a miracle indeed that both my bus and I have managed to arrive to this point without breaking down.

Still, I yearn for a reprieve, even momentarily, from India's incessant trials. I long for a sanctuary of Western culture in this desert of unfamiliar customs, an oasis that serves bacon-burgers, curly fries and chocolate shakes. I pine to climb the Golden Arches, to dive headlong into a sea of special sauce, and have whatever I want, *my way*. I whip out the guidebook and flip madly for Pondicherry, when I'm struck by "Auroville" - an experimental international community just outside of Pondicherry designed by a French architect, dedicated to harmonious living and universal oneness. Sounds to me like an excellent place to get a fresh croissant and a good cup of coffee.

Quickly, I inquire of the locals who have drawn about me as to the whereabouts of Auroville and am directed to a road off the highway, well, not quite a road, more like a chopped up dirt path through a ploughed field. Not deterred, I walk several difficult miles in the scalding sun until I reach a small village of primitive one-storied buildings. Surprisingly, there is not a soul around. I remove my sweaty backpack and search about, finally discovering a community mess hall, empty save for three white men and one white woman, seated silently at the far end of a long, wooden table.

"Hello," I bellow excitedly, bounding up to the other Westerners. "Excuse me. Is it possible to rent a room?"

I am met with cold and distant stares. The four foreigners turn to themselves and speak rapidly in French. I don't have to be born in Paris to glean they are annoyed by my presence. Finally, the woman faces me and without the faintest inkling of a smile, mutters, "Oui." She leads me to a one-room hut, quickly rattles off the schedule of meals and departs, grumbling something in French under her breath like, "Ah, if only Napoleon had won."

Before long it is time for dinner. I return, ravenous, to the mess hall, grab a tray and get in line, smiling warmly at the Western man ahead of me. He scowls and looks away. I nod to a white woman in a stained apron. She greets me with a grimace worthy of the Grinch at Christmas. Okay, what is it? Do I smell that bad? Finally, I reach the front of the line, salivating wildly. My thoughts race with visions of French cuisine - duck a l'orange, thick creamy sauces, strawberry-filled crepes, sorbet, vin rouge! I am practically drooling as I hold out my plate, only to receive a bland serving of brown rice and boiled veggies.

"No baguette?" I whimper to the cook, who frowns at me with disdain. I seat myself dejectedly at an empty table and pick at my food, dreaming of french fries, when all of a sudden, an alarmingly thin girl in her twenties joins me. Hey, maybe I don't smell that bad after all.

"You are new?" she inquires with an Eastern European-sounding accent.

"Yes," I reply.

"You like it here?"

"Well, except for the fact that no one will talk to me, I like it fine."

"They will not talk to me as well, but I am also new."

"How long have you been here?" I ask.

"Six months."

"Six months?" I say. "And no one talks to you?"

"One day, I know, they will welcome me to their community."

"Yeah, when you're eighty-five years old, maybe they'll throw you a bone and snarl *bonjour* at you."

"You don't understand," she says. "They are creating here an example to the world of cooperation and peaceful interaction."

"Yes, I find being an outcast quite peaceful."

"They don't like newcomers. I probably shouldn't be talking to you." Abruptly, she picks up her tray and moves to another empty table.

Later, as I rise to leave, she is still alone, her food practically untouched. I try to connect my eyes with hers, but she is lost in months of imposed isolation. I return to my hut, bewildered, and sadly welcome sleep. It's been a long day.

The next morning, I awaken to a rooster crowing and a sensation of dire necessity to empty my bladder. I crawl groggily out of bed, check my watch, and hurry to the toilet. It is five A.M. and from the bathroom, I can see the first light of day softly inching its way over the treetops. I stand and yawn, waiting for the tinkle of pee to signal the relief of pressure building in my bladder. I wait, but hear nothing. I bear down, but witness no penile emission whatsoever. And then it hits. A blade of pain so vicious it cripples me to the floor.

"Oh no!" I cry. "Not again!"

Forcing myself to my feet, I hurl myself into the bedroom, faltering like a pinball from furniture to wall, wailing like a castrated dog. I charge for the door, erupting from my hut, cracking the silence of early morn.

"Help!" I cry. "Please, please help!"

But the neighbours I wake say, "No doctor resides, return to your bed, the pain will subside."

"Taxi!" I plead.

"The road is too rough for a taxi," I am told as I'm ushered back to my room and left alone. Pain lacerates my left side. For the next six hours, I vomit, I sweat, I spit, I shit, but goddammit, I can't pee! Finally, at three P.M., I flounder desperately from my room to the mess hall, demanding some attention.

"Je suis mal!" I shout.

Everyone in the mess hall agrees - if it means my departure, they'll be more than glad to help. I am escorted back to my room, my belongings are packed, and I am ushered to a taxi at the edge of the village.

"I thought you couldn't get a taxi!" I scream. But with no explanation and not so much as an *au revoir*, I am dumped in the backseat of the cab, left to watch as my "fellow" Westerners return to their snooty obscurity. I turn to the driver. "Doctor!" I beg.

The taxi ride is excruciating. I feel like I'm in a dryer, spinning and crashing against rooftop and doors, each jolt a catalyst for a searing lash of pain, a surge of fever and the urge to go stark-ravingly insane. Finally, the taxi reaches Pondicherry. The driver pulls up screeching to a white building. He helps me from the cab, carries me through the front door, down a hallway and into a dreary office. The walls are lined with glass cabinets, shelves crammed with beakers and jars. There's an unshaven man sweeping in the corner. He and the driver exchange words. The driver sighs heavily and motions for me to sit.

"Doctor not here," he says. "He come back tomorrow."

"Tomorrow?" I gasp. "I can't wait until tomorrow!"

The driver once again converses with the sweeper then looks at me.

"This man, he help you," he says.

"Who? The janitor?" I say, but before I can object, the man lays down his broom, opens one of the glass cabinets and produces a long syringe.

"Wait a minute -" I say, but just then a bolt of pain slices through me, shoving me from the chair to the floor - which I must say, despite the pain, *is* nicely swept. The janitor approaches. I'm too weak to resist. He stabs me with the needle, injecting me with *Javex* for all I know. Within moments, I become woozy. The pain decreases and with it all bodily control. The two men lift me off the ground, but not before I've left a yellow puddle on the once clean floor. They wipe me off - discreetly - then carry me out to the taxi.

We drive away. In a daze I watch the sights of Pondicherry whisk by - pastel pink buildings, French-style terraces from colonial days. We stop for petrol at an Indian Oil station. A sign reads:

I swoon from the heavy dose of drugs, thinking, what if I die? "Don't let them take my eyes!" I cry to the driver. He shimmies his head nervously, cooing in a tone as though he were calming a lunatic, "No eyes. No eyes, Baba."

Once more on the road, we pass another sign:

"I can?" I think in my delirium. "How?!"

Some time later, the taxi stops at the Hotel Surguru. The driver once again bears my limp body, this time to the reception, then to a room, laying me gently to bed before retrieving my luggage. Upon his return, I manage to regain just enough coherence to pay the man generously. He exits quietly, leaving me to wallow in a drugged-up euphoria. Finally, once again, I pass out.

Another two days lost to unconsciousness. That Javex sure packs a punch! I wake with a bruising headache, a dull throb in my side, and - ow! - I seem to have developed a hemorrhoid. I stagger to the bathroom, nearly frightening myself in the mirror. It's always alarming to realize you look as bad as you feel. I'm as pale as a ghost - almost as though I'd been bleached from the inside.

I drag my body out of the hotel in search of food and water. It is a gray, oppressively muggy day. A strong wind kicks up dust in the busy street. My head feels like it's inside a tuba, the roar of the traffic pulsating against my temples like a horn section gone mad. I stumble back into the hotel, purchase a bottle of water from the front desk and return to my room. The city is too hectic. I need a place to retreat and recover but feel too weak to endure another brutal bus ride. Once again, I consult the guidebook. Luckily, not far away, in another part of Pondicherry is a guesthouse run by the Sri Aurobindo Ashram with balconied rooms facing the sea. Sounds heavenly!

Within an hour, I arrive at the Park Guest House and settle in to the peaceful routine of ashram life. All day long, I lie in bed or sit cross-legged on the balcony trying to meditate, listening to the crash of the waves. I am hoping to recuperate on my own. The last thing I want is to seek out further janitorial - or should I say, medical - attention. By late afternoon, ominous clouds have begun to darken an already turbulent sea. Thunder rumbles like distant drums. By night, the rains begin. Next morning, I awake to pounding from outside. I look out the window. Rain is crashing down upon the ocean. Waves are bucking and heaving. The wind is ferocious, bending trees in half, gusting with un-restrained fury. I open the door. It is almost ripped instantly from its hinges by the wind. I wrestle the door shut then curl up cowering on the floor.

For seven days, the storm rages. Hour after hour, all I can do is witness the beating inflicted upon Pondicherry. I am restless, claustro-phobic, but at least I have a safe haven. Luckily, the restaurant attached to the ashram remains operational. At meals, I try to converse with some of the other residents but they seem more interested in silence. I'm beginning to think Pondicherry is not a very friendly place. Finally on the tenth day, the demon wind dissipates and clouds disperse. A crack of blue appears in the sky. An eerie calm accompanies the first hazy rays of sun. I pry my door open and walk tentatively to the sea. The waves ripple harmlessly on the shore. The wind is now a soothing breeze. You would think nothing had happened.

The scene in town paints a different story. Shingles from rooftops litter the streets; metal debris like shrapnel covers the ground. Roads are mined with puddles and potholes, wreaking havoc on vehicles and pedestrians alike. Pastel homes that appeared so colourful only days before are now muddied and gray. Whole shanties have been washed away. Everywhere I look, people scrounge for remnants of their scattered lives. A family displaced, huddles in the doorway of a torn-apart building warming by an open fire, but their eyes are cold. I walk by them with my head down, afraid to look, afraid to really see the destruction, the eyes of the beggars all around, their ragged clothes, matted hair, their misery, their anger. In Canada, I'm not a rich man, but in India I might as well be Norman Rockefeller. How do the people here see me as I pass them by? How do they feel when I avert my eyes? How many before me have refused their cries?

I am deep in thought, when all of a sudden a violent thud crashes down on my back, dropping me to one knee. I look up, alarmed to see an old beggar standing over me, eyes wild, fists in the air, hissing at me, spitting at me, threatening me in his native tongue. My heart beats furiously. I rise in defence and yell sharply, "Get away! Get the hell away from me!" I prepare to strike, but before I do the old man retreats, still muttering. In a panic, I run and flag down a rickshaw. In the backseat, I am shaking, sweating, enraged and ashamed. Can't I just have one moment's peace? Is there no escape? What did he want? What have I done? Then it dawns on me - it's bad enough to flaunt clean clothes and money, but it's worse to try to hide from the reality of poverty. Did the old man want money? Maybe. But I figure, even more, he wanted to be seen. India demands to be seen. The more I veil myself, the more she will slap me in the face, open my eyes.

I didn't want to acknowledge India's anger. Anger has been the greatest curse on my life. My father was a volatile man, torn between great love and terrible anger, and I have been my father's son: compassionate, soft-spoken, but all too ready to thrash out like a caged tiger. My anger has hurt more people than I dare to admit. It has scared away just about anyone who has ever tried to love me. No wonder I'd rather bury my head than risk even the possibility of confronting anger.

But there is no hiding in India. There is no fantasy burger stand waiting for me around the corner, no haven of Western culture. Only India. She is all that exists for me now.

Next morning, I pack my life on my back once again and head to the bus station, destined for the temple-town of Thiruvanamalai. This time though, I'm driving straight into the heart of the city. No more detours.

Chapter 7

THE DEEP PLUNGE

When I said "no detours," perhaps I should have added, "within reason." Had I known the direct course to Thiruvanamalai would take my bus and I not *over* but *through* a rushing river, I probably would have been more careful with my intention.

Not an hour out of Pondicherry, my bus encounters a slight road-block. A section of the highway has been completely washed out by the recent tropical storm. Where once was a paved roadway, now roars a frothing, white set of rapids. The bus slows to a halt, parking uneasily at the edge of the torrent, revving in indecision. All chatter stops, suspended by an ominous silence, as my bus-mates and I inch forward to assess the situation. It doesn't exactly look like smooth sailing, especially for a bus.

The driver lights a cigarette, burns it to a butt. He prays feverishly to the altar arranged on his dashboard, kisses the cartoon image of his god and wraps an extra wreath of flowers round the rear view mirror. My bus-mates collectively stifle their breath awaiting his decision, tension dripping from each brow, eyes glued to the driver's hand shakily gripping the gearshift. Hmm... if the locals are afraid, I should be terrified.

Suddenly, the driver cranks into first gear, lurching the bus into motion, perilously submerging the vehicle into the raging rapids. The bus teeters as it touches the first rock. Water crashes against the tottering wheels. A slip forward almost tips us over, but our grip is regained at the last possible instant. Slowly, but never surely, the bus turtles its way to safety on the opposite shore, followed by an eruption of cheers, claps, sighs! The driver wipes his forehead with a hankie. A fat man hugs me, a thin man kisses my cheeks, until with relief, we all settle back in our seats for the ride. The rest of the outing is uneventful, relaxing... just the usual amount of near accidents and reckless speeding.

We arrive at the Thiruvanamalai bus station at three in the after-noon. I never thought I'd be this overjoyed to see a chaotic Indian town.

The insanity is downright charming. I positively welcome wading through masses of people, revel in the sticky compression of bodies and happily agree to pay a rickshaw driver many times what I know I should. Hey, I'm lucky to be alive!

"Take me to the Udupi Brindhavan Lodge," I say to the rickshaw driver, randomly selecting a name from the guidebook.

Once out of the bus station, I am amazed at how congested the streets are, countless times as dense as Madras even. Thousands upon thousands of people pack the way, impeding the progress of my rickshaw, indifferent to the danger of being run over. A lone policeman in full uniform and bare feet tries hopelessly to direct the onslaught of traffic. My driver honks and toots incessantly at the throng, which strangely does not disperse, but continues unfazed by the possible threat of an oncoming vehicle. The rickshaw bleats aggressively, until almost sleepily, the throng ebbs as one mass to the side, allowing us a few inches, then to our frustration oozes back to the middle, plugging the road once again. At this pace, it takes forever to reach the Udupi Brindhavan Lodge, whose vacancy is disappointingly filled by the time we arrive.

"How about the Trishul Hotel?" I ask, but we battle traffic only to find there's no room at that inn as well. Hmm... I never thought of making a reservation. Finally, I beseech of my driver as to whether *he* may know a hotel. An eternity later, we putter up to the doors of the Hotel Chicken (it's true), which sure enough has one room available, the size of a small coop. The Indian men who hang around the reception resemble gangsters and I think better than to inquire of them as to the unique name of their establishment, though it is pecking at my curiosity.

I drop my bag in my room and proceed outside. There is a jovial spirit in the air, a carnival atmosphere. People are grinning, at ease. Even in the near dark, I feel secure for the first time since being in India. I pass by an endless procession of carts selling bananas, peanuts, hankies and wristwatches. At one intersection, a crowd gathers tightly to partake in a raucous game of chance. At another, I purchase a green coconut that the vendor cracks open using a veritable machete, allowing me to suck up its sweet, tender milk through a thin, pink straw. This is just like a Fall Fair back in Canada - albeit slightly more sweaty - and I find myself searching the grounds on the off chance someone might be selling cotton candy. No such luck.

I enter a restaurant and check out the menu. The choice is limited to masala dosa, idli or thali. I never thought I would say this, but I'm getting just a little sick of thali. I decide upon masala dosa. In minutes, I am served a giant, hot, greasy rice pancake, wrapped around a savoury centre of curry-flavoured potatoes. The waiter hovers above me as I chew my meal, observing each bite with growing fascination as if he's never seen a white person eat - and maybe he hasn't. Finally, I feel obliged to speak, if only to momentarily disrupt his relentless scrutiny.

"Are there always so many people in Thiruvanamalai?" I ask.

"Oh no, tomorrow is very big festival," he answers. "Big festival. Rath Yatra. People come from villages far away to see."

"Rath Yatra? What does that mean?"

"Rath is like car, giant car," he explains, describing a massive vehicle of some sort to be driven through the streets the next day by a number of highly powerful gods - sort of like the "H-Indi 500," I think, trying to imagine the god Shiva behind the wheel of a gigantic, souped up Ferrari. In the past, he tells me, devotees were actually known to willingly lay themselves down on the road to be buried beneath the wheels of these cars in order to die auspiciously in the presence of their gods. Hmm... some kind of spiritual road-kill, I presume, thinking of all the racoons and skunks that have gone to heaven suffering the same fate.

"You like sweet?" my waiter asks as I finish my dosa.

"Sweet? Now that you mention it, I'd love something sweet. What have you got, cake?"

"Better," he says. "I bring."

I watch as he hurries over to a counter supporting two large uncovered trays buzzing with a frenzy of wasps and flies. Shooing the insects, he carves a square of something sticky, places it on a plate and delivers it to my table. Some of the flies follow. I look down at the beige, gooey treat then up at the waiter.

"Taste," he says.

"Oh, yeah. Right."

I raise the dessert to my lips then take a cautious nibble off the edge. Instantly, I am struck by a sickly sweet sensation so repulsive it causes an involuntary spasm in my stomach.

"It's good," I fib, trying not to regurgitate my dosa. "What do you call it?"

"Barfi!" the waiter exclaims.

I should have guessed.

The next morning, I arise early, leave the Hotel Chicken and take to the street, encountering wall-to-wall bodies eagerly anticipating the coming of the "car." Within moments, around a corner appears a colossus on wheels. This ain't no Chevy Van! Standing at least fifty feet tall, this "car" is comprised of a wooden platform high atop four stilt-like legs, pulled along by hundreds of men heaving on thick braided ropes, rolling forward on rounded rock tires reminiscent of vehicles in The Flintstones. It is spindly, gawky, off-balance and ready to tilt at the toss of a turban. The high platform is draped in ribbons, strewn with garlands of flowers and packed with whooping and hollering worshippers huddled around bronze and stone statues, waving to the crowd down below. Well, I suppose it's not everyday one gets to sit with their gods on a throne fifty feet from the ground.

I follow the parade for about an hour before it disappears round a bend amidst drumming and revelry. The crowd then begins to disperse, moving like small armies in every direction. I join the flow that is heading back towards my hotel and surrender to its pace, easing comfortably into the merry masses. Rickshaws toot. The crowd and I slowly ooze to one side then back to the middle. A taxi honks. The throng seems disinterested, but finally acquiesces, temporarily allowing passage. I continue, almost lulled by the comfort of warm bodies about me, when all of a sudden, I hear a call from behind, "Hello!"

I yawn, carry on, not even bothering to investigate.

"Hello!" I hear again. Yes, yes, alright, all in good time.

"HELLO!" the voice barks. Okay already! Don't you know how this works? I turn sharply as if to rebuke the outrageous impatience, only to find myself nose-to-trunk - yes, trunk - WITH AN ELEPHANT!!

"Aaaaaaah!" I leap backwards. What the heck is an elephant doing in the middle of downtown? I look up at its master, seated between massive ears.

"Hello," he grins.

"Yeah, hi," I reply, certain that the next time a taxi toots, I'll be the first aside.

Later that day, I decide to visit the Arunachaleswar Temple, hoping for a place to unwind after that morning celebration. As I approach, my jaw drops. This is not just your average temple. The structure looms above me like a mountain, ascending skyward to heights of worship heretofore reserved for the birds, spectacularly decorated with elaborately sculpted figures covering every square inch as far up as my eye can see. It's a high-rise apartment for the gods.

It costs me two rupees to enter the temple grounds. I pass through a gate, anticipating a quiet refuge. Immediately within though, I am taken aback with a barrage of sights, sounds and smells more akin to a Super Bowl rally than an austere religious haven. The temple confines are bursting with people of all ages, rich and poor, villagers and city folk alike. There are those tattered in rags and those elegant in silk saris. There are true devotees, bowing and chanting, and others not quite so pious, squatting, spitting or selling souvenirs. An offensively blaring loudspeaker barks out rapid fire announcements, almost crushing my eardrums with tin can tones, its short, staccato delivery reminding me more of a call to war than a prayer for peace. "GOD IS COMING" I imagine it saying. "THE WORLD WILL END TOMORROW! SHOP NOW AND SAVE AT SEARS!" - or something like that.

I wander about, collecting quite an adherence of admirers. People seem to follow me wherever I go in India, fascinated by my every move, by my hair, my green eyes, my clothes, and certainly by my camera. A man stops me, begging me to take his photo. His smile is so sunny, how can I resist? Eagerly he poses, grinning happily, slicking his hair, but just as I bring the camera into focus, his glowing disposition disappears. He turns deadpan. His torso tenses abnormally still, arms by his sides at military attention. It seems that in India, having your snapshot taken is very serious business. I feel like he's expecting me to shoot a gun, not a picture.

"Uh... smile," I say, trying to coax the cloud from off his face, but his lips remain rigid, cheeks remain taut. "Cheese," I say, but his sober expression only hardens. Finally, I sigh and snap the camera, when all of a sudden he begins smiling, laughing, congratulating himself on his dignified behaviour, gushing with relief at the release of tension. "Wait," I call out. "Don't move, let me take another." But no sooner do I point the camera than his face flops into an un-photogenic frown. I try everything to get him to smile, but it's no use. He seems determined to appear as if he were attending a funeral - that is, until after, of course, I have snapped another somber souvenir.

I continue my tour of the temple, my flock of admirers growing, lagging behind me as though I were a Hollywood celebrity or circus attraction, I'm not sure which, but I am developing a slight Messianic complex from all the attention. The leader of my admirers is a bald-headed, trident-toting, orange-robed man who speaks little English but manages to communicate with a complex series of hand signals. If he had a sock on his fist, he'd make one helluva puppeteer.

"Me Sadhu!" he says.

"Hello, Sadhu. Me - I mean - I'm Stew."

"What is your name?"

"Uh... Stew."

"Me English... very good, yes?"

"Oh, yes, very good -" I say, when abruptly he turns away from me, hailing my flock of admirers in the local dialect. Ten minutes later, he is still babbling excitedly, gesturing wildly in my direction. What could he possibly be telling them? I only said three things to him - hello, my name, and how good his English was - hardly enough material to create a theatrical event. Still, he circles me dramatically, pausing for effect. Who is this white stranger, I imagine him saying, where did he come from? Who cut his hair? He seems to be acting out my life story. The audience oooh's as he sobs at some tragedy unknown to me; aaah's as he laughs at some obscure comical event. I only wish my life were half as exciting as his portrayal. He is particularly enthralled by a small band-aid of mine, appearing almost frightened by the sinister plaster cloaking my middle finger. "It's a cut," I want to say, but I don't want to dampen the moment with anything as drab as the facts. Finally, I decide to leave my devotees to their imaginations and wave goodbye, eager to terminate our association. But hardly to my surprise, they follow behind. I rove about the temple, admirers in tow, wishing I had a better understanding of these strange religious rituals, wondering how this worship of idols translates so readily to so many as a path to higher spiritual ground. I turn to Sadhu to enlighten me, but he is still staring at my band-aid.

I pass a sign that reads: DARSHAN TWO RUPEES.

"What's darshan?" I ask Sadhu.

"Me look in god's eye, god give very good blessing."

"That's darshan?"

"Yes, Baba."

"You look in god's eye?"

"Yes, Baba."

"But, where's god?"

"In there!" he points inside a cave-like shrine.

"You mean the statue?" I ask.

He looks confused. "God," he says.

"So, you look at the statue and you get a blessing? That's darshan?"

"Me look god in god's eye, god give very good blessing," he says again, slower this time. It seems not even Sadhu's theatrics can decipher the deeper meaning for me. I decide to pass on the darshan, saving my two rupees for something a little more concrete. Maybe somebody here is selling cotton candy.

Suddenly, Sadhu becomes quite excited, dragging me over to where an even larger crowd has gathered. Squeezing to the front, I am shocked to find myself once again, closer than I ever thought I'd be to an elephant. Aaaaaaah! Now there's a place to keep a wild animal - in the temple! Actually, the beast looks quite docile, probably because it's chained to a post. Its body is adorned with elaborate red and yellow designs, its forehead painted with three white stripes. My guess is I'm looking at the largest worshipper of Shiva in all of India.

I watch, fascinated, as the crowd lines up, one by one eagerly presenting money to the immense creature. The elephant then gently, with its trunk, removes the rupees from their fingers, and pats each person in turn lovingly on the head.

"You go, you go," Sadhu urges me towards the front of the line. Well, two rupees to be blessed by an elephant - now there's a bargain not even I can resist.

The crowd is boisterous, applauding as I step before Jumbo. At first, I'm distracted by the attention and commotion, but then I notice the elephant's eyes; tranquil eyes, sympathetic eyes, captivating eyes. I watch, mesmerized by the elephant's soft stare, as its trunk sails through the air, resting with a mother's touch upon my hair. Suddenly, I am flooded with flushes of warmth, blissful sensations sweeping to my feet with intensity so unexpected as to wobble my knees. For a long moment, I seem suspended in a surreal silence, cocooned from the din outside, swimming in a calm so deep it tingles my fingertips and toes - so surprised, I could almost cry. In a daze I step back, light-headed and sit down. It is then I hear a whisper, and looking up, find Sadhu's smile.

"*This* is darshan," he says, and finally, I understand. To look in God's eye is to see God in all things - a statue, an elephant, or even a fellow human being - and perhaps this, above all else, is the greatest blessing.

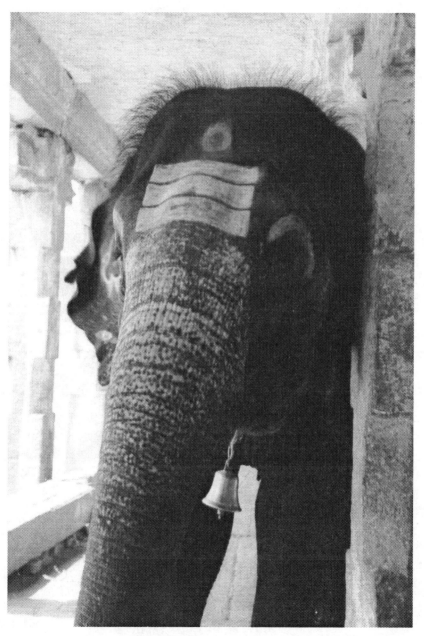

The largest worshipper of the god Shiva in all of India.
(Thiruvanamalia)

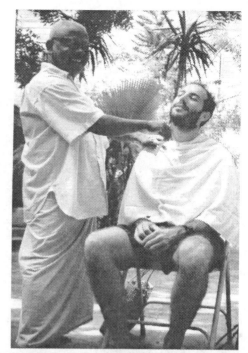

"Uh, excuse me.
Do you think you
could stare at the
camera *after* you've
removed your razor
from my neck?"
(Mahaballipurum)

"Hey! You! Eat my nuts! Eat my nuts!
Hmm... I wonder why business is so slow."
(Thiruvanamalai)

Shiva in "Wonderland."
Hanging out with the
Cheshire Cat.
(Madras)

And you think *you*
have a lot on *your*
mind!
(Pondicherry)

II

A
WORLD
TURNED
UPSIDE DOWN
IS BEST VIEWED
STANDING ON
ONE'S HEAD

Chapter 8

A GOD BY ANY OTHER NAME

I arrive in Kanchipurum, drawn by its description in the guidebook as being home to some of the holiest temples in all of India. Temples are to South India what castles are to the English countryside, casinos to the Riviera at Monaco, or canyons to the sprawling American Southwest. They're everywhere, defining the culture, shaping the economy, drawing tourists by the thousands to places that otherwise might never be visited. There are temples built before the time of Christ, temples carved into the walls of caves, temples towering over traffic and modern life, even temples where pilgrims have to line up in a cage.

In a shop in Kanchipurum, I discover a whole other kind of Indian temple. There, I find postcards depicting photos of religious carvings taken in temples in the northern town of Khujaro. The first image is of a buck-naked man with a salami-sized erection about to "mount" a young woman from behind. She is bent over a basin washing her hair. A second postcard portrays a relief painting of a buck-naked man with a salami-sized erection about to mount a *horse* from behind. (I'd hate to see the saddle sores after that excursion.) Though obviously unorthodox from a Western viewpoint, I can see how these sculptures would arouse worship in even the most atheistic of men. I know for myself, if only the synagogues in Montreal had been decorated more like these Indian temples, I might have grown up attending a lot more Jewish services than I actually ever did.

My first morning in Kanchipurum, I have barely emerged from my hotel, when I am beckoned over by a swarthy, young Indian man, leaning against a beaten-up rickshaw, eyes hidden behind dark glasses. Running a slow hand through his greasy black hair and smoking a bidi - a popular, slender, brown cigarette rolled from the cheapest and smelliest of tobaccos - he solicits me to take his whirlwind tour of the city's sacred sites: seven temples in two days for only a hundred rupees. He reminds me a little of an Indian James Dean, a rebel perhaps without cause, but not without charm, and I agree to take him up on his offer.

I am picked up that evening to visit the first of the temples. Though it is well past dark, James Dean is still wearing sunglasses. Looking cool is one thing, but I'm a little concerned when he speeds down an alley nearly careening headfirst into a wall.

"Are you sure you can see through those glasses?" I ask.

"No need to see, Baba, I am knowing the way," he says. Not surprisingly, this does little to comfort my nerves. The drivers in India are either the best or the worst in the world, I'm not sure which, but somehow, every time, I do seem to reach my destination in one piece.

At the temple, I leave James Dean to explore the inner sanctuaries. The ambiance at night is creepy. Sculptures peer out at me from behind pillars, coming to life in the surreal play of light. To my right is a figure with six arms, dancing. To my left is a demon in obvious need of orthodontistry. Looking down at me is an elephant-headed man with a size-able potbelly. All around me are grinning faces. I feel as though I am touring the disturbed mind of Salvador Dali, no longer able to discern between fiction and reality, gripped by the fear that if I linger, I might slip into a Kafkaesque nightmare and metamorphose into an Indian-sized cockroach. And if you haven't seen the size of cockroaches in India - they're frightening.

I cut my visit short and walk rapidly back to my rickshaw, recalling the first time I encountered strange images like those in the temple. It was in Toronto. I had just started psychotherapy and was being encouraged by my therapist to explore new venues of spirituality. She recommended yoga. I thought it sounded promising, meditative, and more importantly, a potential way to meet girls. That weekend, I entered the Sivananda Yoga Centre. Removing my shoes as the sign requested, I waited in the hallway for further instructions, but no one was around. Incense burned my nostrils. I tiptoed nervously in my stocking feet, cracking open a door to see if a class was in progress. Unwittingly, I stepped into an empty, candle-lit room. In one corner was an altar with flowers arranged around a black and white photo of a serene but shirtless elderly man. On every wall hung framed pictures of the most bizarre characters I had ever seen: a blue-skinned man playing a flute; a woman decked out in gold jewelry with multiple arms and a halo of light; a half-man, half-elephant, balancing on one leg in silk pajamas. This was too weird. I immediately fled the Yoga Centre and headed for the YMCA, deciding to seek both spirituality and girls in the safe context of an aerobics class.

That night, lying in bed, I am plagued by those same disturbing images and decide that at the next temple, I will hire a guide, someone to explain to me once and for all the meaning behind these extraordinary Indian characters. Bright and early, James Dean is waiting outside my hotel. At the first temple's gates, much as I expected, there is no shortage of willing guides. At least twenty children and adults inundate me, more than eager to escort me by the hand around the temple. I settle upon a barefoot young man in neatly pressed slacks who speaks a reasonable English. He sets his price for a guided tour at one hundred rupees, but I haggle him down to fifty, feeling proud of my newly honed bargaining skills. He proceeds to shepherd me through several different areas of the temple, pointing out a range of architectural anomalies of varying levels of interest. Finally, I indicate a statue of that ever-present pot-bellied, elephant-headed man.

"Okay, just who is that?" I ask.

"Baba Ganesha," he says.

Sounds like a Lebanese eggplant dip.

"Baba ganoush?" I say.

"No, no, not ganoush. Ganesh. Ganesha. This Hindu god of good fortune, remover of obstacles and god of telling stories. Ganesha, he told story of Mahabaratta."

"Mahaba... whatta?"

"Mahabaratta! This most excellent epic of Hindu literature."

"Okay. Who is that?" I refer to another statue.

"This Shiva."

"Alright, who exactly is Shiva?"

My guide proceeds to bestow upon me an invaluable lesson on Hindu deities. Apparently, there are an astounding number of Hindu gods - *three hundred million*, give or take a few. What's more astounding, I think, is that someone actually counted. Now, all Hindu gods, I am told, spring from an eternal, formless source known as Brahman. Of all the gods, there are three main ones: Brahma, Vishnu and Shiva. Brahma is considered the creator of life, Vishnu the sustainer of life and Shiva, the destroyer. The three together maintain and oversee the worldly cycle of life and death.

Interestingly, Hindu gods do not necessarily have just one name. That would be too simple. Shiva, for example, has *one thousand and eight* names, including Pashupati, the champion of animals and Nataraja, Lord of the Dance. He is also Lord of Yoga, Master of the Himalayas, the source of the holy river Ganges, a lover of marijuana, and the ideal husband. He is often portrayed carrying a miniature hand-drum and a three-pronged trident, with blue skin, four arms, long matted hair and a wardrobe consisting of nothing but a tiger-hide loincloth. Well, I guess that's somebody's idea of an ideal husband.

The god Vishnu, on the other hand, has only twenty-two names, but lest he get an inferiority complex, his incarnations are amongst the most important in Hindu lore. His alter egos include Rama, Krishna and Buddha.

Prince Rama is the bold hero of the mythological literary epic, The Ramayana, revered for valiantly liberating his princess Sita - with the aid of Hanuman, the monkey-god - from the evil clutches of the demon-king Ravana. In the course of The Ramayana some fantastical events occur. At one point, Rama leaves behind his sandals - yes, his *shoes* – to govern over his kingdom while he is off on his rescue mission, authorizing them not only to *stamp* out crime but also to *put their foot down* if necessary to ensure social order. At another point, Rama's brother, Lakshmana, does not sleep for *fourteen years* while on guard duty - and that without the aid of a single cup of coffee. And still at yet another point, Hanuman, the monkey-god, unsure as to which Himalayan herb might redeem Rama's faltering health, incredulously single-handedly carries the *entire* mountain through the air in order to deliver the correct cure. In the end, good eventually triumphs, evil is appropriately vanquished and plausibility is often stretched.

Krishna is the eternal flute-playing romantic, usually depicted serenading beautiful shepherdesses or "gopis" who don't seem at all put off by his blue skin or by the fact that he is loosely committed to his main girlfriend, Rada. Such is the magnitude of Krishna's love, too grand to be limited to one woman. Krishna and Shiva seem to be the most popular of all the Hindu gods. Their images pervade the cultural psyche of India the way Star Wars or Batman dominate the West.

And in case they get lonely, many of the Hindu gods have female consorts, filling the role of heavenly wives. Brahma's consort is Saraswathi, not only the goddess of learning, but also reputedly the most beautiful goddess of them all. Vishnu's wife is Lakshmi, no slouch herself. She's the goddess of wealth and by anyone's estimate, though not considered the *most* beautiful, is still pretty darn sexy. Shiva's wife is the powerful, popular and pretty Parvati. Parvati is a force in her own right and is worshipped in many different forms. Her multiple personas include: Devi, Mahadevi, Shakti, and Durga, to name but a few. Depending on the time of the month, Parvati can either be Devi, known as the great mother; Shakti, the creative, sexual force; or Durga, the fierce destroyer whose gruesome slaughter of the buffalo-headed demon Mahishasura is a well-known Hindu myth. Talk about PMS!

The goddess Kali, "the black one," luckily never got married. She's fickle, bloodthirsty and downright fearsome. She has coal-black skin, a blood-red tongue, wears a necklace of human heads and has a penchant for dancing on Shiva's dead body. Not exactly the cover girl for Bride's Monthly. What's more, her devotees throughout history have been known to appease her legendary hunger for carnage with, believe it or not, *human* sacrifice - a rite that was only outlawed as recently as the early nineteenth century. Now, *that's* scary.

My guide is prepared to expound further, but I'm beginning to get a headache. After all, I've had enough trouble in my life wrapping my mind around a single Judeo-Christian God, let alone three hundred million Hindu ones.

"You know story of Ganesha?" my guide entices me with one more tale.

"Uh, no, I don't."

"You like to hear?"

"Aw, sure, go ahead." I suppose my brain can handle a bit more information. What he tells me goes something like this...

One day, while the god Shiva was away on business, his wife Parvati decided to have a son, and, being a goddess, conveniently skipped not only the act of conception but the nine months of pregnancy as well, conjuring a young boy out of thin air and affectionately naming him, Ganesha. So pleased was she with her accomplishment that she chose to celebrate with an aromatic bath, enlisting Ganesha's help in guarding the door while she soaked inside.

"Don't let *anybody* in," she commanded.

Soon after, Shiva unexpectedly returned home. "Where's Parvati?" he asked of the strange boy.

"In the bathhouse," Ganesha answered.

"Well, get out of my way and let me in," Shiva demanded.

Ganesha, being the dutiful son, followed his mother's instructions to the letter. "Sorry," he said, denying Shiva entry.

"Sorry?" Shiva questioned.

"Sorry," Ganesha repeated.

"Why you little upstart!" Shiva bellowed and without a moment's hesitation, brandished a gleaming sword and lopped off the rude boy's head with a single swish. Parvati, hearing a thud, came running.

"What have you done?" she shouted at Shiva. "That is your son!"

"It is?" Shiva exclaimed. "Why are fathers are always the last to know?"

"Don't just stand there, do something!" Parvati wailed.

Quickly, Shiva ordered a number of his attendants off to the woods to retrieve the head of the first being they found. After an hour, they returned with an elephant's.

"Not exactly what I had in mind..." Shiva thought, but he knew he had to act fast. With lightening speed, he performed a miracle of surgery, grafting the elephant's head onto the dead boy's body. Within moments, Ganesha regained consciousness.

"My baby!" Parvati cried.

"Uh, hello, son," Shiva said, staring into the eyes of the elephant-headed boy. "Uh... want a peanut?"

"I'll give you a peanut," Parvati scolded. "You're just lucky my baby's still alive!"

"That's some story," I remark to my guide.

"Ganesha is very lucky god."

"Yes, I can see that."

"You like I show you something," my guide asks suddenly.

"Uh, sure."

Without further elucidation, he grabs me by the hand and begins leading me down a series of narrow passageways. For twenty minutes, we twist and turn up dilapidated stairways, squeeze past barriers of rubble, until finally we reach a dead end. Propped up against a wall is a decrepit wooden ladder.

"Come, come," my guide says, encouraging me onto the first rung of the uncertain ladder. "Go, go," he eggs me upwards, until I emerge in some sort of attic whose floor is like a well-baked pie crust, seemingly solid, but dangerously on the verge of crumbling. For a long moment,

I'm too afraid to move, cringing in terror at the steepness of the route I've just traveled. How am I ever going to get back down?

My guide scoots up the ladder behind me and bounds into the attic, scurrying across the room to an open window. "Baba, look see," he calls out, motioning for me to join him. I hesitate. "Baba, come, come!" he urges me, until tentatively, I crawl across the creaking floor and lean past him, when all of a sudden, I lose my balance and nearly fall out the window.

"Not so far!" he cries, pulling me back from a potential plummet hundreds of feet to the ground below.

"Why didn't you warn me?" I shout.

"I said *look*, not jump!" he says, wiping his brow with a hankie.

After a few deep breaths, we both settle down. It *is* a marvelous view - once I get over my high anxiety - a panorama of lush, green countryside and a velvety, blue sky.

"Okay. Time for going down," my guide decides abruptly.

"Going down?" I shudder at the thought.

"Yes, but first you pay. One hundred rupees."

"One hundred rupees? We agreed on fifty!" I protest.

"Okay, see you at the bottom."

"Wait!" I screech, begrudgingly handing him a hundred rupees - so much for my brilliant bargaining. Shakily, I am aided down the tenuous ladder, led past the labyrinth of stairs, until once again on level terra firma, I burst out of the temple into the sunshine, so thankful for my life, I consider kissing the ground – but hey, this is India, let's be reasonable.

Chapter 9

Sikh And Ye Shall Find

Across the street from my hotel, a man is renting bicycles. I am terrified of bicycles. I have only been on a bicycle once in my life. That was at the age of eight. My father took my brother and I out to an empty shopping mall parking lot with the intention of teaching us to ride. After a few attempts, my father prematurely released the bike and I crashed to the concrete, scraping my belly. That was it for me. I never rode again.

My father encouraged me to go out and practice on the street in front of our home, but I was too afraid. The outside world was a dangerous place, filled with menacing dogs and the cutting ridicule of neighbourhood kids. In retrospect, I was scared of almost everything growing up. I was petrified of drowning, frightened of cats, apprehensive about sleeping because of vampires in my closet. I never learned to skate or ski. It's a wonder I ever left the house, let alone learn to ride a bike.

But my childhood home itself fostered an atmosphere of fear. My earliest memories have me cringing before my father's frightening outbursts of anger. I vividly recall the way his cheeks would puff out and redden, the terrible heat his body would exude, the way his shouts alone could wound me, the way his belt felt upon my cowering back. My childhood offered no refuge of safety. Taunted at school, terrified at home, my small world became a breeding ground for adult phobias. Fear of abandonment, fear of rejection, fear of the future, I've got them all. And now here I am in India. What a place to try and run away from fear. Each day of my travels, terror presents itself in an array of subtle manners - queasiness at arriving in an unknown town, anxiety over having to speak with strangers. But that's the challenge of traveling. My inner resources are constantly being tested, building confidence in my innate ability to transcend any obstacle. Life at its best is a series of risks. Life at its worst is routine, boxed in at the edges by fear.

And so, spying those bicycles for hire, I become determined to "feel the fear and do it anyway." I march straight over and pay the vendor for half a day's rental, then walk the bike out of view, not wanting him to see that he's just entrusted his livelihood to a rank amateur. On the next street, I climb onto the seat and grab the handlebars, quickly realizing that I haven't the slightest idea how to start this thing. Every time I raise one or both feet off the ground, I lose my sense of balance, the bicycle wobbles and I must catch myself before crashing to the ground. I feel like a child again, afraid of being teased by curious onlookers. But at least here I'm a tourist and tourists are expected to act strangely. I ignore the stares and soon to the testament of my resolve, I am triumphantly coasting, managing to steady the bike almost into a straight line - that is, until I find myself swiftly approaching a congregation of reclining cattle and it dawns on me, not only didn't I know how to start this thing, I have no idea how to stop! I can just see it now, page one of the Times Of India: CANADIAN BEATEN TO DEATH AFTER REAR-ENDING REAR END OF INDIAN SACRED COW.

The bike accelerates out of control, propelling me into a near nose-to-rump altercation with the first bovine, when at the very last moment, seeing no alternative I leap recklessly from my seat, barely averting an international incident. If I were eight years old, that would be it. I would probably quit. But I am a man, gosh darn it! I will not be deterred. I dust myself off, hop back on the bike and after several tries, am pedaling down the lane again, this time gaining not only control and confidence but also speed. That is, until I spy a trinket-cart, way on the other side of the road, being pushed along wearily by a very old man. For no reason I panic, gripped by the irrational fear that I may lose command of the steering, and before you know it, I am doing just that. I am veering drastically and incomprehensibly completely out of my way, headlong into a totally avoidable - if only I were more competent - collision with destiny. CRAAAAAAASH!

When my head finally stops spinning, I find myself sprawled on the ground, legs tangled in bicycle bars, chest covered in trinkets and cheap jewelry, the cart completely upended, the owner standing over me, yelling in disbelief. But then a man from a nearby restaurant comes running to the scene and begins shouting at the cart-owner, seemingly accusing *him* of negligent responsibility. A heated war of words ensues, a crowd predictably gathers, and soon everyone is screaming, taking sides in the debate.

Dazed, I crawl out from under the wreckage and try to sneak away, but the man from the restaurant immediately comes to my aid, supporting me with his body as I limp into the relative sanctuary of his nearby cafe, away from the mob that by now is nearly brawling. For almost an hour, I hide inside the cafe, nursing a swollen knee and cold bottle of Limca, the Indian equivalent of Fresca (which is the American equivalent for what, I don't know). Finally, the cart is restored, trinkets replaced, and crowd dispersed. It now seems safe for me to return to my hotel, but then I realize to do so, I have to get back on that bike - with everyone watching. If I don't make them believe I can actually ride this thing, there will be no doubt how the accident really happened, and I'll probably have to fend off a lot of angry people. I'm sweating nervously by the time I lift the bicycle off the curb and balance myself uneasily on its seat. So far, every time I've wanted to get it started, it's taken me several aborted attempts, but now I don't have that luxury. I have to take off smoothly on the first try. "Feel the fear and do it anyway," a voice inside my head says. "Ah, shut up!" I say back to that voice. With all eyes upon me, I suck in a deep breath, and with a single, graceful, miraculous thrust, for the first time ever I'm able to set the bike rolling on my initial attempt!

Once out of sight though, I slow the bike down and dismount. Sometimes when moving through fear, it just makes more sense to walk.

Back at the hotel, James Dean is waiting to take me on the rest of my temple tour.

"Not right now," I say. "I'm a nervous wreck. Do you know a good restaurant? I'd like to buy you lunch." Nothing works up a better appetite than a morning of near-death experiences. James Dean drives us to a clean, no-frills establishment that offers the abundant choice of thali or thali. Being chronically indecisive, I enjoy the simplicity of dining in South India. "I think I'll have the thali," I say. James Dean orders the same.

Before our meals arrive, a child in a waiter's uniform appears and wipes our table with a rag so gray, I wonder if he's not actually making the table dirtier. As he's about to leave, I stop him. He looks at me with alarm.

"No, no. I have something for you," I say smiling, removing a packet of crayons from my bag.

The boy hesitates.

"Go ahead, take them. They're for you."

With a bow, he accepts my gift, racing off to the kitchen before I can change my mind. I glance over and notice James Dean pouting behind his dark glasses.

"What's the matter?" I ask.

He shakes his head frowning.

"What is it?"

He shakes his head again. How do you like that? Here I am buying him lunch and he's angry, possibly with me. Just then the child waiter skips by our table, enthralled with his crayons, grabbing James Dean's attention. An expression of terrible sadness falls on the rickshaw driver's face.

"WHAT?" I beseech of him. "WHAT?"

He looks at the boy then at me, when finally I realize - of course. *He* wants crayons! I reach down in my bag. "Here," I say, slipping James Dean my last packet. "Better put those away before the cook sees them."

I am losing my appetite watching the man at the next table devour his food with all the manners of a baboon. Eating with your hands is one thing, but witnessing someone lick gravy off their elbow is simply nauseating. Finally, our lunches do arrive. James Dean ravenously attacks his meal, polishing off a second helping before I'm even halfway through my first. I am amazed at how much food Indian men seem capable of consuming, especially considering how emaciated everyone looks. Then again, diarrhea does make the best diet. James Dean is well into his *third* portion, when it occurs to me that maybe he doesn't get to eat out in a restaurant very often. Carefully, I pry into the young man's life, wondering what he does for fun, how he spends his money.

"Money?" he laughs. "All money is to feed my wife and four children!"

"Four children?" I exclaim. "How old are you?"

"Twenty-three," he says.

"Twenty-three, and you have four children? How old were you when you got married?"

"Sixteen," he says matter-of-factly. "My wife, she was fourteen, the daughter of my father's friend."

Sixteen! Imagine that. All that responsibility at such a young age, and here I am over thirty without a care in the world.

"You are marriage?" he asks me.

"Married? Me? Oh, no. Not me."

"No wife? No children?" He looks at me as if *I'm* the strange one, and I realize how different our cultures are: he, a boy, prematurely made a man, and me a supposed man still playing like a boy.

After lunch, I treat James Dean to an ice cream and watch as he sits outside on the curb by the restaurant, gliding his tongue thoughtfully around the edges of his cone while rolling each one of those crayons I gave him slowly in his hands, lost in this rare opportunity to forget everything for a moment and once more be a child.

It is a busy afternoon visiting the last five temples on James Dean's tour. By the time we reach the final temple, I'm exhausted and would actually prefer returning to my hotel, but being obsessively value conscious, I am determined to get my full money's worth. So, leaving my sandals on the rickshaw floor - temples request bare feet as a show of respect - I drag myself once more through another temple door. When I return shortly after, I'm shocked to find the rickshaw gone. Anxiously, I search the temple's exterior, but James Dean has vanished and with him my shoes. For two hours, I wait, barefoot, alone, warding off beggars who smell easy picking. Finally James Dean putters up in his rickshaw. By this time though, I'm quite irate, not only dealing with hunger and sore feet, but irrational feelings of abandonment. It's one of those situations where irritation blends with relief, as I'm happy he's back and at the same time, pissed off that he left.

"Where were you?" I shout, feeling like a heel when he explains he was just at the doctor's, and really feeling small when for the first time since we've met, he removes his dark glasses, revealing pussy red eyes that squint from the glare of the sun. I slink into the rickshaw and sit low in the backseat. James Dean says nothing, just stares straight ahead and drives off. Fifteen minutes later, he pulls over in an unfamiliar neighbourhood.

"Aren't we going back to the hotel?" I ask.

"Come," he says, getting out of the rickshaw.

Oh, no. I shouldn't have yelled at him. Now he's probably mad at me, and here I am, totally at his mercy. I always thought this could happen, getting into strange rickshaws. What's to stop him from beating me, robbing me and leaving me for dead?

"Come," he repeats more forcefully, but I grab the door from the inside. If he wants my money, he's going to have to drag me out of here.

Then, I hear him laugh.

"What's so funny?" I ask defensively.

"You tourists, very strange," he says, explaining, to my embarrassment, that for keeping me waiting back at the temple, he's decided to surprise me with a visit to one of the living saints of India, the Shankarcharya of Kanchipurum.

"You mean you're not going to kill me?" I say.

"Not now, maybe later," he grins.

How do you like that? I yell at the guy and in response, he takes me to see a saint. If I felt small before, from now on just call me "Stuart Little."

I follow James Dean through a battered gateway into an open-air garden, where about a hundred men, women and children are sitting cross-legged, focused intently on a stage obscured by a thick maroon curtain. There is a low murmur of anticipation, when suddenly, the curtain is opened, revealing, to my surprise, a withered old man in orange robes, lying immobile on a hospital bed, flanked on one side by a man in starched white clothing. "Which one's the saint?" I wonder, fully expecting the man in white to perform some miracle healing on the grandfather in the hospital bed. But instead, one by one, members of the audience begin approaching the stage, bowing in reverence and making offerings to the grandpa. *He's* the saint. But he can barely move! He certainly doesn't appear to have the energy to bless anyone. Some devotees stop to ask questions, but the ancient saint can hardly speak. He seems to whisper to his attendant in white, who then conveys the saint's answers to the crowd.

Soon it is my turn to come forward, but I'm a little reticent. I'm all for being blessed, and I have no problem paying my respects, but inside I can't help pondering what's the point. The grandpa can't even lift his head off the pillow. The woman behind me though, urges me on, handing me an apple so I won't have to face the saint empty-handed. I thank her and advance towards the stage, bowing as I arrive within a few feet of the Shankarcharya. With great strain, the saint manages to turn his head on his pillow then whispers something to his aide. From then on, the aide acts as translator between me and the saint.

"What country?" the saint inquires through his aide.

"Canada," I answer.

"Good, very good country. What god?"

"Sorry?"

"What god are you believing?"

What god? Now there's a question I didn't expect to hear. While I do believe in God, I'm not a particularly enthusiastic fan of any of the world's religions. I just believe in a non-descript, universal, intelligent life force that exists within each person. How do I answer his question?

"Uh, I don't know the name of my god," I finally respond. "I just think that every time we humans behave with, say, compassion and generosity, we become more like, you know, God."

There is silence.

Hmm... perhaps I should have just said my god was "Ganesha." Before I can amend my response however, the aide has turned to the Shankarcharya, supposedly explaining to him what I just said. After several prolonged moments, the aide faces me once again, and smiles.

"The Shankarcharya says, if this is your god, then, you are Hindu!"

"Hindu? Me?" Something definitely must have gotten lost in the translation.

The aide continues. "Every Hindu, much like you, wishes to attain the saintly qualities of his gods, Rama, Krishna, Vishnu, Shiva. As you say, when you are generous, you are like god, like Rama. When you are wise, you are like Vishnu. When you are love, you are like Krishna."

Well, how do you like that? Forget Stuart Little and just call me Hindu Stew! I look up at the Shankarcharya in his hospital bed. His eyes are penetrating and I feel suddenly like a small child before him, just grateful to be basking in the warmth of his attention. Though obviously frail, incredibly, he seems to be beaming compassion, not only at me but beyond me, beyond his devotees, beyond this garden, beyond Kanchi-purum even. I feel, strangely, yes, as though I am in the unlikely presence of "God" - no, not *one* God, it's more powerful than that. I feel as though I am in the presence of three hundred million gods, all at once.

Back at my hotel, my cheeks are still tingling. I can't wipe the grin from my lips. Though the day has been stressful, I find myself peaceful, as though all tension has been washed from my soul - now that's what I call "Darshan." James Dean, as ever in dark glasses, leans on his rickshaw, smoking a bidi, our tour now over. I thank him sincerely and bid him farewell, paying him the hundred rupees I owe and slipping him an extra two hundred for some much needed medicine and perhaps a restaurant outing for his young wife and rapidly growing family.

Chapter 10

FOR RICHER OR POORER

Even though I swore in a million years I would never return to Madras, wouldn't you know, I find myself back on a bus, heading nowhere else but straight there. I really have very little choice in the matter. Madras, being the largest population centre in South India, also offers the only bus and train connections to the destinations I hope to visit next.

So, from Kanchipurum, I travel an uncomfortable six hours only to return to somewhere I can't wait to leave. Sitting in my seat, I can feel my anxiety escalating with each moment that brings me closer to the city where I first landed as a cultural virgin in India. I remember with dread the alarming shanties, the mobs of pedestrians, the aggressive street urchins of Madras, and as I enter the city limits, I am a nearly certifiable nervous wreck. But the thing that truly shocks me, as the bus indeed passes by those familiar mobs and shanties, is that I am actually not at all shocked. I seem to have developed a hardened outer shell of sorts. I may actually be getting used to India. This time, upon my arrival in Madras, to my surprise, I'm familiar enough with the guidebook to choose a clean and reasonable guesthouse - The Broadlands - and astute enough in warding off the masses to attempt an exploration of Madras' downtown core.

And imagine my delight, after having given up all hope of finding a haven of Western culture in India, to discover just that in of all places, Madras. Imagine my glee, stumbling upon magnificently decadent Western-style five star hotels, patio restaurants canopied by palm trees, evening performances of Indian classical music and dance, waiters in black ties and red jackets, delicious continental cuisine. Veggie Burgers. Time Magazine. Maybe that travel agent from Toronto was right. Madras really does seem like the Paris of South India.

I'm having fun! People here are downright amiable, warm, willing to go out of their way to be helpful, always eager to offer directions - okay, usually *wrong* directions, but nonetheless, their intentions seem sincere. I can't believe this is the same Madras. Everything seems so different. But then I think, wait, maybe it's *me* who has changed...

Naah, it must be Madras.

That night, I venture out to a posh, five-star restaurant wearing my fanciest clothes: a white t-shirt with a yellow curry stain on the collar, blue baggy pants with a draw-string not only around the waist but around both ankles, and my Birkenstocks, no socks. It's not exactly evening wear. I'm not even sure it qualifies as casual attire. But it's the best I own, having packed more for comfort than for style. Still, I enter the restaurant, hoping to be seated but preparing myself for the embarrassment of being turned away. The maitre d' eyes me up and down, taking in the full extent of my wardrobe. He settles his gaze upon my face. I am about to save him the trouble and show myself to the exit when to my surprise he leads me graciously to a choice location in the dining interior. He bows as he hands me a menu. The waiters all treat me with the utmost respect. There can only be one explanation. I am white. Though I am dressed like a slob, I am treated like royalty by the grace of my light skin.

I peruse the menu. *Two hundred rupees* for vegetable curry? Good thing I am treated like royalty. Only a king could afford these prices. Just then, I hear a voice from behind and turn to see a young Indian man smartly dressed in an expensive cashmere sweater.

"Excuse me," he says. "I couldn't help but notice your shirt. You are from Canada, are you not?"

"Uh, yeah," I say, looking down at my t-shirt. The logo depicts a Toronto rock 'n' roll band, The Skydiggers. "You know them?"

"Oh yes, I have seen them many times at the Horseshoe Tavern. I am from Toronto as well."

"Really?"

"Oh, yes."

"Who would have thought? Small world, eh?" I say.

"Oh, yes - *eh*?" He shimmies his head.

"Come, join me," I say.

"Thank you." He pulls up a chair. We order two beers. "Actually, I am really from Madras, but am presently making my studies in computer sciences at the University of Toronto. One day, I hope to be a Canadian citizen."

"I wish you luck. What brings you back to India?"

"My best friend's wedding is tomorrow. He only met his wife for the first time yesterday, but I hear they are getting on very well."

"Arranged marriage?" I ask. The young man shimmies his head. I must admit, I find the concept rather perplexing. I can't imagine marrying someone you've just met, but then again, I can hardly imagine marrying anyone, period.

We dine together, myself on Aloo Gobi, or potato and cauliflower curry, my new friend, Raja, on chicken tikka and vegetable pakoras. Over coffee, Raja announces a brilliant idea. "Perhaps you would like to attend tomorrow's wedding as my guest? Meet my friends?"

"Oh, I couldn't. You don't even know me."

"Come, come, you must. We are practically brothers, countrymen. You will find it quite interesting. Good music, good food. I won't let you refuse. Nine o'clock tomorrow morning, I will pick you up at your hotel."

Indian hospitality is definitely grander than any other I have encountered, reaching far beyond the protective nature of Westerners. Well, how can I say no? It's not every tourist who is invited to witness a traditional Hindu wedding, and besides... did he say free food?

The next morning, I purchase a spiffy outfit, my own Salwar

Kameez, so that I may be dressed presentably for the wedding. I also decide to treat myself to a five-rupee shave. The barbershop I enter is like most in India, a dirty stall plastered with posters of Bombay movie starlets and *Baby* Ganesha. It is exceedingly busy and I'm about to leave when the owner rushes up and begs me to stay, insisting upon finding someone to cater to my needs. He disappears briefly into a back room, emerging with a nine-year-old boy carrying a broom. Not the janitor again! The broom is whisked out of the boy's hand and replaced with a freshly loaded razor.

"I don't think so," I say, but the owner assures my satisfaction if I stay.

It starts off well enough. The boy seems competent, if unsure. He swirls up a hearty lather, slops it onto my face, then slowly runs the razor across my Adam's apple, seeming to linger an excessively long time about my jugular. "Hey," I'd like to say. "I only wanted a shave, not a game of Russian Roulette." But I hold my tongue. No sense in startling the boy when my throat is on the line. After several tense seconds, the boy miraculously manages to remove most of the stubble without severing my neck. He lets out a huge sigh. I'm not sure who's more relieved - me, or the boy. From there, things proceed relatively smoothly up along my cheeks... that is, until the boy arrives at my upper lip. Then I see his hands begin to shake. My immediate instinct is to leap to safety out of the chair. But before I can act, the blade jerks clumsily up towards my nose, scraping ruthlessly that sensitive area of skin, instantly causing me to wince in pain. The boy looks panicked, but instead of stopping, he scrapes again. Now I'm the one who's panicked. I look in the mirror and notice a stream of red blending with the white lather. I'm bleeding! I peer over at the boy who is readying himself for another swipe.

"STOP!" I cry.

The owner runs over. "Very sorry! He is still learning."

"So what am I, his guinea pig?" I say.

"Oh no, Baba, you are no pig," the owner quickly qualifies.

Well, I may be disfigured, but at least I'm respected. I'm just glad I didn't ask him to trim my nose hairs. Ouch!

Back at my hotel, at two minutes past nine, Raja arrives to take me to the wedding. We drive across town, Raja chattering excitedly, finally parking before a large arena-like building. He escorts me inside into a grand hall decorated in the richest of gold and red hues. There must be over four hundred guests present. There is a band playing a joyful melody on flutes and drums, incense is smoldering, a feast is served. The actual wedding ceremony proceeds the entire morning on an elevated stage, orchestrated by a bald-headed Brahmin priest who chants mantras, performs pujas, burns offerings. Everyone is dressed in luxurious silken ceremonial clothing. The bride and groom are elegantly handsome. The groom's cheeks are flushed from all the attention. The bride's hands and feet are painted in burgundy swirls. Her long eyelashes flutter under her veil.

Raja introduces me to ten of his good-natured friends who immediately embrace me as one of the gang. We are just becoming acquainted when without warning one of them drags me protesting into the centre of a frenzy of dancing. Hundreds of people surround me. Everyone is clapping, prodding me to show them some fancy Western steps, but I feel embarrassed, self-conscious. I politely attempt to leave the circle, but the crowd won't let me, crossing their arms, laughing, obstructing my way. Finally, I think, "Ah, what the hell!" and decide to join the party. Abandoning all inhibition, I begin twirling recklessly, twisting with delight, hands in the air, creating an original choreography somewhere between Fiddler On The Roof and The Arabian Nights.

After the wedding, Raja invites me back to his sister's apartment. All of his friends are meeting there for an after-wedding celebration. When we arrive at the apartment, to my surprise, it resembles any two-bedroom flat you might find in downtown Toronto. I am told to make myself comfortable while Raja, his sister and their friends change from their formal outfits, but instead of donning saris or the skirts I'm used to seeing men wear in South India, they all recline in blue jeans and sweat-shirts advertising American Universities. It seems that all of Raja's friends have studied in North America. Most of them are computer programmers. One friend is an architect. Raja's sister is a psychologist, and his cousin, also a woman, a fashion photographer. This is a whole new side of India to me. All of Raja's friends speak with a liberal usage of slightly outdated American slang. One, in particular, Shoshidar, is always telling me to "Check this out!" or claims he might, "Freak out!" he's so excited. Shoshidar lives in nearby Karnataka State in the city of Bangalore, which just so happens to be exactly where I'm heading next, so we agree to travel there together by train - first class.

The next morning, Shoshidar picks me up in a taxi and we proceed through traffic to the hectic Madras train station. Emerging from the backseat, I am perturbed to find that we literally have to step over hundreds of people camped on the hot concrete in order to enter the terminal. Now I've seen street people back in Toronto, sleeping on sidewalks, wrapped in old newspapers with seemingly nowhere to go, but I've never witnessed desperation of this magnitude in one place. It leaves me rather shaken. Thankfully, I am with Shoshidar. He leads me through the sea of bodies without incident, finds our seats without interference, but as we wait for the engines to engage, it seems the street people have entered the train.

One by one they parade by me, a procession of the downtrodden and the deformed, tapping me on the knee or grabbing at my hand, begging rupees. An emaciated boy, crawling on the floor, wipes the area beneath my feet with a filthy rag then meets my eyes, hoping for money. As he moves on, a sad-eyed girl performs listlessly on a battered old hand organ, while her sister who's only three sings a melancholy melody. Next, a man dressed unconvincingly as a woman, with exaggerated rouge-circled cheeks, invites charity but receives mostly ridicule as he sways clownishly down the aisle. Just behind him, a boy with lifeless legs wrapped over his shoulders, slithers by me on his chest. But the most disturbing is an obviously distressed, pretty teenage girl with a sharp stick impaled through her lower lip, through her tongue, and further, through her upper lip, forming a sort of shish-kebob of her tongue, so she can't even close her mouth, let alone utter a plea. All she can manage is to moan, hand outstretched.

But Shoshidar dismisses the beggars, telling me that for the most part they are organized, belonging to a mafia, under the direction of sinister crime lords. If given the opportunity, Shoshidar informs me, most would choose begging over the chance at finding honest work. Parents, he claims, are actually known to deliberately mutilate their children at birth so that later they will invoke greater sympathy and thus perversely increase their value as beggars. Shoshidar seems to take their distress in stride, cynicism curbing any inclination towards sympathy. But I find it impossible to be so callous. I'm more troubled than ever that such broad affluence can coincide so casually alongside such debilitating poverty.

The train finally begins to move, prompting the beggars to hurriedly return to the platform outside. Shoshidar shakes his head with disgust then buries his head in a local newspaper. I sit quietly the entire distance to Bangalore, staring out at the passing countryside, preparing myself for arrival in another worn-down Indian town.

But India has a way of constantly keeping me off balance. In some ways, I am more bowled over entering Bangalore than I was upon my initial visit to Madras, but for completely opposite reasons. Some parts of Bangalore actually resemble a cosmopolitan, Western city! Situated at a higher elevation than Madras, Bangalore enjoys a cooler, more bearable climate. Traffic is organized; roads are paved. Residential neighbour-hoods are interspersed with parks. The main street, Mahatma Ghandi Road (or M.G. Road) is a boulevard lined with upscale boutiques, shaded by tropical trees. Shoshidar tells me that Bangalore is the "Silicon Valley" of India, accounting for nearly one third of the nation's two billion dollar a year software industry.

Over the next few days, Shoshidar treats me to a view of Bangalore that compared to most of my trip so far, feels like an episode of "Lifestyles Of The Rich And Famous." We have dinner at Chung Wa, a delicious Chinese restaurant rivaling any in Toronto. We have banana splits at the Ice Cream Parlour And North Indian Restaurant, where the waiters race up and down the aisles, shouting, "What do you want? What do you want?" But they never actually stop long enough to take your order. Hmm... ice cream and North Indian cuisine. Can you imagine if Dairy Queen served Indian food? Sinking that little plastic spoon into a Peanut Buster Thali, Tandoori Blizzard, or Aloo Gobi Brownie Delight? Curried eats and cool treats, they can't be beat. Hard to believe not long ago my only choice was thali or thali.

And if the radical change in menu isn't enough, we see a Holly-wood movie, "Dick Tracy," in English with Hindi subtitles at a local cinema. I enjoy a swim in a heated pool at an exclusive health club, and finally, I'm introduced to the latest rage in Bangalore, an authentic English-style pub, with not only real draft beer but also dartboards. At times I completely forget I am even in India.

One morning over breakfast with Shoshidar, I mention how worn out I am feeling from all the non-stop sightseeing. "I need a break," I say. "I am thinking of going next to an Ayurvedic Hospital to totally relax and regain my strength. My travel agent back in Toronto told me the best one is in Phaikattussery. Have you heard of Phaikattussery?"

"Sorry," Shoshidar shrugs.

"It's in the state of Kerala."

"Never heard of it."

"It's supposed to be near the city of, uh, Trichur."

"Sorry."

"I have a phone number. Do you mind if I call?" Shoshidar is rich enough to have his own phone.

"By all means, go ahead," he says.

I dial the number, but the person on the other end has never heard of Phaikattussery.

"Try the operator in Kerala," Shoshidar suggests.

No luck. I'm beginning to wonder if this place even exists. I ask Shoshidar if mailing them a letter would be a better approach.

"You have an address?" he asks.

"Uh, yeah."

"You didn't tell me you had an address. Just go! This is India! You don't phone. You go! Just show up!"

"Just go?"

"Just go!" he waves his hands as if I'm crazy if I don't.

And so, that very evening, I reluctantly bid farewell to the world of the wealthy and board the overnight train bound for the city of Trichur in Kerala State. I must be insane, I think, heading off to a place I'm not sure even exists, but then again, insanity in a world gone mad might just be the most logical course of action.

Chapter 11

DOCTOR HEAL THYSELF

India boasts one of the world's oldest civilizations. Four thousand years ago, at a time when many of the earth's continents were still in cultural diapers, India enjoyed advances in arts and science, dance, music, literature and sculpture. The Hindu sacred scriptures, "The Vedas," were written 1500 years before the birth of Christ, impressively contributing to the development of such diverse modern disciplines as astronomy, mathematics, linguistics and medicine.

The Vedic system of medicine is known as Ayurveda, a deeply complex method of natural healing that focuses on balancing every aspect of one's life into harmonious existence. And if there is one thing that becomes achingly clear on the long, long, *long* train ride to Trichur, it is that both my health and sanity are in dire need of balancing. The idea of admitting myself to a hospital becomes more and more appealing with every hour spent in the cramped quarters of my third class compartment. I am more than ready to give Ayurveda a try.

Finally, I arrive in the city of Trichur and hop a cab to a nearby hotel. Once there, I immediately inquire of the clerk at the front desk if he has heard of a place called Phaikattussery. I may as well have asked him if he knows the way to San Jose. He calls upon the manager who is equally baffled. A map is pulled out, a crowd gathers, all to no avail. No one has heard of Phaikattussery. I am beginning to think I have come a long way for nothing, when someone walking by overhears. He is unfortunately unfamiliar with Phaikkattussery, but he knows of a remote village several miles from town called *Thaikattussery*. Coincidence?

"Does it have an Ayurvedic Hospital?" I ask. He's not sure, but he's more than willing to take me there in his taxi. Ah, the old taxi scam. Take the tourist on a magical mystery tour to a place that doesn't exist. I get it. But really, I have nothing save some rupees to lose, and he is after all my only lead, so I agree.

Next morning, my eager driver is waiting for me and an hour later, I find myself in a village so miniscule, I'm not surprised it missed the attention of the mapmakers. But sure enough, there on the right-hand side is a sign denoting an Ayurvedic Hospital.

"Thaikattussery," the driver announces. I thank him profusely, tip generously and enter the hospital door. Behind a desk is a man in military uniform, who with moustache and chubby cheeks appropriately reminds me of "Dr. Bombay" from the old Bewitched television show. He seems very surprised to see me.

"I would like to check myself in," I say.

"Oh, do you have reservation?"

"A reservation? I must be in the wrong place. I'm looking for the Ayurvedic Hospital."

"Yes, yes, this is Ayurvedic Hospital," he says. "It is just we have so few rooms to accommodate patients, we require reservation."

He pauses, smiling awkwardly.

"Oh," I groan, unable to mask the weight of disappointment and exhaustion in my voice. "Does that mean there's no room for me?"

"No, no!" he laughs, fumbling for his glasses. "You are very lucky. Most lucky! Patient just checked out this morning."

"That's great!" I say, perking up.

There is another long pause as Dr. Bombay eyes me up and down.

"Do you want my name?" I finally ask.

"Oh, name, yes, so sorry."

Another pause.

"It's Stew."

"Sorry?"

"My name. It's Stew."

"Oh, Sa-too, yes."

Still another pause. He is looking at me from different angles now.

"Is something wrong?" I ask.

"Oh yes, well no, you see... we don't receive many foreign visitors here. In fact, you are the first."

"Really?"

"Not many tourists in Thaikattussery."

"Well, perhaps if the town were on the map or if the telephone operator knew you existed, business would pick up," I say.

"Oh, telephone is more often out of service than in, and well, we like to keep our little village quiet."

"Of course," I say. "I'll try not to make too much noise."

"Oh, noise! Yes, ha, ha," he chortles. "What country?"

"Canada."

"Oh, Canada people are most funny. Please, allow me to tend to administration. I will inform the doctor of your arrival."

"You're not the doctor?"

"Me? Doctor? Ha, ha, Canada people very funny."

I am asked to wait in an adjoining office, a gray room, painted, like most Indian buildings, once long ago and never again. Half an hour later, a thirty-five year old man appears at the door. He has a black, shaggy beard, a round pot-belly, and is wearing a sweat-stained blue dress shirt over-hanging a long white skirt, which by now I have come to know is called a "dhoti." He stands there puffing on a cigarette, sipping from a steaming hot coffee.

"Uh, hello," I say.

"BUUUUUURP!" he belches loudly in my direction. At first, I take offense, but then reconsider. You never know in India, this may be some strange local greeting. He moves behind a desk and shuffles through a stack of papers, never taking his eyes off of me.

"Coffee?" he offers.

"No, thanks," I say.

"Cigarette?"

"Uh... no."

There is a prolonged silence as he searches his drawers for something, probably a lighter. "Are you the doctor?" I say finally.

"Oh, yes, doctor, doctor," he mumbles.

"And this is the Ayurvedic *Health* clinic?" I ask, starting to wonder.

"Oh, yes, very healthy, very healthy," he grumbles, sucking another drag off his cigarette.

"Uh, perhaps it's not my place to say so, really, but don't you think you're setting a bad example for your patients, drinking coffee and smoking cigarettes?"

"Oh, this?" he looks up at me and laughs. "Everything in moderation, my friend, everything in moderation. Especially if it helps you have a good bowel movement!"

Moderation. Well, it's hard to argue with logic like that. Lord knows I've done some pretty *extreme* things in the past in order to get my bowels moving. Maybe a little moderation wouldn't hurt.

"You know what?" I say. "I think I will have that cup of coffee."

"Excellent! Milk?"

"Sure."

"PARVEE!" he suddenly shouts at the top of his lungs, nearly shocking me out of my chair. "MILK COFFEE FOR OUR GUEST!"

"Acha," I hear a young girl's voice respond from the other room.

"Coffee coming right away," he smiles, turning back to me. "Now, what is your sickness?"

"Well, I'm actually not sick, really."

"Hmm... not sick, very interesting."

"I am exhausted, stressed out, and oh yeah, I've had two kidney stone attacks in the past month."

"Oh, kidney, very serious."

"Really?"

"Well, I cannot give you complete diagnosis. That is the job of Senior Doctor."

"You're not the senior doctor?" I ask.

"Ha, ha. Me? Oh, no," he says. "First there is Senior Doctor, then his son, Senior Junior, then there is me."

"You're not the janitor, are you?"

"Ha, ha, janitor," he laughs. "What country?"

"Uh, Canada."

"Oh, yes, ha, ha, Canada people most funny. Ha, ha. No, I am Junior. Junior Junior."

"Is it possible to see the *senior* doctor?" I ask.

"Oh, yes, all in good time, but first I must give you list of dietary restriction, foods you must certainly abstain from eating if you are to avoid painful kidney." He hands me a faded paper containing an inventory of over a hundred items. Red meat, dairy products, tomato, spinach, spices, pepper, and at least a dozen foods whose names I've never heard.

"I can't eat dairy?" I ask.

"Milk, butter, paneer," he answers.

"Paneer?"

"Cheese."

"I was afraid you were going to say that. I love cheese. No butter?"

"Sorry."

"Is there anything I *can* eat?"

"Um, rice."

"Great."

"Mild curry."

"Even better."

"And, oh, yes!" he says. "Beer! You must drink as much beer as you can."

"Beer?"

"Oh, yes, it will increase your urination and you must urinate to eliminate!" he sings as if chirping out some ad agency ditty.

Beer, rice or curry. Well, if those are my choices, it's a liquid diet for me. Meanwhile, a young girl has entered the room, placing before me a glass of cream-coloured coffee. I smile and thank her, raising the glass to my lips, when - "NO, NO! DON'T!" Junior Junior cries out, grabbing the beverage from my hands. "You must not drink that, Baba! It has *milk* in it. No dairy! Here, let me drink it for you. Mmm… yes, very good, very fine. Super-fine."

So much for moderation, I think, watching Junior Junior light up another cigarette to go with my coffee.

Next, I am escorted by Junior Junior out of the office and into a pale blue room buzzing with overhead fans. There I am led before the oldest-looking man in the world, seated high above me on a throne.

"May I present, Senior Senior," Junior Junior says.

Now, if I thought the Shankarcharya of Kanchipurum was old, this Senior Senior looks frail enough to be his grandfather. In fact, he looks old enough to have been a baby at the time of India's ancient Vedic civilization. Senior Senior gazes down at me absently then closes his eyes. After a prolonged moment, he appears to be snoring.

"And may I present also his son - Senior Junior!" Junior Junior announces abruptly, indicating a jittery man in his late sixties, nervously clutching a clipboard.

Senior Junior bows his head. "Welcome, welcome," he says then leans closer to his father. "Pssst! Wake up, Daddy."

"Huh?" Senior Senior's head snaps back. He looks around the room, stares at me for a couple of minutes, then croaks out three barely audible syllables - ugh, ugh, and ugh. In response, Senior Junior, as though having taken a cue from his father, immediately launches into an interrogation probing every facet of my life. Age, date of birth, country of origin, daily exercise, dietary habits, emotional state, and finally, and seemingly most importantly - bowel movement. Colour, consistency, frequency, odour - everything, I'm relieved to say, short of taste.

Just as I think Senior Junior is finally done, he then undertakes the lengthy process of translating this encyclopedia of information to Senior Senior. Junior Junior stands to one side through all this, chewing his nails, looking painfully bored. After an agonizing forty-five minutes, Senior Senior again mumbles three barely audible syllables - ugh, ugh, and ugh - in response to which Senior Junior immediately prescribes a treatment plan so complex, I am amazed he could decipher it from the limited utterances of his father.

For the next fourteen days - I am told - I am not to leave my room here at the Ayurvedic hospital, to ensure full and complete rest. I am to receive a hot oil massage every morning (sounds good), a hot bath massage every afternoon (even better), while specially prepared herbal remedies and a personally designed diet will be delivered directly to my door. I could get used to this! Lastly, alternating super and regular bustees will be performed daily upon my body.

"Uh, bustees?" I ask.

"Enemas," Senior Junior clarifies.

"ENEMAS?"

"Herbal enemas, super and regular. Very therapeutic," Senior Junior says.

"Even better than coffee and cigarette!" Junior Junior pipes in for the first time in two hours.

"Is it too late to get the next taxi out of here?" I moan.

"Oh, ha, ha, next taxi," Senior Junior laughs.

"Ha, ha, next taxi," Junior Junior joins in.

"Ha, ha, what country?" Senior Junior asks.

"Canada," I groan.

"Oh yes, ha, ha, Canada people -"

"I know," I sigh. "Canada people most funny."

"Oh yes! One more thing," Senior Junior exclaims. "Absolutely no fried foods. No fried foods whatsoever!"

This should be a change. I didn't think it was possible to eat in India without ingesting fried foods.

That afternoon, I am assigned *a man* to be my personal masseur and administrator of enemas.

"This is your man," Junior Junior proudly proclaims.

He is in his sixties, thin and shirtless, wearing nothing but a checkered skirt or "lungi." His hair is ridiculously greasy. He has a frenzied moustache, two front buckteeth, and seems entirely unable to speak, responding to my every query with nothing but a silently demented Bugs Bunny grin. I am increasingly overcome with the sinking feeling that I have landed in a situational cliché - the lunatics have taken over the asylum!

Worse yet, I've never had an enema before, and even under the best of circumstances would be leery if not severely disturbed at the impending invasion of my privacy, but the thought of receiving such a delicate procedure from someone as potentially crazed as Bugs Bunny has me sleepless my entire first night. The next morning, Bugs returns carrying a bulging black sac attached to a hose that narrows to a thin metal tip. I'm not sure if he's going to give me a "bustee" or play the bagpipes.

Now it is very difficult to accurately describe the experience of having an enema. Suffice it to say that once you have recovered from the initial discomfort of having your, ahem, anus penetrated, the subsequent cramping caused by water grotesquely distending the normal limits of your intestines makes one feel, without exaggeration, like a bloated balloon about to burst. But that's not the worst part. What really starts you perspiring is the irrational fear that if and when you do implode, everything and everyone within a ten-foot radius will be instantly plastered with flying fragments of your unrestrained feces. Somebody could lose an eye!

Frankly, I'd rather have that coffee and cigarette.

Having survived my morning enema, Bugs then motions for me to don a slinky piece of cloth.

"You want me to wear *this*?" I ask.

He stares at me grinning.

"How?"

Bugs gleefully cups the material under his genitals, securing it with a string around his waist.

"You want me to wear a loincloth?"

He nods vigorously, buckteeth protruding enthusiastically from behind his upper lip. Now, I must say, I'm a little self-conscious about being naked save a G-string in front of Bugs Bunny, but then again, he has just given me an enema, so I quickly shed my shyness and comply with the dress code.

"What now?" I ask warily.

Bugs then seats me on a low stool and begins massaging hot oil in sweeping strokes all over my body. At first, I must admit, I am a wee apprehensive - this is Bugs Bunny after all - but soon I relax, drifting off into a daydream in which I imagine myself to be Tarzan on a steamy jungle night, Jane by my side, her hands dripping with hot oil, caressing my biceps, fondling my chest, buffing my belly, searching beneath the folds of my loincloth - whoa! Wait a minute! This is getting a little *too* relaxing! I don't want Bugs getting the wrong idea. From then on, I make sure to think of nothing but boxing, baseball or bullfighting whenever Bugs' hands are snaking their way all about me.

That afternoon, Bugs leads me from my room to a basement chamber resembling a medieval dungeon. The walls are cool stone, the ceiling low. Bugs indicates for me to slip on my loincloth once again, only this time I am to submerge myself in a deep, recessed tub. I sigh as I sink to the bottom, but then to my surprise, Bugs' hands are with me in the water, rubbing my thighs - "Hey! What's the idea?" I exclaim. But soon the pressure of his fingers and the heat of the water combine to send me into a reverie of sensual sensation - uh, tempered, of course, by images of John Wayne, Clint Eastwood and Ernest Hemingway.

On day seven, I am disturbed to discover that I have developed a heat rash of sorts on my - well, how do I put this delicately - on my crotch. I reveal my symptoms, but not the location, to Junior Junior, who that evening returns with a remedy in the form of a yellow, oily paste.

"What is it?" I ask guardedly, holding it up to my nostrils.

"Ayurvedic cream. Mostly made from ghee," he says.

"Ghee?"

"Butter."

"Butter?"

"Yes, yes. Apply three times daily. Soon all itching will disappear."

"Let me get this straight. You're saying I can't *eat* butter, but it's okay to rub it all over my, uh… skin?"

"Yes, yes," Junior Junior asserts. "Rub all you like!"

Rub all you like. Precisely the words every man longs to hear about his genitals.

"Alright," I say. "I will."

I decide to follow the doctor's advice and for the next three days saunter about in the intense Indian humidity with butter smeared generously between my legs, after which, I am disappointed to say, not only has my itching persisted, but I believe I've sautéed my testicles! Well, it appears that butter does not make *everything* better, as the ad campaign used to claim.

Food at the Ayurvedic clinic comes straight to my door three times a day. When Senior Junior originally told me I would be receiving a personally designed diet, I had visions of succulent, exotic homemade recipes. What I get though is worse than prison rations. After a week of nothing but boiled rice in water, boiled rice in milk, boiled wheat in milk (I thought I wasn't even supposed to have milk) and boiled bananas, I am desperate for something tasty, something spicy, something fried. I recall Senior Junior's strict instructions, "No fried foods!" But at this point I no longer care.

The man from the kitchen who brings me my food is obviously unaware of my prescribed menu as I beg him one day to add something tasty to my dinner and he complies. That evening, he arrives with the usual bland, boiled fare, but this time he slips me an extra container filled with crispy, spicy, salty, fried pappadam crackers. I thank him profusely and so pleased is he to see my satisfaction that from then on, each meal includes a surreptitious packet of deep fried pappad.

One night though, as I am sucking the grease out of a particularly oily cracker, Senior Junior and Junior Junior barge into my room unannounced. Their greeting smiles immediately disappear as they spy me red-handedly about to devour an illegal pappad. Senior Junior, in particular, appears as if he is about to suffer an epileptic fit. His face turns purple. His shoulders vibrate. His lips quiver.

"N-N-N-N-N-" he stutters, trying to form with his tongue unspeakably angry thoughts. I know the timing could not be worse, but I find it almost impossible not to laugh.

"N-N-N-N-N-"

I chomp heavily on my lip.

"N-N-N-N-N-"

Tears well at the corners of my eyes.

"N-N-N-N-N-"

"Spit it out, man!" I think, barely stifling a guffaw.

"N-N-N-N-NO FRIED FOODS!" he finally shrieks, words now rolling off his tongue with the aggression of a rockslide. "Fried foods are absolutely forbidden! These bananas, are they boiled?" He grabs one of my bananas and crushes it between his fingers.

"Hey, I was going to eat that!" I protest.

"These bananas are not properly boiled!" he fumes. "What did you have for breakfast? For noon-time meal? Describe to me in detail your bowel movements!"

Question after question is fired at me without pause enough to answer.

"How could you allow this?" he barks at Junior Junior.

"It wasn't me," Junior Junior replies impotently.

"Aaaarrgh!" Senior Junior growls. He throws his arms up in the air and storms from the room.

Silence. There is a long pause as Junior Junior and I stare at each other not knowing what to say. Suddenly, Senior Junior reappears!

"WELL?" he ogles furiously at Junior Junior.

Junior Junior looks confused.

"COME ON! IMBECILE!" Senior Junior screams and departs once again, sheepishly followed by Junior Junior who by this time is also struggling not to giggle.

I sit, waiting, expecting them to return, but after awhile it becomes apparent they have gone... having left behind the contraband canister of pappad! Now what do I do? I know full well that I shouldn't, that it's better for me if I don't, that the success of my treatment could depend on it, but I'm like a fried food addict. I take one small bite, then another, then another, then greedily devour every last crumb of salty, oily cracker.

By the end I'm sweating with satisfaction.

There's nothing better than grease to douse the fire of a guilty conscience.

Day twelve. I am beginning to go a little stir crazy and decide to sneak out of my room, knowing full well that I am once again breaking the rules. I slip through my door, dart past the office and dodge down a nearby path into a grove of palm trees and downy grasses. Within moments, I am completely alone, having entered a zone of calm and tranquility I have seldom before known, far away from the electric sizzle of the city, far away from the yoke of responsibility, far away from the world of expectations and demands. I sit amongst fruit trees and flowers, swept gently by the warm breeze, surrendering to the perfect silence. For the first time since being in India, I truly allow myself to unwind, merging a growing sense of peace within with the almost surreal quiet outside. Time stops, boundaries become blurred, all thoughts pass. For a long, succulent moment I feel expansive, open hearted, free.

After awhile, I rise as if in a trance and wander amongst the beautiful scenery of Thaikattussery. It is like a dream, the serene, smiling faces, children playing cricket in an emerald field, women picking mangoes from their own gardens, the sun sleepy and low, the clothes bright purple and blue, the whites of teeth against ruby red lips, and nature, brilliantly displayed in a kaleidoscope of green. This is the India I have longed for, the India I have imagined. This is my India now.

By the time I reach the hospital, I am floating in an altered state of calm. I actually feel love glowing from within me - I think I may be having a New Age moment. It is then I pass a room whose open door reveals to me a young Indian girl apparently asleep on a bed. Her breath is laboured. Her family is gathered tightly about her, faces weary, sick with worry. And I want to rush in, share the peace I am experiencing, but I shrink from their pain. I return to my room, despondent. Later, I ask Junior Junior about the girl. She is in a coma, he tells me. Not even Ayurveda has been able to wake her. And suddenly, I am gripped by a terrible sadness, becoming acutely aware of the pettiness of my problems. A heat rash? A kidney stone? What stress do I know? What suffering have I to compare with the anguish of that dying Indian girl? What concerns do I have that hold any weight when measured against the tragedy of her family?

Then I remember, fighting back tears, that once it was me searching for answers round a hospital bed. Once it was *my* father dying, ravaged with cancer, suffering in agony and I could do nothing. I couldn't even tell him how much I loved him. Even on his deathbed, I was paralyzed by fear. I just watched him slip away, and with him all sense of life's meaning.

Now I see my father in that dying Indian girl. I see myself in the eyes of her family. And I realize we are all God's creatures subject to misery. We all bear the same trials. We all share the same woes. We all yearn to be loved. We all pray for serenity. All of us in our hearts are one and the same, just trying to live and die with a semblance of human dignity.

A seedling of compassion is planted within me in Thaikattussery. I sought out Ayurveda for physical healing. Little did I know it would take place on the level of my soul.

Chapter 12

HELLO, MANGO?

After fourteen days of imposed relaxation, I bid farewell to the Ayurvedic Hospital. I'm not sure my stay has cured my kidney, but I definitely feel rested and raring to go. Senior Senior, Senior Junior, Junior Junior and "my man" all congregate outside the hospital to wave me goodbye as I climb into a taxi headed for the train station in Trichur. Once there, I appreciate, perhaps for the first time, how peaceful the Ayurvrdic Hospital actually was. The noise of the station is an abrupt shock. The crowds feel like an unwanted intrusion. Waiting for the train, a man in thick glasses hurries towards me, stands altogether too close for my comfort, and asks excitedly if I am familiar with Archie Comics. "You, meester! You look just like Archie - in profile!" he tells me. I'm not sure whether or not to take that as a compliment.

I push my way up to a snack counter selling greasy egg omelettes and two types of almost identical deep fried snacks.

"What is that?" I ask, pointing to one.

"Bada-bada," the vendor says.

"What's the other one?"

"Badee-badee," he replies.

"Hmm... if I take one of one and one of the other, does that mean I'm getting Bada-badee?"

He just stares.

"Yabadabadoo?"

He just stares.

"I'll take both," I say. Some people have no sense of humour.

The train arrives and soon I am heading south through the state of Kerala en route from Trichur to the city of Trivandrum. Kerala is a paradise of rich green hills, miles of sandy beaches, tropical rivers and acres of palm trees. It is unique to India as the only state to have elected a local communist government. It is also the state with the highest percentage of literacy and university graduates per capita. Unfortunately, it is not unique to India in terms of unemployment. Like most other Indian states, Kerala's jobless rate is astronomical.

A young fellow seated by me on the train tells me he has just received his Bachelor's Degree in English Literature. Hey, that's the same degree I have. "What's your prospect of getting a job?" I ask.

"None," he answers.

Funny, that's exactly how I felt when I graduated with *my* Bachelor of English.

In Trivandrum, I am not ten minutes at my hotel when a car with a Soviet flag parks outside and begins blaring propaganda on a deafeningly loud sound system to all who may or may not want to hear. It's not very subtle, but neither are the building-sized murals of Comrades Lenin and Marx. Being a staunch capitalist myself, I feel slightly uneasy, leaving Trivandrum after one night and heading for Kovalum Beach, a short bus ride from town. Now, if I've wondered before where all the Western tourists have been in South India, and believe me I have, I no longer need to quandary. They're all here. Kovalum Beach is teeming with tanktops and tanned bodies, guys tossing frisbees, girls in bikinis. I've died and gone to Club Med!

Kovalum is a magnificent, golden crescent beach, backstopped by a string of adjacent ocean-facing restaurants and guesthouses. I find myself a room at the Sea Flower Guesthouse whose owner, a jolly fellow named Thumpi, reminds me of the A&W Root Bear. For some reason, he takes a particular liking to me, confiding in me gleefully every time he has just outrageously overcharged some new guests.

"Uh, how much should *I* really be paying?" I ask Thumpi one day.

"Ha, ha, ha, ha," he laughs and then immediately changes the subject. Oh well, whatever I'm paying, it's worth it. For the next ten days, I luxuriate in living the good life. I laze on the beach, swim in the surf, and stuff my face with excellent Western food - they even have french fries! For breakfast at the Volga Restaurant, they actually have cornflakes with banana and honey. For dinner at The Sea Fish Restaurant, I order from a selection of fresh seafood caught that very day by local fishermen. One night, I have red snapper, the next night swordfish. On the third night, I can't resist trying the shark - well, I figure it's about time somebody was biting *them* back. All the main courses at The Sea Fish Restaurant are marinated in mouth-watering tandoori spices, skewered then lowered into a pit dug into the sand, where they are barbequed on a bed of searing hot coals. I can enthusiastically claim that it is the most succulent cuisine I have ever tried, and what makes it even tastier is that I can literally feast for less than four dollars a meal.

I am feeling so merry, and it's not just because it is Christmas during my stay at Kovalum Beach. Blinking lights decorate the palm trees and beachfront restaurants. Guesthouses shimmer in the night. A group of young carolers serenade me with Indian-style Christian hymns and demonstrate Michael Jackson "moonwalks" for me - at the low cost of just two rupees for each lunar stroll. Later, I find myself singing my own Indian-style versions of the hymns, like, "Deck the halls with bowls of curry, fa la la la la…"

My favourite pastime in Kovalum is bodysurfing for hours in the rough waves. With each passing day, I linger in the ocean longer and longer, sometimes dreaming of dinner - should I have shark tonight or snapper? Until one afternoon, while swimming, it dawns on me: if I am *eating* shark, well then…

I decide after that to spend all my time *on shore*, tanning.

I am having so much fun at Kovalum! But alas, nothing is ever perfect. My first day, I have barely laid myself down on the sand with my tanning cream and a sex-filled crime novel, when I hear a shrill voice above me: "Hello, mango, papaya, coconut, pineapple, watermelon, banana, cold drink, sir?" I look up to see a young Indian woman with a huge Carmen Miranda fruit basket balanced on her head.

"Hello, mango, papaya, coconut, pineapple, watermelon, banana, cold drink, sir?" she repeats.

"Uh, no thanks," I say.

"Hello, mango, papaya, coconut, pineapple, watermelon, banana, cold drink, sir?"

"Uh, no," I say again.

"Hello, mango, papaya, coconut, pineapple, watermelon, banana, cold drink, sir?"

"No, thank you," I say a third time. Maybe she hasn't heard me.

"Hello, mango, papaya, coconut, pineapple, watermelon, banana, cold drink, sir?"

This is bizarre. Maybe she hasn't understood me. "Nahin," I say, hopefully in Hindi. "Nahin, thank you."

"Hello, mango, papaya, coconut, pineapple, watermelon, banana, cold drink, sir?"

This is mad! I'll just ignore her.

"Hello, mango...?"

I'm not going to look up.

"Hello, mango...?"

I'm just going to read my book.

"Hello, mango...?"

Sweet Lord! This is outrageous! I try to focus on my book, but it's impossible. I'm sweating and it's not from the heat. "Excuse me miss," I say, gritting my teeth. "I don't want mango, I don't want banana, I don't want watermelon, and anything else you may have, believe me when I say... I DON'T WANT IT!"

"Cold drink?"

"NO!"

Finally, there is silence. But she doesn't leave. She just stands there, watching my every move, blocking my sun. After fifteen minutes, finally she gives up, strutting on down the beach. What a relief! But not thirty seconds later, another young woman takes her exact place.

"Hello, mango, papaya, coconut, pineapple, watermelon, banana, cold drink, sir?"

Dear God, if this is a test of patience, I am failing miserably. "My dear lady," I say. "If I didn't buy something from your friend, what makes you think I will buy anything from you?"

She pauses to seriously consider my argument, then after a moment, responds. "Hello, mango, papaya, coconut, pineapple, watermelon, banana, cold drink, sir?"

Surely, this is some cruel form of tourist torture.

After another grueling fifteen minutes, just as I am about to weep, she suddenly abandons her efforts to pester me into succumbing and slowly saunters away. Thank the Lord. But sure enough, thirty seconds later, *another* woman takes *her* place! And then another, then another, on and on, until I am practically a blathering idiot. I just want some peace. But what's worse, each of them in turn manages not only to annoy me, but to stand directly in my sun as well. They're compromising my tan!

And, God forbid, I should actually relent and buy something - well, there's a mistake. Immediately, a dozen women surround me, crowding my space, whining in perfect harmony, "Hello, mango, papaya, coconut, pineapple, watermelon, banana, cold drink, sir?"

"My dear ladies," I plead. "I *have* mango. I just bought mango. I am eating mango! What makes you think I want more?"

"Hello, mango…?"

"Aaaaaaaaah!" I scream, but it's no use.

And! If it's not a mango, papaya, coconut woman hovering above me, it's a boy pitching beach mats or a man hawking lungis!

"Beach mat, meester?"

"Lungi, meester?"

Finally, I find I have two choices: either I go completely insane or take my leave, deciding - possibly too late - upon the latter. Goodbye, Kovalum Beach! Goodbye french fries and bikinis! Tomorrow it's back to curry in Kanyakumari. Hmm… it could be a long bus ride to Kanyakumari. I might get hungry. Maybe I should buy a mango for the journey? Papaya? Coconut? Pineapple?

Naah, I didn't think so.

Chapter 13

YOUR LIPS SAY NO, BUT YOUR EYES SAY VIDEO

Traveling in India is like riding a roller coaster, full of lulls and perils, exhilarating fun and stomach turning bends - and that's just the bus rides.

From Kovalum Beach, I head further south to Kanyakumari. But not one hour into the journey, my bus grinds to a sudden halt. Looking out the window, I am alarmed to discover a riot in progress. Buses are being overturned. Vehicles are being burned. People are engaged in wrestling holds and hand-to-hand combat. Men wielding clubs run by my window. Guns are going off. I have no idea what to do! Luckily, I am led by a fellow passenger through the crossfire to an opportune taxi driver eager to whisk us to safety - for a premium.

"What's going on?" I ask the driver as we speed down a deserted side road away from the melee.

"Oh, communists," he says. "Always fighting. Bad for people, but good for taxi business!"

The taxi excursion lasts for hours, swerving through an incessant series of detours trying to avoid the raging masses. By nighttime, I am not only fighting terror, but the worst diarrhea I have experienced since being in India. "This is my vacation?" I keep thinking to myself. It's challenging enough suppressing waves of the runs without the added pressure of being shaken like a jackhammer on some gravel back road. But it does give me the idea for a movie sequel to Bruce Willis' popular DIEHARD series, set somewhere in rural South India. I call it: DIARRHEA HARD: WITH A VENGEANCE. Before I can laugh at my own sick humour though, the driver suddenly cringes, ducking his head.

"Get down! They're shooting at us!" he screams.

"What? Where?" I shriek. Then I realize we're not under attack at all. It's just my bowels. I'm shooting gas so hard it sounds like machine-gun fire.

When we finally do arrive in Kanyakumari, I beg the driver to take me to any hotel as long as it's close. Each moment now is agony as I try, perspiring, to hold back the flood of my intestines. The driver drops me at the Lakshmi Laundry And Guest House. I register quickly, race up the stairwell, fumble with the key in the door then barge through my room to the toilet with an effusive, flatulent sigh of relief.

The next day, I manage to reach my mother by phone in Canada.

"Are you having a good time?" she asks.

"Well, that's a matter of opinion," I moan. "Mom, I have diarrhea."

"Really? You have diarrhea?" my mother confirms. "You're so lucky! I'm so constipated, I wish I had diarrhea!"

And I thought it was a bad thing. Which just goes to show: one man's illness is another woman's cure.

Kanyakumari reminds me of a spiritual Disneyland. Tens of thousands of Indian tourists congregate to this remote locale every year. But they don't come to holiday at a theme park. They come to visit of all things, a gigantic rock, floating in the ocean a short distance off shore.

As the story goes, the great Swami Vivekananda once meditated for years on this rock and pilgrims still flock here to experience his legendary lingering energetic presence. Intrigued, I take a ferry out to the rock and jostle for position with hundreds of others for the chance to enter a dark cave and meditate. It strikes me that while Westerners are willing to spend hours in line to ride Space Mountain or The Haunted Mansion, these Indian tourists gladly queue up to sit on a stone floor and feel a Swami's spiritual vibes.

When I emerge from the cave, to my surprise I actually do feel considerably calmer, more peaceful. I break away from the crowds and climb to a lookout, where I am content just to stare off in a dreamy haze. I am now on the very southernmost tip of India. Before me lies nothing but the meeting place of three great bodies of water - the Indian Ocean, the Bay of Bengal and the Arabian Sea. Amazingly, in the distance, each visibly moves to its own individual current, but at this point off Kanyakumari, they all appear to embrace in a perfect flow of waves. It must be the unifying influence of the Swami.

Later, at my hotel, I decide to head back towards the beach for sunset, drawn by the allure of a spectacular, golden horizon. I hurriedly navigate the alleys of Kanyukamari, until finally, I reach the edge of the beach. Eagerly, I clamber over some rocks and descend towards the sands, nearly colliding with a man going the other way, fiddling with his pants zipper. Intent on the sunset, I think nothing of him, until I notice the smell. Then, looking down, I see a fresh runny turd at my feet, then another, then another, until I realize the *whole beach* for miles is revoltingly peppered with land mines of human feces. Well, that's India, I think - the grotesque and the sublime.

I decide to watch the sunset from my relatively sanitary hotel.

The next morning, I attempt to purchase a bus ticket to the city of Mysore and am informed by the ticket agent that there is no direct bus. He gives me two options. One, I take a bus to a village sounding something like Smumblemumblebelagola, or two, I take a bus to the equally unpronounceable village of Chanrayamumblebumbleputna. From both, I may or may not be able to transfer to Mysore. There is no guarantee. I flip a rupee and decide upon Chanrayamumblebumbleputna.

"I have just one question," I say to the man behind the counter before agreeing to buy a ticket.

"Yes, yes, what is it you like?" he says.

"Does this bus play videos?"

"Yes, yes," the agent says. "Very good video."

"Oh. Is there another bus I can take?"

"Why? You no like video?"

"Not really," I say, having endured the agonizingly loud "video bus experience" far too many times now.

"Oh, well, then there is no video," the agent says. "No video on bus."

"You just said there was a video."

"No, no. Definitely no video."

"No?"

"No."

I eye him suspiciously.

"Music?" I say.

There is a pause.

"You like music?" he asks.

"No."

"Oh, then definitely no music."

"You guarantee - no music and no video?"

"Guarantee, yes, yes, I mean, no, no," he says.

I'm so exhausted, I actually believe him. I purchase a ticket and step up to an idling bus.

"Is this the bus to uh, Chanraya, uh, chanrayamumble, uh, bumble, uh, whatever?" I ask the driver.

"Yes, yes," he says. "Chanrayamumblebumbleputna."

I climb aboard and take a seat. Shortly after, another tourist enters, asking the driver for similar confirmation.

"Yes, yes, Chanrayamumblebumbleputna," the driver shimmies his head. The tourist, satisfied, enters the bus.

A third tourist appears.

"Chanraya, uh…"

"Chanrayamumblebumbleputna?" the driver says.

"Yes. Is this the bus for, uh, there?"

"No," the driver says.

"NO?" the rest of us on the bus overhear and demand in unison.

"No," the driver says with a grin, telling us that the bus is in fact going somewhere not only completely different, but to a place whose name contains at least fifty syllables. I can't even begin to repeat it!

"But you said -"

The driver just shimmies his head, pointing to another vehicle.

The other tourists and I resignedly gather our backpacks and march over to the new bus, only to find that every seat there is already taken. We now have to stand. And then, to make matters worse, not five minutes later, the driver pops in a video of a Hindi musical, cranking the soundtrack so loud for the next twelve hours that I think my ears are going to bleed. This is arguably my most aggravating bus ride yet, which is saying a lot, considering the competition.

I do actually make it to Mysore, a city famous for its sandalwood crafts, with shops and emporiums stocking just about anything that can be manufactured from the sweetly aromatic tree. It's almost intoxicating to walk down the streets of Mysore, inhaling the delicious odour of sandalwood. Quite the change from the more usual stench of pee.

While in Mysore, I witness a bizarre sight: a group of men and women walking down the road wearing hospital masks, sweeping the path before them with miniature, half-size brooms. They look like a surgical team sanitizing the road for an outdoor operation. But really, they're a collection of monks and nuns of the little known "Jain" religion. Jainism is an ancient theology so dedicated to non-violence, it instructs its followers to sweep the street before them and cover their mouths while walking to avoid stepping on, swallowing or hurting any living thing - even insects. Curious, I follow the monks and nuns to their Jain temple, side-stepping ants and shutting my mouth for once along the way. They allow me into their inner sanctuary, where I stand, a little uncomfortably, before an extremely tall, anatomically correct statue of a naked Jain saint. Apparently, another tenet of Jainism is nudism. On my way out, I am proudly shown a photograph of a prominent Jain businessman, sitting buck naked in an audience with a very serious looking Prime Minister Indira Ghandi (she, thank goodness, is clothed).

Of all the institutions I've visited in India, the most stupefying in its procedure has got to be the State Bank of Mysore. One morning, I go there to complete the supposedly simple transaction of changing a traveler's cheque. Still, I am fully prepared for the usual exasperating wait. But after *three hours* in a line that seems to never move, my patience has gone far beyond any allowance for bureaucratic delay.

Finally, I make it to the wicket and present my traveler's cheque. The bank clerk slowly inspects my passport, filling out form after form of paperwork with little interest and no hurry. Twenty minutes later, I am verging on outright annoyance, when the teller actually removes a wad of rupees from a drawer. But instead of handing them over, he proceeds to count every bill individually, wetting his thumb thoroughly before letting each note drift lazily down into a neat pile. Funny thing about Indian money: if there is even the slightest rip at the edges, it's considered worthless, but a huge hole in the middle is perfectly fine. As with so many things in India, if there's logic to these matters, I just don't see it.

Once counted, sorted, checked, inspected, and rubber-banded, the teller at last reaches out to give me my rupees. But just as they are about to make contact with my fingers, another clerk taps him on the shoulder and offers him a glass of tea. Before I know it, my teller has revoked my cash, replaced it in his drawer and has headed off to the back, where I can see him laughing, drinking tea! A *half hour later*, he returns, sits down, reaches into his desk and with no other forms to complete, nothing more to be signed, nothing further to be counted, hands me the rupees. He could very well have just given me the money and *then* had tea. But that's not how things work in Indian bureaucracy.

As I leave the bank, I notice a uniformed guard sitting calmly outside the door, looking bored. This is nothing special. What *is* unusual are the THREE massive beehives buzzing directly above his head, swarming in a turbulent swirl around his turban. The guard amazingly doesn't even flinch! I figure he's either extremely enlightened or dreadfully hungover to maintain such composure. If I were him, I'd be running down the street screaming - or at least searching out the nearest sandalwood emporium for an industrial-size can of aromatic Raid.

One other thing about Mysore, I am shocked at the overpriced coconuts. Five rupees instead of two! Which of course is only fifteen cents instead of six cents, but everything is relative. When does something become expensive or I become cheap?

One afternoon, at the Chimundi Temple in Mysore, a man with ankle-length dreadlocks approaches me.

"You take my photo?" he says. "Only ten rupees."

He is an interesting character, dressed in an orange robe and carrying a three-pronged trident. Well worth the ten rupees. I gladly snap a picture.

"Me Sadhu," he says.

Hey, just like the guy in Thiruvanamalai. "Sadhu, is that a common name?" I inquire.

"This not my name," he says. "Me Sadhu. Me holy man!"

Sadhus, I come to learn, are wandering ascetics, worshippers of Shiva who have renounced all worldly possessions in search of higher spirituality. I have seen them everywhere in India. They are easily recognizable by their outrageous personal attire. Usually they are wrapped in saffron, toga-like robes, but some I've seen have been completely covered in ash, others naked as a jaybird. I had no idea they were spiritual seekers. I thought they were merely costumed to enhance their appeal as subjects for photography.

"You want puja?" he asks.

"You know what, I think I'll skip the puja."

"I give you blessing."

"That's okay."

"Free blessing."

"No, thanks."

But he continues anyway. "Blessing to your family. Blessing also to your home country. Blessing to your children, blessing to your dog - you know, one tourist, he gave me one thousand rupees for puja! Blessing to your aunty - donations are most welcome - blessing to the uncle..."

So much for free - one thousand rupees? My puja back in Mahaballipurum only cost me ten.

"I'll tell you what," I say. "Here's ten rupees. Put in a good word for me with Shiva, will you?"

He smiles broadly. "You are good man. Shiva like you very much."

"Thanks," I say, feeling relieved. I certainly don't want to get on the wrong side of Shiva.

I am dreading another bus ride, but there's no other way from Mysore to the temple town of Sringeri. I am hardly enthusiastic when purchasing my ticket. I don't even bother asking about videos or music. But I am comforted by the assurance of the agent that at least the bus will be "Super Deluxe" and I will be guaranteed a reserved seat. Of course, when I arrive at eight o'clock that evening, I not only find the oldest, most broken down vehicle in the fleet, but every splintered, wooden seat is taken and the aisle is already crammed. Well, I have no intention at this point of standing. I engage in a petulant exchange with the passenger presently occupying my pitiful portion of plank, finally convincing him that not only does my ticket entitle me to the seat, but that I won't stop whining until he vacates it - all those years of training in inflicting Jewish guilt finally pay off. Exhausted, I settle in for a long, uncomfortable journey.

The heat in Mysore has been stifling and even now, at eight-thirty in the evening, I'm perspiring heavily though wearing practically nothing, only a tanktop, sandals and lungi. At nine P.M., the bus pulls out of the station. As expected, the ride is brutally bumpy. Still, I manage somehow to sleep. But sometime later, I'm suddenly jarred awake as the bus rounds a sharp corner at an alarming and dangerous rate. I notice immediately that the vehicle is now rising in altitude. I am no longer perspiring. In fact, it is surprisingly frosty. The window beside me won't close. A brisk draft blows in my face. I'm absolutely freezing! My tanktop does nothing to warm me. My sandals don't cover my toes. I may as well be traveling naked. My mouth chatters so hard it sounds like Fred Astaire tapping a dance routine on my teeth. I can just hear my friends in Toronto now - "Only Stew can go to India and die of hypothermia!" The bus speeds from one switchback to another, tossing me relentlessly until dizzy. Damn that ticket agent! This is what he considers Super Deluxe?

At three A.M., the bus mercifully pulls over. The driver yawns, "Sringeri."

"What?" I sputter, staring out at a frightfully dark, deserted street. "This is Sringeri?"

Abruptly, I am left on the roadside, completely alone, shivering. The bus disappears. It is the middle of the night. What am I supposed to do now?

Wandering the lonely laneways of Sringeri, the wind is frigid, sensation ebbs from my fingertips and toes. I search vainly for a hotel. Finally I come across another lost soul unfortunate enough to be outside at this time of night. He is crouched in a corner, wrapped in a thin blanket. All I can see are his bare feet.

"Hello," I say. I am sorry to wake him, but I'm desperate.

His eyes peek out from under the blanket. To my surprise, it is just a young boy.

"Please, can you help me find a room?" I beg.

He struggles to rise as if all his joints are frozen. It is only when he is standing that I notice a hunch protruding from his right shoulder. Now I really feel bad I bothered him. The boy hobbles, leading me to a motel-style building. He knocks on the nearest door. An irate man appears who begrudgingly shows me to a bleak cement cell furnished solely with a metal cot.

"I don't suppose you have something with a king-size bed?" I say.

He just stares.

"Free HBO?"

I decide not to press my luck. "I'll take it," I say.

I hand the little hunchback ten rupees and enter the room. The custodian slams the door. I lie down. A spring in the mattress sticks in my back. I am shuddering uncontrollably. I suffer through the longest night of my life, counting each excruciating moment until morning.

Finally, through the slit beneath the door, I glimpse the first hint of daylight. Immediately, I rush out of bed and emerge from the dark, like Dorothy after the twister, taking those first tenuous steps from black and white Kansas to the unpredictable technicolour of Oz. To my relief, I find no wicked witches in Sringeri. The sunrise casts a golden hue. The town is just waking. Shopkeepers rub their eyes, unlocking heavy metal grates. A sleepy street vendor sells me tea and round rice cakes called "idli." All is calm - quite the contrast from the hysteria of the previous night.

I stroll out of town. A river flows beside me, the melody of which sweeps away any remnants of tension from my body. I overhear a schoolroom bursting with the joyous songs of children and am suddenly filled with glee. Outside a temple, I see the hunchback boy again, begging rupees. He recognizes me.

"Hallo, meester!" he calls. "You are sleep good?"

"Never better," I fib. Who am I to complain to a homeless hunchback? "Here's something to thank you for last night. You saved my life." I slip him a hundred rupees.

"Ha, ha, now you are save me," he laughs.

Seeing this boy, I can't help but think of myself growing up. No, I wasn't a hunchback, but I was equally visibly grotesque in others' eyes. I was obese. I know what it's like to be different. I know what it's like to be shunned. I remember when I was twelve years old, at a high school dance, standing off in a corner, reflecting on how I had the biggest breasts in my class - and that included the girls. My whole childhood, I was taunted, ridiculed, isolated. I was self-conscious, angry and afraid. Those childhood scars have led to chronic insecurity. I've spent my whole life neurotically trying to be skinny. I've been to years of therapy to repair my broken self-esteem. Transcending others' opinions of me has been a constant effort. But I've learned that approval from others is just as superficial as their disdain. I must focus on what I think of myself. And I must think of myself in a more loving way.

I must be more like this boy. Here he is, a hunchback, a beggar, and he's so cheerful, so accepting. I am amazed at his attitude. He doesn't seem the least bit self-conscious. He has nothing and yet finds reason to smile. I suppose it is all perspective. If life is indeed a roller coaster then perhaps I should just relax and enjoy the ride. The choice is mine. Heaven or hell.

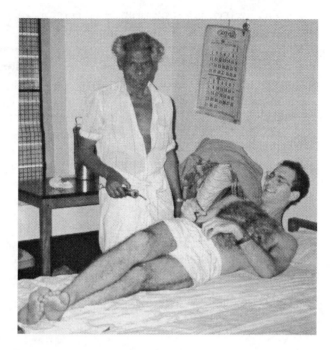

My "man," Bugs Bunny, prepares to bustee my butt - or administer an enema - at the Ayurvedic Clinic. Youch! (Thaikattussery)

Rumplestiltskin. Last seen at a corner shop near the Mysore Bus station.

The dining in Madras
is excellent, even though
the ambiance is a little
trashy.

Everyone says my
girlfriend is two-
dimensional, but I
don't know, I think
she's a cutout – I mean
a knockout!
(MG Road, Bangalore)

"I missed the bus, so I had to take the elephant to work."
(Thaikattussery)

The Kovalum Kids, undercover spies on a mission to save the world. Mondays at 8:00 on Bombay Channel One.

Where better to escape the heat of day than on a rooftop under an elephant? (Kanyakumari)

Slave to fashion.
(Kovalum)

Roadside holy men, or Sadhus. Five rupees for a photo, ten rupees for
a blessing. They also do weddings and Bar Mitzvahs.

III

You Can't Always Want What You Get

Chapter 14

LOVE IS THE DRUG

My next stop is the coastal state of Goa, infamous on the traveler's circuit for its outrageous, Western-influenced, Sixties-style, hippie, party "scene."

As history will no doubt recall, Goa was invaded twice in recent times. Once by the Portuguese in 1510, and secondly in the late 1960's by a new brand of interloper, not as interested in overturning government institutions as they were in transplanting the Haight-Ashbury subculture of San Francisco to the tropical sands off the Arabian Sea. The hippies had landed, and Goa was never to be the same.

Anything goes in Goa. It's the place to do your own thing, let it all hang out, leave your judgments behind, man. A place to live in the past, forget about the future and revel in the present. A place to dress like a freak, act like a geek and think you look chic. A place to try some hashish, lay on a beach and speak Portuguese. Anything you can imagine, you can get it, you can do it, in Goa.

I arrive in Goa from Sringeri via the coastal town of Udipi, where I stay in a four-star hotel for only three dollars - that's less than one dollar per star. It is January, Goa's high season, and so I decide to bypass the hectic resort-oriented beaches of the south and take a bus to the less populated village of Chapora further north. Chapora is a slow, lazy tropical paradise. Everyone moves at a pace dictated by the scorching heat. All through town, tourists stroll by, glazed by the sun, beers in hand, wearing wardrobes so outlandish, they are easily more bizarre than anything I've seen in India yet. Tie-dye is definitely not an anachronism in Goa.

I wander aimlessly through pathways of palm trees. I sit at a restaurant for hours, unperturbed by the slow, carefree service. I inquire leisurely into suitable accommodation. Many travelers, I discover, rent long-term for reduced rates, securing the best of places, but I don't know how long I'll be around - not to be morbid - and decide to seek a guesthouse where I can pay daily. Finally, I find a quaint villa hidden beneath lush foliage with a seemingly quiet room for rent.

My first night in Chapora though, I have just tucked myself cozily into bed, when the room next door erupts with loud music and hyena-like laughter, the noise of which easily penetrates the thin walls. Well into the wee hours of the morning, the people in the next room party with absolutely no regard for those of us trying desperately to snooze. On the second sleepless night, it occurs to me that maybe I am actually the only one in all of Goa who prefers to doze at night. On the third restless night, I decide to respond with some loud noise of my own, quickly finding though that not only is it difficult to maintain a disturbance as a party of one, but even more deflating, I'm far too Canadian to actually upset anyone past eleven o'clock.

On the fourth day, sauntering exhausted through town, I notice a sign that may as well be from God, so stricken am I with the urge to drop to my knees and pray in gratitude. No, it's not a sign advertising earplugs. It's potentially even better. There is an Indian man with beatific eyes standing next to the sign.

"Uh, is this your sign?" I ask, barely able to coax the words past my trembling lips.

"Yes."

"Does it, uh..."

"Yes?"

"Does it, uh, really say..."

"Yes?"

"Bakery?"

"Yes."

"German Bakery?"

"Yes."

"With... bread?"

"Yes."

"And... CAKE?"

"Oh yes, many kinds of cake."

"Lord, I have truly on this day been blessed with a vision!"

"What would you like?" the proprietor asks.

"What *wouldn't* I like is more the question!" South India may offer a world of riches, but a decent dessert has not been among them. "I'll have one piece of chocolate cake, one carrot cake, one macaroon, and one, uh, what's that, walnut strudel? Two of those! Don't bother wrapping, I'll eat them here."

I seat myself down directly in front of the bakery and greedily devour my treasures. Each swallow is so divine, so heavenly, I suggest to the Indian man that he rename his business "The Born Again Bakery." Communion with a crust of strudel - now that's my kind of religion.

On a sugar high that rivals any hallucinogen, I venture out in search of the beach. Just beyond the village, I discover a secluded Eden of white sands and warm water. Over the coming days this becomes my refuge of private rapture. Foreigners seldom frequent these shores. Indians hardly ever appear at its rocky edges. But one afternoon, as I'm tapping on a hand-drum, I become conscious that I might not be alone. Far down on the other side of the beach, a large shadow is protruding from behind a boulder. I have the sinking suspicion that I am being watched. I return to my drumming but out of the corner of my eye I am scrutinizing the shadow. For the next half-hour it doesn't even waver. Maybe it's just the sun playing tricks, I think - when suddenly a cow incongruously appears. Now this is India, I shouldn't be surprised at seeing a cow, but a cow on the beach somehow strikes me as stranger than a cow on a busy city street. There's no grass to chew on a beach, no piles of garbage to sift through, nothing really to attract a cow except the possibility of tanning its already leathery hide. But this is Goa. Acceptance is the rule. Whether or not I believe there should be a cow, the fact is, there *is* a cow and this cow is charging in a beeline straight towards me! I don't know what to do. It seems imminent that I am to be trampled when suddenly the cow stops dead in its tracks and plops itself down right beside me. It looks at me, then at my drum, then back at me.

"Uh, you want me to play?"

The cow snorts.

"Okay," I say. I must have heat stroke. I am talking to a cow. Without further delay, I begin to weave a pattern of sound on my drum in synch with the rhythm of the waves. The cow seems to be drawn by the beat into a deep relaxation, sitting there the entire time I play. How do you like that? A cow in India. My very first groupie.

From then on, every day the cow comes to visit, and though I always welcome her presence, soon it dawns on me the perils of sharing one's beach with a bovine. One morning, while swimming in the ocean, I notice the cow standing directly over my belongings. Frantically, I splash out of the water. You never know when a cow will unexpectedly unload a saucer of soup-like poop. Any moment might deliver a mess I don't ever want to have to wash out of my sarong. Desperately, I lean on the cow's substantial behind in a futile attempt to drive her away, but she won't budge. Urgently, I scramble to gather up my books, my lotion, my bag, my drum, managing to clear the area just as the cow releases a splattering of liquid-y excrement exactly where moments before I had been lying. Gross! You've heard the expression "Cowabunga?" Well, this is "Cowadunga!"

Another day, again while swimming, I catch the cow munching on chapters one through three of the book I'm reading: Tom Robbins' Even Cowgirls Get The Blues. I don't know if she's attracted to the title, but the next day, I find she's returned to chew on chapters four to six! Now I've heard of devouring a novel, but this is ridiculous.

Most days though, the cow just stands in one place, morning to evening, barely breathing, and I think she must be in some deep form of meditation. Perhaps she's a reincarnated yogi, able to transcend tedium into trance-like bliss. Perhaps she is a saint, practiced in the delicate art of serenity. I have longed myself for such detachment. But then, alas, I'm only human and not holy, like a cow.

Late one afternoon, I am feeling a little bored with so much tranquility and seclusion and decide to wander from Chapora to a nearby beach known as "Little Vagator." To my surprise, the sands are crowded, mostly with hippies - this is obviously where all the action has been. Joints and chillums are being passed about freely. Thick tufts of marijuana smoke mingle with the fresh sea air. Topless girls dance to music only they can hear. A man in a G-string juggles spears. Another man swordfights an invisible foe, while a girl doing yoga balances on her big toe. And in the midst of it all, amazingly undistracted by the madness that surrounds her, a lone girl sits in perfect lotus posture, remarkably composed, incredibly still.

I soon forget everyone else and am content just to stare at this girl's back as she faces the sea, meditating. She is like an angel, long dark curls cascading over the tanned slopes of her shoulders, the sunset like a halo outlining her hair. An hour goes by and I am still enthralled, when suddenly the girl rises and turns towards me. My star-struck eyes follow her graceful body as she approaches and slips serenely by me. Longingly, I smile, but she, like that "Girl From Ipanema," doesn't even see.

Day after day, I return to Little Vagator, hoping to meet this gentle, tranquil - not to mention curvaceous - soul. But each time the moment appears ripe I become fearful. I'm not that bold. Then one afternoon, as I'm settling into my regular spot behind the girl, I notice the beach is particularly chaotic. There are the usual flame jugglers, spear dancers, and cannabis consumers, but today they are joined by a raucous pack of stray dogs, kicking up sand, toppling over the topless and snatching people's snacks. I have decided to be a hippie myself this day and have brought along my hand-drum. I begin beating a gentle rhythm, when to my amazement, within minutes, all the wild dogs are either asleep on my lap or curled at my feet, blanketing my body with love. Just then, the girl stirs, stands and again passes close beside me. But for the first time, she stops to gaze in my eyes.

"Nice trick with the dogs," she says, and walks by.

That night, I can't sleep with the thrill that she actually knows I'm alive. Next afternoon, I am back at Little Vagator, but to my grave disappointment, she is nowhere to be seen. Neither are the dogs, neither is the magic. Dejectedly, I return to Chapora for dinner, resigning myself to yet another lonely meal of mixed vegetable curry, when who should enter the restaurant but the girl. She is stunning in a white, sleeveless sundress, hair flowing like soft rapids about her cheeks, teeth bright as moonbeams. She walks over, recognizing me.

"Hello," she says.

"Uh, hi," I gag, choking on a curried pea. "P-please, ahem, won't you join me?"

"I'd like that," she coos, seating herself confidently across from me.

"Uh, what's your name?" I ask timidly.

"Shakti," she says.

"That's an unusual name," I laugh awkwardly.

"It embodies sexual energy," she says.

"Oh -" I choke again.

"Shakti is the Hindu goddess of feminine creative urges."

"No kidding!" I blurt out in an embarrassingly high, squeaky voice, feeling sweat begin to gather in places I'd rather not mention.

"You might say, she's the Goddess Of A Good Time."

"Ack!" The pea that was lodged in my larynx comes flying out of my mouth, barely missing Shakti's left shoulder.

"Charming," she says.

"Sorry. Uh, I'm Stew."

"Well, how do you do, Stew?"

"The name embodies chunks of beef and vegetables in broth."

"Tasty. Are you Hungarian?"

"Hungarian Stew?"

"Yes."

"No, Romanian, actually."

"Too bad."

The waiter arrives and takes Shakti's order.

"Where are you from?" I ask her as the waiter leaves.

"Here and there," she says.

"Have you been traveling long?"

"All of life is a journey."

"No, I mean, where have you been before Goa?"

"The places are unimportant, the moment is what matters."

"I'm from Canada," I say.

"That explains your politeness."

"How so?"

"Most other men would have introduced themselves the *first* time they spent hours staring at me from behind."

"Oh... I didn't think you'd noticed."

"They say if you meditate long enough, you develop a third eye behind your head."

"That happened to Superman once," I say. "Only his third eye was caused by prolonged exposure to kryptonite."

"I tried kryptonite," she says. "It didn't work."

Her food is served. Several moments of silence elapse as we eat.

"So, tell me," she finally says. "Why didn't you just say hello to me at the beach?"

"Uh... the truth?"

"Of course."

"I think you're incredibly beautiful."

"Well, that's obvious. But it certainly doesn't mean you have to be unfriendly."

"You looked so peaceful, I didn't want to disturb you."

"Well, I'm glad I disturbed you," she says. "You're very sweet."

"Really?"

"I'm a Buddhist. I never lie."

"You're amazing," I say, starry-eyed.

"On my good days," she answers.

"Hey, you wanna *blow*?" I say with exaggerated inflection, getting into the hippie vibe.

"Blow?"

"Uh, leave."

"What do you have in mind?" she inquires, taking her last bite.

"I know a beautiful bench overlooking the sea -"

"I've got something better," she smiles. "But you'll have to trust me."

"That's easy. Lead the way. I'm all yours."

As we rise from the table, Shakti hesitates then gently takes my hand, running her fingers along the flesh of my palm, raising my temperature to fever pitch, spinning my senses, flushing my cheeks. Let me tell you, they say a lot about the drugs in Goa, but none compares to that first, tentative touch of love.

Outside, by moonlight, Shakti steers me silently through the back roads of Chapora to a small, one-room house nestled within a thicket of palm trees. Quietly, we slip through the door.

"Don't speak," she whispers.

She guides me through the dark, lowering me to a plush cushion on the floor, then flows all about me, sparking candle after candle, emerging from the shadows into flickers of faint light. The fire dances on her body, skipping where my hands long to follow. All around me she coils, weaving a spell, in then out of darkness, until I'm weak with desire, burning with restraint. Then suddenly, she stops, and slowly begins un-buttoning the spine of her dress, the fabric slipping from her shoulders, sliding past her nipples, revealing the round edge of her belly, resting on the sensual crevice of her hip. Gradually, she frees the white cotton, allowing it to slither past her thighs, stroke her milky calves and gather in a pool at her feet.

I am trembling as she touches me, tracing a line from my forehead, across my temple, down my cheek, placing a long finger on the ledge of my lip, inviting me to taste her. She searches my eyes with her blue, crystal gaze, searches my mouth with her hot, probing tongue. Then she undresses me. She's like an animal, thrusting herself upon me, digging her nails in me. Her hands are through my hair. Her breath is in my ear. I am swimming the sea of her, caressing the waves of her skin, chewing the salt from the nape of her neck. She is unquenchable. I am insatiable. Until finally hours later, our hungers subside. We drift off to sleep amidst half-melted candles. I am wrapped in her heartbeat. She is wrapped in my arms.

Chapter 15

WHATEVER GETS YOU THROUGH THE NIGHT

"Well, well, well. Look what the cat dragged in."

A voice awakens me and I realize I'm stark naked. A remarkably thin girl stands above me, ogling. "Where's Shakti?" I say, fumbling for the covers.

"Gone to freshen up."

"Who are you?" I ask.

"I'm Pritti."

"Well, you're not that modest, but you are kind of cute," I say.

"Not pretty. P-R-I-T-T-I. It's a Sanskrit name meaning, well, actually I haven't a clue what it means, but you must admit, it sounds rather groovy, doesn't it?"

"Uh, groovy was definitely the first word to come to mind," I say.

"So, are you new to the neighbourhood?" she asks.

"You might say that. Listen, uh, do you think you could do me a favour?"

"Maybe."

"Do you think you could stop staring long enough for me to get dressed?"

"Come on, this is Goa!" she says. "The body is sacred, express yourself. Let it all hang out!"

"If you don't mind," I say. "I think I'll let it all hang *in* this morning. Could you pass me that sarong?"

"Man, you're so uptight. Where did Shakti find you?"

"It's a long story."

"I've got time," she says, planting herself cheerily on the edge of the bed.

"The sarong?" I say.

"First the details, then the clothes - and don't leave anything out."

"Hi, everyone!"

"Shakti!" I cry, relieved to see her entering through the front door.

"Hey, Pritti!" Shakti says. "I see you've met Stew."

"We're like best friends. He was just going to explain to me how he got into your bed."

"I was not," I say. "Could someone please pass me that sarong?"

"Oh dear," Shakti says, giggling. "You must feel so exposed. Here."

"Thanks," I say, dressing under the covers.

"He's so modest," Pritti says.

"Canadian," Shakti says.

"That explains it."

"Uh, could you tell me where the bathroom is?" I interrupt.

"It's outside round the back of the house," Shakti smiles.

"You're in a good mood," Pritti teases.

"Oh, Stew! Don't forget to flush," Shakti calls after me, laughing.

"Yeah, don't forget to flush!" Pritti bursts out giggling.

I really don't see what's so funny. I leave the girls and stumble around the house to a broken down cubicle-sized shack with a grass roof. It's the only structure around, so I pry the door open and realize what prompted the girls' hysterics. There's no way I could possibly flush, because there is, in fact, nothing to flush. But I feel so good this morning, no hole in the ground is going to spoil my day. Gleefully, I raise my sarong and squat, trying to relax, when all of a sudden I hear a noise... beneath me. Dismissing it as my imagination, I return to my business, when suddenly, I hear a grunt... beneath me. I freeze. If there *is* someone down there, the image is so revolting, I'm not sure I want to know. Then I hear a squeal!

Instantly, I jump up in alarm and holding my breath, look down into the hole, almost falling in from the shock of finding a pig rummaging around beneath me. A pig! A huge, black, fat, crap-covered hog, foraging in mounds of feces for undigested morsels or other tasty tidbits. Snorting up at me as if it were saying, "Come on, come on! On with your business, out with your poop! I'm hungry! Oink, oink. Hmm, yes, what have we today, vegetable curry, mmm, very good, very tasty, spicy! Huh? Come on, come on. Out with your poop. I haven't got all day. I have many other toilets to visit. Everyone thinks he is so special, thinks he is the only one. Huh? What is this? Mmm, Masala corn niblets! Oink, oink, yum, yum..."

Now there have been many things in India that have disgusted me, but this takes the proverbial cake. In fact, I can't even *think* of cake, having now associated it with this swine-y mess. I hurry back to the house.

"Did you know there's a pig in your toilet?" I ask Shakti.

"Oh, you've met Arnold," she laughs. "He does take a little getting used to, but he's really quite likeable - once you get past all his shit."

"Funny," I say.

"I think he's a *boar*," Pritti says. "But he is cuter than some of the dates I've had lately."

"Not feeling well?" Shakti asks me.

"It'll pass," I say, remembering the large portion of *pork vindaloo* I ate a couple of nights ago. I suddenly feel the need to sit down, collapsing on a pillow next to Pritti.

"You may not want to sit too close to me," she says.

"Oh?"

"I think I may have lice."

"Oh!" I shift quickly to another pillow.

"Yeah, a bit of a nuisance, scratching all the time, but nothing compares to what happened to me this morning."

"I'm afraid to ask."

"Well, I woke up with severe - and I mean, *severe* - abdominal cramps, and not to bore you with the details of my subsequent trip to the toilet, let's just say I found a squirming, living being swimming in my stool."

"You sure it wasn't a pig?"

"It had horns."

"Lovely."

"Parasites. Lice. It's all just part of traveling in India," Pritti sighs. "Hey! Anyone for breakfast? Bacon and eggs?"

Shakti, Pritti and I decide to hike over to the neighbouring village of Anjuna and have breakfast there, although I must admit, my appetite has been somewhat curtailed. It is Wednesday, the day of Anjuna's famous flea market. On our way, we pass by my groupie, the cow at the beach in Chapora.

"I'd like you to meet a friend of mine," I say.

"A friend of yours?" Shakti asks.

"More than just a friend," I say. "A great teacher. Shakti, Pritti, allow me to introduce you to Morris."

"You've named the cow, Morris?" Pritti asks.

"Morris the saintly cow," I say.

"This is ridiculous."

"Wait, I want to find out more about this," Shakti interjects. "You say this cow is a great teacher? What exactly are you learning, cud chewing?"

"No, meditation."

"From a cow?"

"Quite revolutionary," I say. "I've been learning to calm my mind by repeating the mantra, moo."

"Moo?"

"See, aren't you calmer already?"

"Don't you mean Om?"

"Om is obsolete. Moo is definitely the way of the future."

We leave the beach with Shakti and I laughing and chanting, "Moo, moo, moo."

"I'm friends with two idiots," Pritti groans.

In Chapora, we come upon the German Bakery. "Wait. Have you tried the walnut strudel?" I ask.

"No."

"Oh my god! You haven't lived until you've tried walnut strudel!" I excitedly buy ten wedges of the pastry.

"Are you expecting to feed an army?" Shakti questions.

"Uh, no."

"I thought you weren't even hungry," Pritti says.

"I'm not. But I believe in the motto: Be Prepared. What if all of a sudden there was no more walnut strudel? What if the bakery burned down? What if all the Germans went home? What then?"

"Uh -"

"Exactly! This is emergency strudel."

"Emergency strudel?"

"For sudden and unexpected strudel cravings."

"You know Stew, if you're logic wasn't so ridiculous, it would be impeccable," Shakti observes.

"Uh, thank you... I think."

And so, with my strudel gingerly packed in my knapsack, we resume our journey to the Anjuna flea market, arriving to a hodge-podge of Westerners and Indians selling clothes, drums, jewelry, fabric, statues, purses, food - everything you can imagine. There are items from Nepal,

Thailand, Bali and even India. I wander amongst the psychedelic tie-dye fashions. It feels like the Sixties all over again (not that I was there the first time). I buy myself a Nehru-style shirt, swirled with purple and blue paisley patterns. Shakti buys a halter-top hand-painted with an image of the Hindu goddess Parvati. Pritti purchases a bikini so skimpy, it's almost invisible.

"I'm getting hungry," Pritti says just as we pass by an Indian man flipping omelettes at incredible speed. We sit down on his straw mat and order breakfast.

"Are you sure you should eat eggs," I say to Pritti. "I mean, considering what happened to you this morning?"

"What happened? Oh, my parasite? Well, I don't see why something like that should affect my diet."

"No, of course not," I say.

"Hey look!" Shakti announces. "Here comes the rest of the gang."

We make room on the mat for Shakti's friends. I am introduced to Tracey, a mid-twenties punk rocker from Australia; Aldo, a sixty year old "Osho" fanatic from Italy; and from London, Stoney. Stoney is in his early thirties with a mess of brown thinning hair, dark sallow eyes and a friendly but rather crooked smile, seeming to correspond to the caption on his t-shirt that reads: I'M MAD. The first words out of his mouth are barely audible. "I have a headache," he groans.

"Sorry to hear that," I say.

"Well, I have one all the time, but now it's particularly sensitive."

"You have one all the time?" I ask.

"Yeah."

"Doesn't that worry you, to have a headache all the time?"

"Yeah, I've been to doctors. I've got enough antibiotics in my room to start my own pharmacy. They don't know what's causing it."

"Could be the mushrooms," Tracey calls out.

"Oh no," Stoney says. "I think the mushrooms make it better."

"Mushrooms?" I ask.

"*Magic* mushrooms," Pritti clarifies.

"Oh."

"I really don't think my headaches are caused by mushrooms. In any case, I haven't done that many mushrooms," Stoney strains to take a mental inventory. "Well, seven out of the last ten days isn't that much, is it? Besides they're chock full of vitamins."

"Oh, yeah, they're bloody health food," Tracey blurts out.

"No. It's definitely not the mushrooms," Stoney repeats. "Could be all the beer, whiskey and cigarettes though."

"How about a joint?" Aldo offers.

"Now marijuana! That's a proven natural healer," Stoney exclaims. "Well, at least it's a sedative. Helps me sleep and we all know how important sleep is to recovery."

Our omelettes arrive. Stoney spits a white ball of mucous into his hanky. "I think I have a fever," he moans. He is indeed a charming breakfast companion.

"You know, Stoney may be right," Aldo says. "Marijuana *is* medicine. I have been smoking it every single day now for twenty-seven years - and I'm still alive! Ha, ha, ha!"

"How's your health?" Pritti asks.

"Well... I'm alive," Aldo says.

"I, for one, admire your dedication, Aldo," Stoney declares.

"I think you like being sick, Stoney," Tracey says.

"Oh, no," Stoney disagrees. "It's awfully boring being sick and doing nothing. At least if I'm doing nothing, I'd like to be able to enjoy myself."

"You're not doing nothing," Shakti laughs. "You're doing a lot of drugs."

"Stoney, how can you not enjoy yourself in Goa?" Aldo remarks. "Even if I were sick, there is no other place I would rather be."

"Look, it's not Goa," Stoney explains. "Goa is a brilliant place. And it's not being sick. It's life. Life is what's boring."

"That's a lovely philosophy," I say.

"I don't want to come off sounding cynical," Stoney says. "Look, the scary thing is, I know there is nothing I would actually rather be doing than doing nothing on a beautiful beach in Goa, sick or not, and I'm still bored! I could understand being bored at a nine-to-five job in a windowless office in London, slaving away, dreaming of a beach in Goa. I could relate to being bored there. But I think it's a bad sign being bored doing exactly what you want to be doing exactly where you want to be. Where do I go from here?"

"To bed," Tracey says. "You're starting to sweat."

"Perhaps," I say, "you're trying to reach such an intense degree of boredom as to elevate yourself into an enlightened state of mind. I read something about that in Andrew Harvey's book, *Journey in Ladakh*."

"Interesting," Stoney ponders. "You mean I may actually be

martyring myself through boredom for the advancement of all human consciousness?"

"Could be."

"Hmm... very generous of me."

"Downright compassionate."

"Well, I don't know," Stoney sighs. "Sounds rather boring, really."

"Here," Aldo says, handing Stoney a cigar-sized joint. "I think you need this."

"Ah, medicine." Stoney brightens. "At least I haven't yet gotten bored of that."

I imagine meeting Stoney five years from now in sunny Southern California. He has opened his own ashram, dedicated solely to the sublime pursuit of boredom. Many followers, from all over the world, flock to his feet, seeking initiation into this radical new path of spiritual attainment. Signs of inspiration are displayed all over the ashram, such as: MODERATION IN ALL THINGS EXCEPT BOREDOM, and, INTEREST IS FINE FOR MONEY, BUT NOT STONEY.

Stoney sits for hours upon end, sometimes in a comfy leather chair, other times reclining in a hammock, entertaining the queries of eager-eyed disciples, hopefully to the point where he is sickly bored of the lot of them.

"Damn, it's boring being so revered," he says.

Periods are set aside to watch British soap operas.

"Now, *that's* boring," Stoney says.

A bell is rung for a half-hour of chanting - how tedious. Snores can be heard from the monks who have fallen asleep.

I enter the grand hallway, march along a red carpet and stand before Stoney. He is staring off into the distance, glassy-eyed, an unlit joint dangling from his lips, his hair a mess.

"Stoney?" I say.

"Yeah?"

"Do you remember me?"

"Of course, you're that Canadian chap," he says. "Forgive me if I don't get too excited. I'm terribly bored at the moment."

"You're quite the success," I say.

"Yes, rather dull, isn't it?"

"Tell me, do you ever *do* anything?" I ask.

"Well," he says. "There is a difference between laziness and boredom, you know. Laziness implies that you *should* be doing something. Mystical boredom insists that you should not."

"How do you survive, monetarily, I mean?"

"This is a non-profit, charitable organization. I never understood it myself, but don't non-profit organizations always make the most money? The ashram just seems to run itself, really."

"Doesn't look to me like anything is *running* anywhere," I laugh.

"A figure of speech," Stoney says. "I'm really trying to cut down on using so many active verbs. I find them quite exhausting. Yes, I suppose I have relaxed into my place in life, though being a spiritual leader does get a little monotonous at times. I've even grown bored of marijuana."

"Now that's enlightened!" I say.

"No, the enlightened part is that I keep smoking it to become even more bored."

"Such discipline," I say.

"Yes," Stoney says. "And I didn't have to sit in a cave for twenty years to figure it all out either. It just evolved naturally. The process was rather boring, really, but what isn't? Care to join me in a smoke?"

"Why not?" I say, recalling the first sign I saw upon entering the ashram: WHY NOT SAY WHY NOT.

With total disinterest, Stoney reaches over and tugs on a velvet rope, ringing a bell and summoning a familiar face from behind a curtain.

"Aldo!" I say. He is carrying a handful of pre-rolled joints.

"Hello, Stew!"

"What are you doing here?" I ask.

"I'm helping out Stoney," Aldo says, smiling broadly.

"He needed spiritual guidance," Stoney points out.

"I don't mean to be critical, but Aldo doesn't look very bored, Stoney," I say.

"He's a slow learner," Stoney says, "but an excellent roller."

Aldo lights up a joint and passes it to Stoney who leans his head back on a pillow, exhales a massive cloud of smoke and drifts off into a serene expression of total emptiness.

"Ah, boredom," he yawns. "It's so bloody peaceful..."

"Hey, Stew!" Shakti's voice summons me abruptly back from my daydream. "Are you finished your omelette?"

"Uh, almost," I say, gulping down my last bite.

After breakfast, Shakti and I bid adieu to our friends, preferring to spend the rest of the day together alone. On our way back to Chapora from the Anjuna market, we pass a huge parking lot filled with idling scooters. The Goa police have blocked the only exit.

"What's going on?" I ask one of the deterred motorists.

"Ah, it's the same old harass the tourist shit," he says. "Everyone in Goa rents these scooters or motorcycles. It's the only way to get around. The roads aren't wide enough for taxis. But you need a special license to drive them, or so the cops say. Nobody has these licenses. Even the people who rent the scooters don't have licenses. So every now and then, the cops form a blockade to check everyone for their licenses, knowing full well nobody's got them."

"What happens if you don't have one?" I ask.

"Well, you have a choice. You can either go to jail or pay the cops an outrageous amount of baksheesh."

"Baksheesh?"

"Blood money, brother. A bribe."

"How much?"

"It changes all the time. Depends on what they ask for," he says.

"So, they're pocketing money from all these tourists trying to leave the market? There are hundreds of people here."

"You got it. Nice day's wages, huh? Still, it's better than having the police plant some hashish on you. Then you're really up shit's creek. You might have to mortgage your life to bribe yourself out of that one. One thing's for sure. You don't want to end up in an Indian jail."

"They plant drugs on tourists?" I say.

"They'll do anything. Most corrupt bastards on the planet. Whatever you do, stay away from the cops in Goa."

"I know all about the cops in Goa," Shakti says. "Last week, my friend Pritti and I got fined five hundred rupees each, just for going topless on Baga Beach. I mean, everyone goes topless here in Vagator and Anjuna. The cops were laughing at us. They knew the fine was outrageous. But what could we do? We paid it and left."

"Jeez," I shake my head. "I never knew."

"Well, now you know," the guy on the scooter says. "Hey, how are you two getting home?"

"Walking," I say.

"Lucky," he grimaces and returns his attention to the long line-up of vehicles ahead of him.

Relieved to be able to bypass the police barricade, Shakti and I leisurely stroll the distance back to Chapora, holding hands. The entire day, we float about in a romantic haze, snuggling on the beach, necking in the shallow surf, nibbling on bits of strudel. Later in the afternoon, we climb to the ruins of an old Portuguese fort, high on a hill overlooking Chapora Beach. We run amongst the rocks, wind gusting through our hair, gazing at the sunset in each other's eyes. It couldn't be better if it were a dream. We cuddle on a bench overlooking the sea, and after an hour of "French" kissing, hurry back to my room, barely crossing the threshold before all clothes are thrown to the floor, lips and tongues feasting on delicacies of the flesh creamier than any custard. The afternoon flies by with passionate cries and the biting of thighs, until with souls satisfied, Shakti and I drift off to sleep.

Around nine o'clock at night, we wake up.

"Just in time to go to the party," Shakti says, jumping out of bed.

"Party?" I yawn.

"Full moon party!"

"Tonight?"

"Haven't you been looking at the moon?"

"Actually, I've hardly noticed anything but you."

"Flattery will get you many places, but not out of going to this party. Get up and get dressed. Stew! You don't want to miss a Goa full moon party!"

Half an hour later, we arrive by foot at a huge, open field just out-side Vagator. The earth is nearly shaking from the half a dozen speakers mounted like monsters on platforms ten feet off the ground. Thousands of people in various states of undress are dancing ferociously to brain-thumping beats. Trees all around are painted in psychedelic swirls, glowing neon under bright, artificial light. Beyond the wild dancers, hundreds of mats are spread on the grass where Indians serve chai and sell snacks. The energy is overwhelming. There are so many people in one place, yet what strikes me is the undeniable, unmistakable presence of peace. Everyone is smiling, reaching out to others with love. There isn't the slightest trace of aggression. No fistfights, no territorial posturing. Personal space seems to have dissolved. People are hugging, sharing mats, patiently waiting for large crowds to pass. This is Goa incarnate. Woodstock. The Sixties. Love. It really is all you need.

"Hey! You guys, come here!" Pritti calls out. She is seated on a mat with Stoney, Aldo and Tracey. "Look what I just scored."

"What?" I say.

"Acid!"

"Really?"

"What's a full moon party without it?"

"Enough for all of us?" Stoney inquires excitedly.

"Oh, yeah."

"Excellent!" Stoney says. "This will definitely help with my headache!"

"Who's in?" Pritti asks.

I look over at Shakti.

"Well, this is Goa," she says. "Anything goes."

Carefully, Pritti distributes to each of us a miniature postage stamp, instructing us to keep it under our tongues a few seconds before swallowing.

"There's no zip code for where this will send you," she says. "It'll take about an hour for it to hit. Let's dance in the meantime."

As a group we follow her over to where thousands of others are already entranced, grooving to the mind-altering, bone-shaking rhythms. I easily lose myself in the music, until some time later I notice I am losing something else. I think it's my mind. Everything is starting to change. My eyes, without warning, pry wide open. Colours intensify. Figures and forms melt and solidify. The very ground beneath me seems to liquefy then reappear whole. Trees sway at the trunk like go-go's on the old Dick Clark show. Groovy - I must be hallucinating!

Rainbows are now streaming all around Shakti, shape-shifting her features, until suddenly, she dissolves right before me, condensing into a luminescent ball of light. There's no trace of her body left, just pure radiating light. I'm starting to get frightened, this is getting too weird, when just as radically, the ball of energy diffuses, once again taking on Shakti's familiar form. My head is spinning. I can hear Shakti calling, but her words are all muffled, as though she's speaking in slow motion.

"Stew - are - you - all - right?"

"I - think - so, - are - *you*?" I hear myself say, but my voice is far away. I'm not sure if I said it or thought it, if she heard it or felt it. I just stagger to my feet and wander away. Everything is altering so rapidly. People pass me by and I can't stop from giggling. But no one seems to care. I make noises like a monkey, faces like a clown and no one even reacts as if I'm behaving strangely. I'm totally free. This is really alive! But then I become anxious. Maybe I'm not alive at all. Maybe I've died. Maybe I'm a ghost. Maybe nobody sees me because I'm not even really here! Where am I? Then I wonder - who am I? Who am I really? I know that I'm thinking, but am I all these thoughts? Because, even though I'm thinking, I now realize there's also part of me watching. Who is it that's thinking and who is it that's watching? Am I being watched or am I the one watching? Then, I become aware of another me watching the part of me watching the part being watched! Where am "I" in this mess? Nothing seems solid. Everything appears to be an illusion. Except for one thing - I feel inexplicably, unconditionally loving. I look out over the vast field of modulating, vibrating flesh, and feel like weeping, so strong is my love for every beautiful, jiggling body. I am swept up in the current of the moment. The music is pulsating. My heart is opening. My mind, though, is overloading. I can do only one thing to ensure my sanity. I surrender all thought, give the "watcher" the night off, merge with the merry masses, and dance, dance, dance until sunrise. Finally, I am completely exhausted, famished and parched. I wander over to the straw mat area and find Shakti and Pritti sitting, having chai.

"Where were you?" Shakti asks.

"Oh, what a long strange trip it's been," I mutter.

"You sound just like Jerry Garcia," Pritti smirks.

Shakti rises and takes me in her arms. We hold each other close for a long moment then I look deep into her blue eyes. "I realized something last night," I say, seriously.

"What?" Shakti asks, concerned.

"I-I love you," I tell Shakti for the first time.

She sighs, relieved. "And, I love you," she smiles, kissing me tenderly.

"Aw, shucks," Pritti grins. "Ain't drugs wonderful."

Chapter 16

PASSING STONES

"Shakti."

"Mm?"

"Shakti, wake up."

"What, Stew? It's the middle of the night."

"Wake up. I don't feel so well."

"What's wrong?"

"I think it's my kidney again."

"Oh, no, Stew."

"I've got a sharp pain in my left side and I think I'm going to throw up."

"Let me take you to the bathroom."

"I don't think I can do it."

"You don't think you can make it to the bathroom?"

"No, I don't think I can vomit knowing there might be a pig underneath me."

"Don't worry," Shakti says. "Arnold doesn't sleep in the toilet, he just dines there."

"Thanks, now I feel much better."

She helps me to my feet.

"Ow! Those pains don't give you any warning," I bawl. "I feel like I'm giving birth!"

"Come on," she says, leading me to the outhouse door.

"I think I've got to go in there alone," I say. "If I'm not out in half an hour, don't bother coming to get me. The smell will have killed me, never mind the kidney stone."

"I'll be out here if you need me," Shakti says.

Over the next few hours I feel as if I'm having a déjà vu of a déjà vu. Once again, I experience the familiar nausea, fever, delirium and crippling kidney pain. Only this time, I've acquired a new symptom, a crushing headache that feels like a herd of Maharaja's elephants stomping on my brain. By mid-morning, I'm frantic, begging Shakti to find me a doctor. She races off to the village, returning an hour later with news that the nearest doctor is forty-five minutes away - by motorcycle.

"No taxi?" I say.

"The roads are too narrow, remember?" she explains. "I've hired motorcycles to take us there. They're waiting outside. We'll have to ride on the back."

Need I say that I have never been on a motorcycle?

"I don't know if I can do this," I whimper.

Shakti assists me in straddling the motorcycle seat, but I nearly fall off the other side. "Hold on," she instructs as I wrap my arms like a vice around the driver's waist. Then, without warning - ZOOM! It's a good thing my kidney is in spasm or I'd have wet my pants for sure. The first few minutes are absolute hell. My stomach immediately rushes to my throat. My heart pounds even faster than the precarious speeds at which my driver swerves around tight corners. He accelerates recklessly at every indication of danger. Where did he learn to drive - from Evil Knievel? By the time we reach the doctor, my limbs are like jelly, my reasoning scrambled, my intestines twisted into miles of pretzel. The drivers carry me inside and lay me on a sofa. The doctor enters, looking very serious in dark slacks and a tie. Methodically, he examines me, prodding my abdomen, listening to my heart and feeling my forehead.

"You have a very high fever," he says. "One hundred and four."

"Oh my God!" Shakti cries.

The doctor sits behind a desk, fills out a prescription.

"You must take these pills," he says. "I believe you are suffering an infection. Drink as much liquid as you can. Water, juice. No milk, no coffee, no tea. Eat only bland foods. No curry, just rice until your stomach settles. Maybe boiled vegetables, but that is all. Do you understand?"

I nod my head dreamily. Shakti thanks the doctor, props me under her shoulder and struggles with me to the door. But just as we are about to leave, I turn back. "Doc!" I say, with sudden intensity.

"Yes?"

"I just have to know one thing…"

"Yes?"

"Can I…"

"Yes?"

"Can I…"

"YES?"

"Can I still eat walnut strudel?"

There is a long, long pause. The doctor eyes Shakti, trying to glean if I am serious. Shakti shrugs, a little embarrassed. "No," the doctor finally replies, rolling his eyes as if I were insane, not feverish.

I droop my head with disappointment. Wow, you know you're *really* sick when you can't even eat walnut strudel.

Back in my room, Shakti tucks me in bed, administers my medicine, cooks me soup, brings me rice, wipes my brow and constantly changes my sheets as they are quickly soaked in clammy, sickly sweat. My left side throbs with no reprieve, my headache has intensified to the point where the very thought of thinking is far too painful a consideration for me. After four days, the fever has still not broken. On the fifth day, Shakti surprises me with a room full of visitors she hopes will lift my spirits.

"God, Stew," Stoney says. "You look even worse than me."

"Thanks," I whisper.

"It's awful bloody bleak in here. Mind if I draw back a curtain?" Tracey asks.

"It hurts Stew's eyes," Shakti says.

"Well, darkness is always nice."

"He's had a headache for five days," Shakti explains.

"You don't only look like me, I think you're becoming me," Stoney says. "Have you tried a mushroom omelette for the pain?"

I smile weakly.

"What do you think is the problem?" Aldo asks.

"Kidney stone," Shakti says. "Maybe an infection."

"I brought with me Louise Hay's book, Heal Your Life," Tracey announces. "Hmm... it says here that kidney stones are actually lumps of undissolved anger, and the affirmation needed to heal them is: I dissolve all past problems with ease."

"I once went to a new age healer," Stoney says.

"You did?" Tracey seems skeptical.

"Yeah, she told me that my constipation meant I was full of shit."

"No affirmations?" Tracey asks sarcastically.

"Oh yeah. The affirmations she said I needed to repeat were: I release all *crap* from my body, and, I resolve to *dump* my problems on other people."

"Don't you ever take anything seriously?" Tracey glares at Stoney.

He reaches into his pocket, revealing a thickly rolled joint.

"I mean besides marijuana," she says.

"You know," Aldo says to Shakti. "I have been thinking and wondering if Stew might like to try some antibiotic pills I have brought with me from Italy. Sometimes these Indian pills work no better than sugar."

"That would be great," Shakti says. "We'll try anything at this point, Aldo. We're getting a little desperate. Right, Stew?"

I nod feebly.

"Hey, let's change the subject," Stoney exclaims. "We've come here to cheer Stew up."

There is silence.

"Come on, somebody say something. Hey, Pritti! Be entertaining."

"Me? Oh, uh, hi, Stew." She is standing off in a corner.

"That's entertaining?"

"How are you, Pritti?" I whisper.

"Oh, I'm okay," she says, stepping forward. "Actually, I'm pretty used to being sick myself, but I get a little queasy around other people's illness."

"Tell him about your love life," Stoney interjects. "That's bound to be entertaining."

"Well, uh…" Pritti says meekly. "Every night I'm being visited by a wet cat. Does that count? Yeah, I know, it's no man, but it's nice to have *somebody* to cuddle up with."

"I don't know. To me there's absolutely nothing smellier than a wet cat," Stoney says. "Well, except maybe a wet cow. And it's not their fur, you know. It's their breath."

"Oh for god's sake, Pritti. Don't listen to him." Tracey interrupts. "Stoney, why don't *you* say something entertaining."

"Oh, well, now that you mention it, this is sort of exciting: I think I've discovered a slight mistake with my visa," Stoney says.

"What do you mean?" Shakti asks.

"It, uh, seems to have run out," he says. "Three months ago."

"Stoney, how could you have let that happen?" Tracey shouts.

Stoney sparks up his joint.

"Never mind," she says. "I retract the question."

"I thought I had a six month visa," Stoney continues. "But the fellow at the airport seems to have only stamped me for two weeks. I don't know how things like this happen to me."

"It's a bloody mystery," Tracey says.

"So what are you going to do?" Shakti asks.

"I suppose I should go to an immigration office," Stoney says.

"They'll probably just fine you," Tracey says.

"Oh dear, how much do you think that would be? Whatever, I'm sure I can't afford it."

"Maybe you should go to the police," Pritti says.

"Don't do that," Tracey warns. "They'll throw you in jail for sure. Look at you."

"Yeah," Stoney says. "I'll probably end up spending the next ten years in an Indian prison, waiting for Amnesty International to raise enough sympathy worldwide to arrange my release."

"Well," Tracey says. "Look on the bright side. If you did go to prison, you could sell the movie rights to your story and make enough money to pay your fine."

"I could get Richard Burton to play me in the film," Stoney says.

"He's dead," Pritti points outs.

"That's okay," Tracey says. "I think Stoney would need someone dead to capture the true essence of his character."

"I could just see Stoney on his first day in prison," Aldo jumps in. "There he would be in a cell with drug smugglers, rapists, murderers, the biggest, meanest, dirtiest convicts, cornering him and asking him what heinous crime he has committed, and all he can say is, 'Well, actually, I sort of fucked up on my visa and can't afford the fine!' "

"That would definitely impress them," Shakti laughs.

"Let me see your passport," Pritti says.

Stoney hands her the document.

"Oh my dear God, Stoney! You better not let anyone see this photo. They'll lock you up for sure. You look deranged."

Pritti passes it around and indeed, Stoney looks more crazed than ever, hair completely unable to decide upon a direction, eyes swollen and glazed.

"I stayed up the whole night before," Stoney clarifies. "It's sort of the reason I'm here in Goa. You see, I'm not exactly on holiday. I kind of had to escape London."

"You're a fugitive?" Tracey asks.

"In a manner of speaking," Stoney says.

"From the law?" Pritti demands.

"Well, not exactly. More like from my best friend. You see, I was up the whole night before, sort of, uh, sleeping with his girlfriend. Well, she wasn't actually his girlfriend. Strictly speaking, they had broken up that afternoon. Although, I did in fact sleep with her several times while they were officially together, but on this night, when we were together, they weren't together - man, I've got to get it together."

"No wonder you've got a headache all the time," Tracey says.

"Anyway, to make a long story longer, I thought it would be more conducive to my good health if my best friend didn't find out, so I left. The country, not his girlfriend, well, her as well, I suppose."

"But, what about this passport photo, Stoney?" Shakti asks. "Didn't you think a clean-cut, close-shaven photo would save you interminable hassles crossing international borders? I mean, you look like a criminal."

"Quite the contrary," Stoney replies. "I think if someone were actually planning something illegal, they would make damn sure they had a decent, respectable photo. The fact that mine resembles a terrorist makes it all the more likely officials will assume that I'm innocent."

"You're as mad as your photo," Tracey sighs.

There is a pause.

"So, you think it's your kidney, Stew?" Stoney says.

I nod.

"Hmm... I heard a story recently about a kidney. It seems this girl with malaria checked herself into a hospital in New Delhi, but after a couple of weeks was actually feeling worse, so she booked herself a flight back to London to see her own physician. When the English doctor examined her, he found a big scar on her back. 'What scar?' she said. She'd never had a scar. The doctor immediately ordered an x-ray and wouldn't you know it, her right kidney was missing - stolen in that hospital in New Delhi!"

"They stole her kidney?" Aldo gasps.

"The black market pays big bucks for dispossessed organs," Stoney says. "I'd stay out of these Indian hospitals if I were you, Stew."

"I don't think you're helping, Stoney," Shakti says.

"Sorry." Stoney reflects a moment. "It's too bad my dear old brother isn't here. He could probably help Stew. He's a doctor... well, a proctologist, actually."

"A what?" Tracey asks.

"A proctologist," Stoney says.

"What's that?" Tracey asks.

"An ass doctor."

"An ass doctor?"

"That's right," Stoney confirms.

"For the love of God, why?"

"Why what?"

"Why, of all the professions in the world, would anyone want - no, choose - to spend his days up other people's asses?"

"For the view?" Pritti says.

"Money," Aldo says.

"Money?" Tracey laughs. "You couldn't pay me enough to do that job. Besides, couldn't you make as much money being an ear, nose and foot doctor?"

"Throat," I whisper.

"Is something wrong with your throat?" Shakti asks.

"Ear, nose and *throat*," I croak.

"Not foot?" Tracey says.

I shake my head.

"Okay, not foot. Whatever. But, money, let's say we rule out money as a reasonable motivation for being a proctologist, why do they do it?"

"Power!" Stoney says.

"Power?"

"Yeah, just think about it. You're invited into a stranger's office, he closes the door, straps you face down, spreads your flabby buttocks -"

"My buttocks aren't flabby," Tracey protests.

"No comment. As I was saying, spreads your flabby buttocks, snaps on a rubber glove which you hope hasn't been used, you can't see his face hidden behind you, you can barely make out his credentials on the diploma on the far wall, you hope there's no hidden video, no secret audience of cheap pleasure seekers, no cleverly concealed two-way mirrors. Sweat drips in your eyes like Chinese torture, your hands are tied down, then - whoosh! - something slimy slithers inside you! You gasp. You are overcome with a hollow feeling in the centre of your soul, a probing deep in the private recesses of your body. Then... everything goes black. You close your eyes, you open your eyes, it doesn't matter. All you see is black, that is, until forms begin to take shape and you recognize your life racing before you. You see yourself as an adult, then as a child, then as an infant spiraling back within the womb. All the pain, all the trauma of all your past lives gets relived and relived until you're nothing more than a burst of light, a SCREAM! And then, like nothing happened, he lets you off the table, sponges your forehead, pulls up your pants and escorts you to the waiting area where a roomful of perspiring, petrified people stare up at you from Time Magazine, wondering who's next. And you swear you hear muffled laughter from the receptionist as she announces your name a little too loudly as if deliberately trying to embarrass you, requesting you snap out of your state of shock, stop walking like you've got a pickle up your rectum, come to your senses and pay for the privilege."

"Wow," Tracey says. "Power."

"Exactly."

"How do you know so much about it?"

Stoney turns a little green. "Let's just say, there are experiences in this life which make you feel your cosmic insignificance on a deeply profound level. Standing in the Himalayas is one of them, having your anus inspected is another."

"Sounds religious," Pritti says.

"Well, it has most definitely taught me humility," Stoney says. "Of course, I still perspire whenever I see an index finger, but it's a small price to pay for such an enlightening experience."

"I don't know about en-*lightening*," Pritti says. "In my experience, there's not a whole lot of *light* down there."

"In your experience?"

"Don't ask," Pritti cautions, raising a finger.

"Hey, put that finger down," Stoney shrieks. "I'll start to perspire!"

"Okay, that's enough," Shakti intervenes. "Visiting hours are over. Stew looks like he's going to pass out."

"You don't think it has anything to do with our conversation, do you?" Stoney whispers sheepishly.

"Are you kidding?" Aldo says. "I was myself hoping to pass out so I wouldn't have to hear anymore about all you people's assholes! Come on. Let Stew have his sleep. Shakti, I will bring you that medicine."

"You're an angel," she says.

"Let's hope it will work."

Aldo's medicine does indeed work. By the seventh day, I am weak but back on my feet. To celebrate, Shakti and I head out to a restaurant for breakfast. When we arrive, Stoney and Aldo are there, but there's no sign of Tracey.

"She left this morning," Stoney informs us.

"Without even saying goodbye?" I ask.

"She just got the feeling it was time," Stoney shrugs.

"But I'll never see her again," I say.

"You don't know that, Stew," Shakti says. "You may see her again, if it's meant to happen. I don't think we ever meet anybody by chance."

"What do you mean?" I ask.

"People come into our lives for a reason. Either we're connected through some past karma or we have something to learn from each other in the present. When the lesson is over, it's time to move on. It's the natural flow."

"But what about mailing addresses?" I ask. "Christmas cards?"

"That's just attachment," Shakti says. "It brings suffering."

"I don't get it," I say.

"Things change," Shakti says.

Over the next few days, one by one our family fragments. First Aldo leaves, then Pritti packs up. Stoney talks about leaving but that would mean becoming sober long enough to sort out his visa. I don't think it will ever happen. Then one night, while Shakti and I are in bed snuggling, the bomb drops.

"Stew, I have something to tell you," she says.

"What's that?" I say, cozy in her arms.

"I know I've been a mystery to you, of sorts..."

"I like that," I say.

"But what I haven't told you is that I am only in India for a total of two months. In three days, I have to leave for Bombay to catch my flight home."

"What?" I cry out.

"It's true. I'm so sorry I haven't told you earlier, but I wanted the dream to continue. I was trying to just be in the present."

"Wait a minute," I say. "You're talking like we'll never see each other again."

"Well, you still have travels ahead of you and after that you'll be back in Toronto."

"So, you can't be that far away," I say.

"I live in Berkeley, California."

"Okay, maybe you can be that far away, but that doesn't mean we can't work it out somehow."

"I really try to live in each moment," Shakti says. "If we're meant to be together, we will, I have no doubt. And if we're meant to flow apart, we'll always have this time together, we'll always have Goa."

"My heart is breaking and you're sounding like Humphrey Bogart in Casablanca."

"In four days, you will be in India and I'll be in California," Shakti says. "Open your heart and trust. Try not to hold on."

"Can I at least have your mailing address?" I ask.

"Of course. Don't be silly."

"I don't want to lose you," I say.

"You never had me," she says. "We only had these moments."

"Will you think I'm less macho if I weep?"

"Stew, promise me one thing."

"What?"

"Whatever you do, choose peace. No matter the circumstance, no matter who is with you or who is not, no matter where you find yourself, choose peace, not suffering."

"Shakti, you're even a better teacher than that cow on the beach."

"Stew, you sure know how to flatter a girl."

"This is even more painful than my kidney stone."

"Everything passes," she says.

For the next two and a half days, we barely leave my room, torn between bliss and sorrow, speaking our most intimate thoughts. I've never been this happy, never felt this dejected. The morning Shakti is leaving, we have one more wild, desperate, clawing encounter in bed. Shakti wraps her long legs about me, pulling me towards her for one last game of "Goddess And Devotee."

Lying there after, Shakti whispers, "That'll be ten rupees."

"What?" I laugh. "I thought sex was free."

"Sex *is* free," she says. "Love is ten rupees."

Finally, the moment arrives when Shakti must go. I travel with her to the train station in the town of Old Goa, my heart growing heavier, my brain growing numb. I help her with her bags and escort her to her seat. She gives me one last passionate embrace, drawing stares from the other passengers. The train's whistle sounds. I grab Shakti's waist. The whistle sounds again but I can't release my grip. Tears trickle, bitter to my lips.

"Go," Shakti says. "Go and choose peace."

The locomotive begins to roll. Reluctantly, I dash down the aisle to the door and leap to the platform below. There I stand, watching the train become smaller and smaller, growing tiny, like a far and distant toy, stealing with it down those forlorn and dusty tracks all my hopes for love, all my dreams of joy.

Later, alone in my room, I stare out the window at the moon. It brings no solace. Shakti's laughter, once robust and alive is but an echo in the silence. I wallow in hollow memory. My bed is empty. My heart is frozen. Sleep brings no comfort. Darkness is no friend.

Chapter 17

HOW DO YOU LIKE BOMBAY?

I abandon Goa two days after Shakti leaves me at the station. On a desperate whim, I follow her by train, hoping to find her again in Bombay before she flies back home to California. It shouldn't be that hard. There are only fifteen million people in Bombay. How difficult can it be to track down one of them with no address or phone number?

I'm an anxious wreck without Shakti. I'm restless, distracted, constipated. Why is it I can never break up without my intestines taking the worst of it? You would think after so many past failed relationships, I would be accustomed to the physical and emotional fall-out. But each time I am left, I sink helplessly further into a pervasive sense of loss and despair. My old insecurity rears its head, shaking an already flimsy foundation of self-confidence. The familiar tape begins in my head. "I am unloveable," it says, and I believe it.

Abandonment is nothing new to me. When I was barely sixteen, I had my first real taste of it when my grandmother unexpectedly passed away. At the time I felt she was the only one in the world who truly loved me. She doted on me. She listened to me. She could hardly speak English, but then I could have said nothing and she still would have heard. Her death broke my heart. And then, two years later, almost to the day, my father succumbed to cancer of the liver. I vividly recall that day, arriving at my father's hospital room with my mother and sister. My brother was already there, standing in a corner facing the wall. My aunt was crouched at my father's side, weeping. My father's withered body was no longer propped as usual on pillows. It laid motionless, stiff, hidden head to toe under a sheet. My mother immediately began wailing hysterically. My brother turned, allowing a torrent of tears to burst free from his eyes. My sister, who was only thirteen, ran off down a corridor, sobbing. But I just stood there in the doorway, white with fear. Suddenly, my aunt grabbed me by the shoulders and shook me viciously, shrieking, "Why aren't you crying? Your father is dead! Your father is dead! Why aren't you crying?"

In retrospect, I can see that life for me froze in that moment. I was abandoned once again, terribly and permanently. I was too afraid to feel. Only rage was safe. Anger kept my father alive.

I wonder as the train barrels through the humid Indian night, how such velocity can generate a complete lack of breeze. A sickly apprehension churns my stomach. The throttle of the engine drives my heart further into a state of nervous tension. Each hour brings me closer to Bombay.

It is six-thirty in the morning when the train finally wheezes to a halt. I step down onto the platform, morning rush hour teeming all around me. From an impatient porter, I find out I'm actually not in Bombay at all. I'm in Dadar, a suburb on the outskirts of the city. I try to discern where to catch the connecting train to Bombay's Victoria Station, but by this time chaos has engulfed me. Though I've traveled the railways of South India for months, I feel as disoriented as a novice. Maybe that's why Westerners refer to Asia as "The Orient" - because of our constant need to "orient" ourselves to what should be familiar.

I am literally spinning, attempting to decipher in the midst of all the confusion which platform leads to Bombay, when out of the corner of my eye I notice a beggar kneeling on the floor not far from me, but quickly realize he's not kneeling at all. He is propped upright on two mangled stumps that were at one time his knees. This in itself doesn't strike me as extraordinary, a shortage of limbs being the least shocking of deformities one is exposed to on a regular basis in India. It's only when I take a closer look that I notice, to my surprise, his calves and feet standing right *next* to him, casually erect and detached to the left of him, appearing as though they followed him of their own accord, or were waiting independent of him for the next train. I stand there for twenty minutes trying to wrap my mind around this anatomical puzzle. Those calves beside him are undoubtedly real. Whether or not they are *his*, will forever, in my sleepless nights, remain open to debate.

Before I can ponder further, a tempestuous surge of commuters sweeps me forward contrary to my will. For a moment, it seems to me that the entire population of India has congregated on this single, narrow platform. Just then, I hear a loud mechanical moan and a locomotive appears speeding around a bend, bursting with an excess of passengers: women dangling from windows, children clinging to rooftops, men in suits with briefcases hanging hazardously by their free arms. The platform crowd immediately tightens its grip about me, forcing me to the track's edge, I wonder how anyone expects to get *on* that arriving train, or *off* the train for that matter, or whether this is even my train!

Before the engine has even barely begun to brake, I have my answer. Bodies begin plunging with abandon from the locomotive's roof into the sea of humanity around me. A child thrown from its mother's arms just misses my head. At the same time, from the platform, Bombay businessmen wrestle for passing iron bars with which they hope to lift themselves onto the train. By the time the train has actually stopped, a titanic battle has erupted between those desperate to flee and those frantic to board. Those wishing to stay on the train are mercilessly thrown off. Those wishing to stay on the platform - namely me - are forced on! Profanities spark the air like firecrackers on the Hindu holiday Deewali. A fistfight breaks out. Still, the throng continues to bloat and ebb and cheer and for all I know even *bet* - but does not miss a beat, just oozes around the combatants like a giant one-celled organism. And then - just as I'm being tossed uncontrollably, my feet literally inches off the ground - everything suddenly stops. I don't understand how. It makes no rational sense. But for a brief, surreal, yet definite and unmistakable moment, the crowd, the fight, the noise, everything actually stops! And in that very moment, an Indian man turns to me, smiles broadly and with utmost sincerity says, "How do you like Bombay?" - at which point all hell breaks loose again and I am briskly whisked away.

Somehow, I manage to finally sever myself from the rush hour melee and escape to relative safety outside the Dadar Station, deciding to taxi my way to Bombay, thus avoiding another muddle with the trains. Now, there are three prices you should know about in negotiating taxi fare in India: 1)"Local price," which refers to what the Indians pay, 2)"Fair price," which is about double the local price and what foreigners should expect to pay, and 3)"Tourist price," which is simply off the scale, basically what people pay when they've just stepped off the plane. On the way to Bombay, I agree upon a taxi price somewhere between "local" and "fair," but halfway there my driver tries to take me for a "tourist" and ups the fee.

"Five hundred rupees, Baba," he says. "Trip cost me much rupees, much gasoline!"

Actually, he used the gasoline driving forty-five minutes out of our way searching for my hotel - The Ganesh View Guest House - despite the fact he swore before we left that he knew exactly where it was located.

"This not it? No worry Baba, I find hotel. I know all hotels in Bombay!"

Yes, and I'd like to sell you swampland in New Delhi.

Bombay, as it turns out, is not the cesspool of humanity my imagination led me to believe, a jungle of decaying bodies and oppressive shanties where beggars cling savagely to ankles and sleeves.

"No, that is Calcutta!" corrects the patron at my hotel.

My hotel, though in the posh "Colaba" business area, is actually a seedy dormitory on the top floor of an obscure building, the entrance being an innocuous stairway hidden behind aggressive street vendors selling luggage, clothes, radios and picture postcards of the Hindu gods. My room is claustrophobic, my neighbour offers to sell me heroin, and with the lights out at night I hear the small scurry of feet and can't sleep. In the morning, I find on my bed a chewed up bone and several large black droppings. In the afternoon, I change hotels.

The Hotel Lawrence is much cleaner but Bombay is already wearing me down. I have a fever of one hundred and two, a dry, hacking cough and diarrhea so bad I'm doing the "Bombay Bolt" to the bathroom every twenty minutes. I'm suffocating in Bombay. I have an overwhelming sense of paranoia, a result of the constant solicitations to buy drugs, change money, eat lentils. I am keenly aware of the possibility of theft and am repeatedly warned against trusting any Indians, but never - "Never!" I am told - trust a Westerner.

I wander the streets of Bombay, hoping to run into Shakti. Maybe she's doing some last minute sightseeing or shopping. I am searching for her outside the famous five-star Taj Mahal Hotel when a turbaned man with excessively large earlobes saunters up to me.

"Clean your ears, meester?" he says, snatching an oversized Q-tip from behind his own ear and twiddling it between his fingers with the dexterity of a martial arts master.

"Uh, no, thank you," I say, wary that he may strike at any moment.

"Feel good. Clean ears. Five rupees."

"Ears already clean," I say, slowly backing away, wondering what other bodily orifices he has cleansed with his Q-tip. I cross to a sidewalk where an obese woman is begging while voraciously stuffing her mouth with pizza. "Ome rubee, ome rubee," she says, spitting pizza dough at me as I pass. I'm not sure she really needs my charity. I stop to consider buying some shelled peanuts from a leper when suddenly I feel a warm hand on my shoulder and turning, find a rotund, middle-aged Indian man perched too closely for my comfort behind me. He is sporting an expensive pink dress shirt, navy pleated pants and shiny, snakeskin shoes. He has a thin moustache and slick black hair that he combs obsessively. His chin doubles as he smiles at me.

"Beautiful day, isn't it? May I purchase you some peanuts?" he says.

Before I can say no, the transaction is complete and he hands me a rolled up newspaper-cone of nuts.

"Thank you," I say, suspiciously.

"What country?"

"Canada."

"Oh, very good. Excellent! Tell me, sir, how long have you been in India?"

"Six months."

"And, how do you like Bombay?"

"Swell," I say.

"You look like a man I can trust," he continues, walking beside me now down the sidewalk, occasionally mopping sweat from his brow with a silk hankie. "You see, I have a slight problem, nothing too important, still I would like to ask your humble assistance."

"No thanks."

"I will pay."

Pay?

"Cash. You would perhaps like American cash, American dollars?" His eyes meet mine. "You see, I am a businessman trying to make a better life for my wife and children, but the government of India has passed laws that are very unfair. I wish to move to London, England, to set up business there with my brother, but the government has passed many restrictions on the amount of money I am allowed to take with me. If you will believe, there is a seventy percent tax on foreign monies leaving the country, but only a one percent tax on traveler's cheques made out to my business."

He hands me his business card: P.T. Govinda - Gems, Antiques, Carpets.

"Here is what I propose. I will give you American dollars with which to buy traveler's cheques at the bank. You then simply sign the cheques over to my business, and for every thousand dollars that you change for me, you will keep one hundred American dollars for yourself."

He moves even closer to me, standing well within my personal bubble. I don't trust him and yet, his plan does sound foolproof. What would I have to lose? He gives me the cash, I go into the bank, buy traveler's cheques - there's nothing illegal about buying traveler's cheques. I sign them over to him and travel a few months longer with the money he pays me. Still...

"Let me tell you," Govinda intrudes upon my thoughts. "I am supposed to meet a man today, right now, from Australia who changed money for me yesterday and seeing how simple it was, has asked to change more. Perhaps you would feel better if you meet him. After all, he is a Westerner like yourself."

I hesitate but then agree and next I know we're in a taxi, speeding through unfamiliar neighbourhoods, screeching to a halt outside a non-descript chai shop. We enter and sit at a table near the back. Mr. Govinda barks at a passing waiter, smiles at me and promises that chai will be forthcoming. I can feel a pit forming in my stomach. Moments later, a burly white man appears and seats himself beside me. He is mid-forties, dirty blonde. A shag moustache shades his lips like a broom.

"G'day mate," he growls in an accent that sounds strangely Germanic.

"Where is it you're from again?" I ask.

"Australia."

"Are you sure you don't mean *Austria*?" I say.

"No, I am from down under."

"Is that near Vienna?"

"I am an Aussie!" he shouts. "Sydney, Melbourne, Byron Bay!"

"Okay," I say. These Arians - I mean, *Australians* - sure are touchy.

Mr. Govinda excuses himself from the table, inviting us to get better acquainted.

"You thinking of changing money?" the Australian says.

I shrug.

"Easiest thousand U.S. dollars I ever made. I'd have to be crazy not to come back for more. Govinda's a nice enough chap, wants to move to London, God only knows why. Did you see this article?" He takes from his pocket a piece of newspaper torn from the Times Of India. "Seventy percent tax to take money out of India. Can you believe that? Government, ha! They're all criminals, I tell you. They're holding the country hostage. Can't even take a vacation abroad these poor bastards. I'm glad to help the old bugger."

Mr. Govinda returns. "So, are we about ready to do business?"

I would answer but the pit from my stomach has now moved to my throat.

"There's been a slight complication." Govinda says. "I was just speaking with my uncle who works at the bank. He is the one who exchanges my rupees for American cash, which then I give to you. He is a dear man, my uncle, but very suspicious. You see, he is not acting strictly legally to give me American money and is most apprehensive as to who then receives the cash from me. Perhaps I don't need to tell you but my uncle and I have been cheated before. A Western man simply took our money and ran. I am afraid my uncle requires proof that you have enough money yourself not to steal ours. What he would like to see are your traveler's cheques, as proof, of course."

"Suspicious bugger," the Australian interjects.

"He would like to see yours as well," Govinda says to the Australian.

"What? I already -"

"I know, I know," Govinda sighs heavily. "There is no other way."

"Well, let's go see your uncle in the bank," the Australian says.

"I'm afraid you can't go into the bank with me. It would arouse a great deal of suspicion. I will need you to give me your traveler's cheques. I will go into the bank and satisfy my uncle, you will wait for me outside. When I return, we will go to another bank to complete our transaction."

"But -" the Australian says.

"There is no other way."

They both look at me. I must look as green as George Washington on the one dollar bill. My mind is a mass of bells, whistles, sirens and sitars, warning me to abort this increasingly suspect venture. But a few hundred dollars - U.S. dollars! - could extend my travels for months, a few *thousand* and my extension could be indefinite. And what, I ask myself over and over, could Govinda possibly do with my unsigned traveler's cheques? Against all better judgment, I comply.

Govinda and the Australian whisk me out of the chai shop into another taxi. We hurtle through a maze of even more unfamiliar neighbourhoods until the three of us are deposited like sore thumbs in the midst of an impoverished section of Bombay.

"My uncle's bank is down the street," Govinda says. He is very agitated. "Quickly, give me your traveler's cheques."

The Australian hands him a bundle wrapped in cloth.

"Wait for me here," Govinda says and with that he disappears.

The Australian and I try to act nonchalant, inconspicuous, but we are the uncomfortable recipients of a growing number of hostile stares. An eternity later, Govinda returns. He is short of breath and temper. He abruptly returns to the Australian his cloth bundle and - I can see - a wad of American bills. Flagging down a passing taxi, he practically throws the Australian into the back seat, shouting to the driver in Hindi. The taxi tears away and Govinda turns to me. My fingers are like a vice around my money belt. I hesitate.

"Hurry! There are a million eyes watching!" he hisses.

The pit in my throat is now in my brain. My fingers numbly release their grip and I watch myself helplessly hand over the entire contents of my money belt - *four thousand dollars* in traveler's cheques, my passport, credit card and a few hundred rupees cash. Govinda grabs the package, turns to leave, then stops, teetering indecisively. Meeting my sheepish eyes, he removes my passport, credit card and cash and returns them to me, keeping the traveler's cheques.

"There is a restaurant on the next corner, wait for me there," he commands gruffly and is gone.

I find the restaurant, sit in a booth in the back and order chai, but I'm unable to drink. A blur of humanity passes on the street outside, but no Govinda. No Govinda.

An hour later, the sun has set, I have yet to touch my chai and the restaurant patron is staring at me quizzically. I have never felt so alone as I do this night in Bombay. I yearn for Shakti almost as much as I do for Govinda. Suddenly, I bolt from the restaurant into the dark street, frantically searching for either. The air is cold but I'm sweating profusely. Faces shun me with alarm. No taxi will stop for me. Finally, I jump in front of a cab and beg the driver to take me to the Taj Mahal Hotel - the only landmark I can think of - and mercifully, he acquiesces. As I ride in the backseat, it is all I can do to suppress the tears. I have just handed over all my money save a few rupees to a complete stranger.

Back at The Hotel Lawrence, I lie in my room in the dark, envisioning Marlon Brando from Apocalypse Now muttering over and over, "The horror. The horror." I know how he felt. What to do now? Go home? No! Determined, I wrench myself from a paralysis of fear and decide to take the one affirmative action that can rectify this entire ugly mess - I'm going to lie through my teeth. I find a nearby police station and file a report of theft, fabricating a story that my money belt was stripped from my body while being jostled by a crowd of commuters at the Dadar train station. The police chief, a swarthy character, is immediately skeptical. He menacingly rotates a dagger in his hands as he reads my report.

"Where were you?" he interrogates. "At what time? Lost all your money but not your passport? Curious..."

He refuses to sign my report on the grounds that the theft occurred in another precinct's jurisdiction. I am near panic when the police chief is interrupted by a phone call of some urgency. Uniformed officers begin to march past us carrying billyclubs and pistols. The chief stares at me momentarily with disdain then begrudgingly signs the report, if only to be rid of me.

The next morning is Sunday, and I must wait a full harrowing day to find out whether the traveler's cheque company will believe my story and refund my money. I read and reread the traveler's cheque agreement, clearly stating that the company is not responsible for any loss that occurs while involved in illegal activity... such as swindling the government of India?

I do not leave my room.

Monday morning early, I walk the few blocks to the traveler's cheque company's office, avoiding contact with anyone, especially Westerners. Seated before a committee of stern company representatives, I recount the alleged details of the theft, trying to look pathetic. I don't have to try that hard. I hand them the police report. I am asked to repeat my story several times, the last being over the phone, long distance, to the president himself in New Delhi, who, after a grueling cross-examination, informs me that ... I will be refunded, in full.

I am on the very next available bus out of Bombay, having given up all hope of locating Shakti.

A week later, in a medieval castle turned hotel, deep in the jungle of a tiger reserve in Rajasthan, I sit down to dinner with two young blokes from the English countryside. After a few beers, one of them looks up at me and inquires, "Have you ever been robbed, I mean, in India?" He and his friend proceed to tell me of their very first day off the plane, how they were approached on the streets of Bombay by an overweight Indian man with a thin moustache, telling them of his hardship with the government and foreign currency. They relate in detail my entire fiasco, down to being left stranded in a remote restaurant, watching the sun set on any hopes of ever seeing Mr. Govinda again.

"But what about the Australian?" I ask. "Weren't you suspicious of his accent?"

"What Australian?"

"The Australian with the German accent?"

"There was no Australian," the British blokes say. "The chap with the German accent was one of you."

"One of me?"

"He was Canadian."

"WHAT?"

Well, I suppose I should be proud of my country's multicultural society. A crook can have any accent and be totally believable as a Canadian.

Chapter 18

BIG CITY BLUES

The train from Rajasthan to New Delhi rages through the arid countryside, scenery flying by in a blur of dust and shriveled trees. A hazy crescent-moon hangs limply on the parched horizon like a wedge of burnt orange. For countless hours now, I have been standing erect on this train, pressed between other passengers, marinating in their sweat to the point of feeling like a curried sardine. Finally, I manage to squeeze myself a spot on the floor by an open door and sit, legs dangling precariously off the edge of the train. I stare down at the tracks whizzing by underneath me, clasping tightly onto an iron bar to secure myself from falling. The speed is exhilarating, the roar of the engine deafening, the passing objects hypnotizing. Suddenly, a hand from outside the loco-motive appears and grabs onto the bar that I am holding - a hand? *Outside?* Who could possibly be outside the train when we're traveling at such astonishing speed? The answer comes quickly. Incredibly, an Indian man swings up and over me, flipping his body into the train. Not only that, but he has a dozen glasses propped under one elbow and is amazingly supporting a huge, scalding metal cauldron in his other hand. Then, once inside the train, as if nothing out of the ordinary has happened, he brushes himself off and instantly begins plowing through the cramped cabin, selling tea.

Cautiously, I lean forward and look both ways out the open door, pondering the enormous scale of the stunt I think I have just seen. That this man could have possibly monkey-ed his way one-handed the entire length of this car, train plummeting at ridiculous velocity, handling an awkward, bulky, metal container of potentially injurious hot beverage in a death-defying feat rivaling any performed by Indiana Jones, all in the name of selling tea! Remarkable, I think, when out of nowhere, more hands appear, more bodies swing acrobatically into the train past my head: peanut salesmen, chickpea salesmen, dosa salesmen. If I didn't see it, I wouldn't believe it, and having seen it, I still don't believe it. Only in India, I think.

My journey from Bombay to New Delhi has been an exasperating trip through bleak topography. If the outer world is truly a manifestation of my inner state of mind, then my emotional terrain must be a wasteland indeed.

My near disaster with Mr. Govinda in Bombay has all but tightened a vice about my heart. I wear a permanent scowl, treating everyone universally with suspicion and disdain. I am a powder keg waiting to blow. Every town I pass through seems devoid of redeeming qualities. Not one person extends even the slightest trace of hospitality. Some people are actually outright nasty. My impatience only serves to exasperate the situation. Travel is never quick in India, but on this particular trip I've exhausted endless hours waiting, spent days being delayed and have endured more than my share of haphazard connections from Bombay to Aurangabad to Fardipur to Jalgaon to Surat to Ahamedabad to Udaipur to Jaipur to New Delhi! If this hell is really the outer expression of me, man, what a cesspool my inner mind must be.

I finally do reach New Delhi, another in a string of overcrowded and polluted big Indian cities. But I figure if there's anywhere in India to get a good smoked meat sandwich, it's got to be in New Deli, right? *Deli*? Smoked meat? Maybe I've inhaled too much smog.

I find accommodation in the Main Bazaar, or "Paharganj" in Hindi, a marketplace with inexpensive lodging conveniently close to the train station. I splurge on an air-conditioned room at the Anoop Hotel; a ceiling fan in New Delhi is simply not enough to cut through the oppressive humidity.

The next day, I am up with the sunrise and New Delhi is ablaze, already ninety-five degrees at six-thirty in the morning. It's so hot that my body keeps on sweating even while I'm taking a cold shower. Out on the street the air is stagnant. The Main Bazaar is a cyclone of curry and dust. Rickshaws and taxis choke me with their exhaust. Cyclists hiss at me as they try to pass. Fruit carts are stacked with produce that has already wizened. Cheap "flip-flop" sandals are piled high in mounds of melting rubber. Women hustle by me in faded apple-green and cherry-red saris. A man with shockingly pink, hennaed hair - an obvious dye job gone bad - beats soot off of bedspreads hung outside his storefront. Everyone is perspiring, but most of all I pity the men deep-frying "samosas," leaning their faces for hours over enormous black cooking drums spitting boiling oil. Even from across the road, the heat from these frying pans hits me like radiation. I can only imagine what it must feel like up close.

In the Main Bazaar, I purchase a set of Indian percussion instruments called "tablas." The storeowner packs them in a box and sends me off to the post office to mail them back to Canada, warning me about Indian postal workers who have a reputation for routinely slicing open packages to rob them of their contents. He advises me to pay a man outside the post office to sew up my parcel in a cocoon of white linen. Boxes sealed with linen are supposedly less apt to be tampered with and therefore more likely to arrive undamaged at your home - a year or two later, yes, but at least in one piece.

Inside the post office, I hand over my linen-covered box to the clerk, knowing full well that there is still no guarantee my parcel will make it all the way back to Canada. The clerk inspects the box, weighs it, then blatantly asks me for a bribe, clearly implying that if I don't hand over a handsome baksheesh, he will personally oversee that my package gets lost right here in New Delhi. I'm outraged, but what can I do? I offer him one hundred rupees.

"Is that enough?" I ask resentfully.

The postal worker shimmies his head.

"Alright, what exactly does that mean?" I snap. "Yes or no?"

The postal clerk shimmies his head once again. "Sometimes yes, sometimes no," he grins, snatching my hundred rupees, "but most certainly always maybe."

Well, that's about as imprecise a definite answer as I should have expected. I guess I'll just have to wait a year or two to see if my package makes it to Canada.

Now, there are a few luxuries I discover in New Delhi that do make my stay momentarily bearable. Some of the food for instance is actually excellent. I find the Lebanese buffet at "El-Arab" exquisite and the ice cream desserts at "Nirula," refreshing. Another feature to New Delhi that makes my stay more pleasant is, surprisingly, the train station, which offers a special service agent upstairs from whom tourists alone are allowed to purchase tickets, thus enabling me to avoid the bedlam of the general reservation counter downstairs.

And there are several decent budget restaurants to choose from in New Delhi's Main Bazaar, my favourite being "Leema's" - mostly for its, uh, *creative* menu. There are so many interesting items listed. For example, for breakfast, how does one possibly decide between *banana cornflags, scrumbied eggs, half fried egg* (what do they do with the other half?), and *banana paincake*? For lunch, the choices include: *italian omlat inside chicken, finger cheeps,* and *sweet and sawar rice.* And dinner offers these enticing dishes: *spegetee chicken buls,* and *chicken katan blue-inside chess*! What the heck is that supposed to be? For dessert, it's *rice fooding* and *jinger tea.*

Actually, the real reason I find myself frequenting Leema's is not the menu, the food, the service or the ambiance, all of which are in their own way lacking, but because I've met a Danish girl who for some reason seems to like it there. Now I know it seems hasty to be indulging in casual dating so soon after I've just left Shakti, but I have never been one to tolerate loneliness well. The sad truth is, my entire life I have been burdened by a crippling insecurity. The only times I've ever approached feeling worthy within is when I have been the recipient of a woman's attention. I have been so desperate to be loved, so desperate for a tender touch, that I have always readily fallen "in love" with any woman that has shown me the slightest kindness or interest. Everywhere I go I am attracted to women, willing for any one of them to alleviate my suffering. It hardly matters whom. Did I really "love" Shakti, or could I have just as easily been smitten with Pritti if it had been she who had joined me for dinner that night in Chapora? Well… maybe not Pritti. But I really do like this Danish girl I've just met. I love Danish. Blueberry Danish. I'd like to learn how to make my own Danish. Maybe this girl will be able to tell me how.

And it's so much easier to meet girls in India. Not only are most girls more relaxed, more open on the road than they would be at home, but right from the start we have something basic in common – traveling.

"Where are you from?" This is usually the icebreaker. Next comes, "How long have you been traveling?" and "How long *will* you be traveling?" followed by, "Where have you been?" and "Where are you going?" Invariably, all travelers have been to some of the same places or have shared variations of a similar adventure. Travel itself is the tie that binds, for at some level, travel is more than just a hobby or vacation. Travel becomes a philosophy, a way of life, a state of mind.

Travelers rely on each other for a vast network of information. If you want to know where to find the best and worst meals, finest and grimiest hotels, where to change money, where's the best shopping - ask another traveler. That's why I'm having lunch with this Danish girl. For the information. I'm hoping to benefit from what she might know about, uh, making Danish... of course, it doesn't hurt that she's gorgeous.

"There is one thing you must do before leaving New Delhi," she says over a lunch of *noodal soup* and *massed potatos*.

"What's that?" I whisper absentmindedly, staring into her dreamy blue eyes. I am hoping she will invite me to marry her and move to Denmark.

"Visit Dr. Triguna, the world-renowned pulse diagnostician."

"Oh," I sigh, disappointed. "Where is his office?"

"Any rickshaw driver will know how to take you to Dr. Triguna. He's that famous."

"Can I see you again later?" I ask.

"Sorry," she says. "I am leaving tonight to go back to Goa."

"WHAT?" There go my plans for our wedding day. Maybe Shakti was right all along. Try not to hold on, she said. Everything is impermanent. Stay in the present. It's good spiritual advice, even when the present, at the moment, sucks.

That afternoon, I head out alone to see Dr. Triguna. At first, it appears my attempt at visiting the famous doctor might turn fruitless, when no rickshaw driver seems to have any idea who I'm talking about.

"Dr. Triguna," I repeat, but am met with uniformly blank expressions. Frustrated, I enter a shop to buy a Gold Spot orange soda and casually strike up a conversation with the vendor. To my surprise, *he* has heard of Dr. Triguna.

"Tell the rickshaw driver to take you to the fat doctor," he advises.

The *fat* doctor? I'm skeptical, but I follow his instructions and sure enough the drivers all respond.

"Oh, the fat doctor!" they exclaim - well, why didn't I just say so in the first place? I hop in the back of a rickshaw occupied by a driver and his young friend. They tell me their names are Prince and Martin Luther King.

"Pleased to meet you," I say. "And I'm Michael Jackson."

They roar with laughter.

It takes a tediously long time to reach Dr. Triguna's clinic, situated in a poor, Muslim suburb of New Delhi. Once there, though, I find out why so many make the trip. Dr. Triguna is indeed world-famous, one of only three Indian physicians closely associated with Transcendental Meditation guru, Maharishi Mahesh Yogi. As a result, Dr. Triguna's services are in constant demand internationally, but it is a testament to his greatness that someone as influential as he has chosen to operate an entirely free clinic in one of New Delhi's most destitute neighbourhoods. My rickshaw drivers refer to him as a saint.

I wait with dozens of Indian patients at the clinic. I am the only white person there. Dr. Triguna keeps the flow moving quickly in and out of his office, seeming to treat whole families in mere moments. From where I sit, Triguna's face remains hidden, but I'm able to catch glimpses of his hands, struck by how big and yet how gentle they seem. Finally, my name is called and I'm ushered into his office, immediately engaged by his humble smile. He is indeed a large man, well over six feet tall and weighing in excess of two hundred pounds. He appears seventy odd years old, except for his eyes, which twinkle with vitality. He greets me laughing and invites me to pull up a chair, then with great care takes my wrist and with fingers like probes tunes into the subtle throbbing of my pulse. Within seconds, he looks up.

"You have pressure in your kidney, yes?"

"Yes," I nod. How could he know that just from my pulse?

He concentrates. "Also sluggish liver. Try not to eat tomato or dairy. Most important, take one teaspoon of this Ayurvedic medicine twice daily with a great deal of water."

"Thank you," I say, receiving a small plastic baggie filled with grainy powder. I bow and turn to leave.

"One more thing," he says.

"Yes?"

"You are a very good man. A very good man with a very good

nature. A simple, good nature."

"Uh, thank you," I say. "Could you tell that from my pulse?"

"No," he says, with a smile. "From your face."

Chapter 19

TAJ MAHAL

As the beautiful lotus sprouts forth from the slimiest dregs of mud, so does the Taj Mahal emerge like a delicate flower from that cesspool of a town, Agra. Why is it that the least attractive parts of India are exactly the places every visitor seems to go? Bombay, New Delhi, Agra, Calcutta, if these have been your only package-tour destinations, then in my opinion, you haven't seen the "real" India.

All through the South, the locals cautioned me repeatedly regarding India's northern big cities. I was told that people in the North would be more aggressive. Every greeting would conceal hidden motives. There would be none of the friendly curiosity of the South. These warnings were not exaggerated. If Calcutta is supposedly the "City Of Joy," then Agra immediately impresses itself upon me as the "City Of Greed." At least half a dozen men claiming to be "my friend" approach me at the train station as I arrive from New Delhi, inviting me back to their homes for tea, but I'm certain they'd just as soon mug me in the next alley. Everyone appears slippery. Salutations seem insincere. If the Taj Mahal is indeed one of the wonders of the world, I think the wonder is that it's situated in as distasteful a place as here.

"Shaleem!" annoying storeowners call to me as I pass, thinking I'm Israeli and mispronouncing the word, "Shalom." "Come into my shop!" they cry out. Everyone it seems either has a shop or knows someone with a shop. "My brother, he has a shop," or "My brother's cousin's uncle, *he* has a shop." Every time I get into a taxi in Agra, the driver refuses to take me where I want to go, neglecting of course to tell me this until we're well on the road. No matter what destination is prearranged, we always end up pulling into some restaurant or hotel or carpet emporium from which the driver stands to earn a commission. "I don't want to eat here," "I don't want to stay here," "I don't want to shop here!" I protest, but where I want to go seems to be last on everybody's list of priorities. Now, it's not as if I'm unsympathetic to these drivers' need to earn a better living, but I feel powerless being led blind through a strange city, unsure of the credibility of my guide.

One particularly shady driver, unshaven and reeking of booze, cautions me sternly not to talk to anyone around the Taj Mahal. "Do not trust anyone!" he warns. He says this, of course, after he has already taken me against my will to every carpet emporium in town. What do you do then, when you don't trust the person who is telling you not to trust anyone else? Who do you trust? It reminds me of a line from an old Elvis Costello song: "When I told you I was lying, I might have been lying." I think this should be translated into Hindi and hung from a banner in Agra's town centre.

And, if that's not enough, one morning, from the balcony of my hotel, I suddenly hear a noise and looking down, notice an old man, obviously unaware of my presence, lifting his dhoti and squatting directly below me, proceeding - by the smell of it - to shit! So much for the fresh morning air. Another day, again from my balcony, I spy a young man this time, pooping below me. Obviously, the hotel owner neglected to mention that for the hefty cost of my room I was not only afforded spectacular views of the Taj Mahal but the public toilet as well. The young boy catches me watching him, but to my surprise doesn't look embarrassed, neither does he stop what he's doing. He merely holds out his hand and calls up to me, "One pen?"

One pen? Good God! What a time to be begging? Maybe he should be asking me for "one toilet paper" or "one pooper-scooper." That would be more appropriate.

I am amazed at the many uses for excrement in India. Children gather it on their heads heaped in silver pans; old women lay it out to dry in gardens, smoothing the dark, slippery patties with the palms of their hands. Dried chunks of dung are later burned as fuel, feeding the fires over which families cook their dinners. I wonder if that also applies to restaurants. I'm not sure I'll ever look at curry in the same way.

One afternoon, I am out strolling, when I literally stumble upon the most shocking sight I have encountered yet in India. I nearly trip over the body of an old man, or should I say, what's left of him. He is armless and legless, barely a lump of flesh thrashing on the street below me, completely naked, covered in weeping, purulent boils. He has a wild, Medusa-like shock of hair, a long stringy beard, and is shrouded from head to - well, pubis - in white powdery ash. My inclination at first is to shriek. My second impulse is also to shriek. I don't wait for a third urge - I just shriek!

But most disgusting of all is what I witness one night. I'm walking behind two young white girls, tourists, when all of a sudden I hear vulgar, sexually explicit shouts in English from a nearby vehicle overloaded with drunken Indian men. The men of these big cities have absolutely no shame. Time and again, female tourists complain to me of having their breasts cupped or asses pinched by anonymous Indian hands. I've seen women pushed with frustration over the edge of restraint, shouting into amorphous crowds, crumbling in hysterical tears from being groped.

India, in my experience, is in many ways a sexually repressed society, treating women as second-class citizens. I've heard of babies being murdered simply because they were born female; women killed so their husbands may collect another dowry. Even birth control, in a country hopelessly burdened with overpopulation, is resisted because to discuss family planning one must first broach the taboo subject of sex.

Now, take this narrow-minded notion of sexuality and add to the mix the appearance of young, exotic, Western women who have been raised on totally opposite worldviews. Take a society with ultra-conservative values regarding modesty, and introduce women in bikini shorts and skimpy halter-tops! It's one thing to bare legs or show cleavage in Toronto, but to do so in Agra is another matter entirely. It sends out the wrong message. It does not represent women as being more liberated or empowered, but is all too easily misinterpreted to portray Westerners as being sleazy.

An Indian man once told me that he simply could not understand the Western mentality. In India, he said, when you are married, you stay married. The family is the cornerstone for a stable existence. He just could not relate to the Western concept of divorce. Sex before marriage, multiple marriages and illicit affairs were all examples of Western moral decay. It's no wonder, he said, that Indian men think all Western women are promiscuous. They advertise as much with their inappropriate clothing. Now, I am personally of the opinion that all Westerners - men and women alike - should dress in deference to the culture they are visiting, but I also challenge all cultures to get with the twenty-first century. Women are not sexual objects, nor are they property.

In contrast, the Taj Mahal itself is a lasting example of one man's respect and devotion for his wife. From the looks of it, you would think the Taj Mahal was built merely as a palace, but in fact, it was constructed as a grand mausoleum by the emperor, Shah Jahan, in memory of his second wife, Mumtaz Mahal, who died in childbirth in 1631. The emperor is said to have been so much in love with his wife that his hair became gray overnight from the sudden tragedy of her loss. The Taj Mahal then, became Shah Jahan's sublime expression of dedication to the woman he adored, beginning possibly as a construct of grief, but transcending soon after into an embodiment of God.

As at most other tourist attractions around the world, the pathway to the Taj Mahal is lined with vendors selling souvenirs. I am attracted to an Indian version of a toy I used to have as a child called, "Spyrograph," which here is named: "Spray Graph."

The toy basically consists of plastic pieces with holes into which you insert pens of varying colours. By holding the pen in the hole and spinning the plastic pieces, you create different images and designs on paper. Sound simple? Well, nothing in India is simple. To prove my point, here are the instructions exactly as I find them inside my "Spray Graph" packet:

> Piece any paper on which you with to drow on a
> Garboard and fixed the yositive and on the round
> Drawing pine, then place any and of the wheels

inside the ring to the paper and by blacniby and co our bellpen point in a hole is the wheel it care fully inside the ring. All the time keep the teeth of the ring Numbers Dialing can be drawn from one wheel by using different holes in the wheel against the ring. You can also draw many more dialings by placing the wheel in contact with the outside tooth of the ring and reating the wheel with different holes. The re in limit to time number of dialings you can dran drow from this.

What language are they speaking? Is that supposed to be English?

Now I must admit, having heard so much about the Taj Mahal, I fully expect to be disappointed, wondering how any man-made structure could live up to the hype afforded India's most celebrated treasure. At first, I think a red stone gateway is the Taj Mahal and feel vindicated. "I knew I wouldn't be impressed," I think. But then turning a corner, I encounter the actual Taj Mahal in full view and am immediately taken aback. It is perfect, absolutely symmetrical, graciously designed, magnificent beyond any photo. Its rounded towers seem to be reaching towards heaven, the shrine itself appearing in a perennial posture of prayer. It is truly one of those rare moments when gratification far exceeds expectation. All clichés apply - my jaw drops open, breath is taken away. I am speechless, spellbound, moved beyond description. I wander the neatly trimmed grasses, appreciate the manicured flowerbeds, lose myself in the soft glare of reflecting pools. Every detail seems to have been arranged as a lavish offering.

I stay all afternoon. I linger through sunset. I return for sunrise. From every angle, the Taj Mahal thrills anew. With each subtle shade of daylight or moon, the Taj Mahal responds shyly or boldly, somberly or with ecstasy. For you don't just see the Taj Mahal, or visit the Taj Mahal, you feel it. It emits energy. It is built with so much love a tangible intensity exudes from each symmetrical stone. It speaks to me in silence. It inspires in me piety. I mourn with it sorrowfully, but ultimately it impels me to surrender with humility, acceptance, and calm.

Chapter 20

BRING OUT YOUR DEAD

Varanassi, or "Benares" as it is also called, is something of an anomaly. While arguably the holiest of Indian towns, built on the banks of the sacred river Ganges, this city of Shiva is at the same time one of the most intensely disagreeable places I have ever visited. It is easily on par with, if not worse than, Agra in terms of acute harassment and blistering heat. As for the heat, luckily, I am here in springtime, when temperatures are only unbearable as opposed to summer when they can easily be fatal, rising sometimes above one hundred and twenty degrees. As for the harassment, after Bombay, New Delhi and Agra, my patience is definitely waning. By the time I reach Varanassi, my motto has become, "Just one day of peace, please!" I never get it. I cannot walk two steps without some Tom, Dick or Rajneesh pestering me to purchase some pitiful bauble. Just as my nerves are nearly completely frayed, I stride by a shop called "Kashmiri Carpets, Fine Arts And Collectibles." Its owner is loitering in the doorway. He resembles a well-dressed human snake.

"Looooooooking?" he hisses as I pass, inviting me to come in and check out his wares.

"No thanks," I say.

"Come, come, just loooooooooking," he says.

"No thanks."

"Just looooooooooking. No buying!"

"No buying?" For a moment my interest has been peaked.

"Just loooooooooking," he says. "Looooooooooking is free!"

"No, sorry," I say, coming to my senses. Loooooooooking may be free, but the hasssssssssling that begins as soon as you step into a shop can be quite costly indeed. I try to escape into Varanassi's old city, but that plan only backfires. The assault of strangers actually intensifies due to the narrowing of alleys. Suddenly not only verbal but physical contact becomes practically unavoidable. Not even a "Bhang Lassi," a yogurt drink laced with hashish, can take away the edge. As a last resort, I head to the holy steps overlooking the Ganges - the "ghats" - but still am unable to find a moment's respite. A Sadhu approaches me and without invitation begins to perform a puja for my benefit while chain-smoking, hacking his way through mantras, coughing up gobs of black mucus instead of prayers. I'm just glad he doesn't dab cigarette ash on my forehead.

I read a sign posted by the Varanassi ghats and am once again bemused by the quirky Indian misuse of English grammar:

NOTICE FOR THE TOURISTS
1. Shoes, sandals & sleeper sare
   to be keep 30 ft. from The Steps
   of the ganges.
2. In Benares area men & women are
   not allowed to kiss & ambrace in public.
3. Half-clothes are not allowed men &
   women please dress respectively.
4. Strictly prohibited are drugs
   alcohol non-veg food please
   respect the Hindu.
   Religion and follow the above
   Regulation.

Who exactly writes these things? I shrug my shoulders, seat myself by the flowing river and am finally enjoying a moment of relative silence when a zealous boy races up to me.

"You want astrology reading?" he says.

"No, thanks," I respond wearily.

"Good astrology. You come see my boss, Neelu Baba."

"No, thanks."

But after half an hour...

"Alright," I say, not really wanting the reading, just hoping to stop the sales pitch. The boy leads me through a series of alleys and into the back door of a dark, dilapidated building.

"Wait here," he says. How do I get myself into these situations?

Finally, the boy returns, joined by a man in his sixties with a mop of white hair and a long grandfatherly beard. He is shirtless, wearing nothing but a white skirt (a dhoti), over which a huge potbelly unceremoniously hangs. Except for his tan and incongruous attire, I'd swear he was Santa Claus.

"Hello!" he exclaims, introducing himself as Neelu Baba. "You are here for astrological reading?" His voice is startlingly high-pitched.

"Uh, I guess so," I say.

"What is your year of birth?"

"1962."

"What is your month of birth?"

"October."

"What is your day of birth?"

"27."

"Oh, Scorpio!" he says.

"Is that good?" I ask.

"Very powerful," he says. "Obsessed with birth and death. Very intuitive, mysterious, magnetic... sexy."

Did Santa Claus just call me sexy?

"What is your time of birth?" he asks abruptly.

"I don't know."

"You don't know?"

"No."

"Your mother has not told you?"

"To be honest," I say. "The way she describes it, you'd think she wasn't even there."

Neelu Baba appears visibly disturbed. "This will make reading astrology very difficult, if not impossible. Still, I can try!"

He seats me down, scribbles for several minutes then begins.

"You... have been plagued by illness," he speaks dramatically. "Kidney."

"Yes, that's true."

"I have perfect remedy. Drink one cup cow's urine every day for three months. All problems will disappear."

"Cow's... what?" I say.

"Urine."

"I was afraid that's what you'd said."

"Not very tasty, but most medicinal."

"I'll see what I can do. Uh, what else do you make of my chart?"

"You... will soon be very bald!"

"Are you sure you didn't just see that from my head?" I ask.

"No, no. Most definitely in your chart. Most positively! My friend, when planets align, you lose hair."

"You're quite the psychic," I say.

"I know perfect cure for baldness!" he exclaims.

"Why am I not surprised? What do I have to drink this time?"

"No, no drinking," he says. "Merely have a cow lick the top of your head twice daily."

"Lick?"

"Top of your head twice daily. Soon, you will have beautiful hair just like mine."

I try to imagine myself with Neelu Baba's hairdo. "You have a thing for cows, don't you?" I say. "What else is in store for me?"

"You... will meet very beautiful woman!"

"Now, we're talking." I edge in closer. "I wouldn't mind *her* licking my head."

"That will not cure baldness."

"No, but it might fix a few other things."

"Oh, yes! Sexy." He grins.

Stop saying "sexy," Santa.

"I see very intelligent woman," he continues, "very much thinking, thinking all the time."

"That's good," I say.

"Not necessarily. She will think too much and you, my friend, will lose a lot of sleep."

"That's in my chart?"

"Planets never lie."

"Do you know any cow remedies to help me rest?"

"Warm milk?"

"I'm not supposed to drink milk."

"Separate beds?"

"That would probably work."

I see myself several years from now, married to a very beautiful, very intelligent woman who sleeps in my house while I am relegated to the barn, cuddled up with a full head of hair and a cool glass of urine next to "Neelu," our family cow.

And speaking of hair, I later read in my guidebook that the Ganges River is said to originate from the supple hairdo of Shiva, seated on his throne high in the Himalayas. Credited with healing, rejuvenating powers, the Ganges's holy waters attract thousands of pilgrims to Varanassi each year. It is said that to die in proximity to the Ganges is to be reborn in Nirvana, or heaven, freed from the endless cycle of reincarnation and suffering. Hindu men and women on the verge of death are known to travel courageous distances for the chance to spend their final days in run-down hotels near the Ganges. Often though, these elderly souls linger in this world longer than expected, and unable to afford the cost of lodging in Varanassi any longer are forced to die with disappointment on the road returning to their village homes. To actually live in Varanassi then, with daily access to the saintly river, is a great and enviable blessing amongst Hindus.

One of the main tourist attractions of Varanassi is a sunrise rowboat ride along the Ganges, and so at 5:30 one morning, I force myself from bed and hurry down to the river. The Ganges at dawn is a mystical place, a sleeping beauty awakening from the serenity of gentle slumber. I hire a rowboat and guide and set sail. There is a hushed, tender silence as we drift in the downy blue of early morn. My guide is an ultra-thin, elderly Indian man rowing two enormous oars. After awhile, I ask if I can row, but am shocked to find I can barely nudge the oars, let alone lift them. I don't know if I'm so weak or my guide is the Indian Arnold Shwarzenegger in disguise.

From the vantage point of my rowboat, I become absorbed in witnessing the ghats, or steps that line the shore of the Ganges. They are a world unto themselves, teeming with the activities of religious worshipers on the one hand, and locals engaged in daily chores on the other. Elaborate ceremonial pujas are performed next to women drearily scrubbing laundry. Clothes are laid to dry on steps where sacred incense is burning. Sadhus submerge in holy water to their waists, next to men in underwear covered with soap, brushing their teeth.

I am amazed at the diversity of uses for this unfiltered river. People drink from the same waters where both garbage and dead bodies are dumped. Yet, such is the mythology of the Ganges, whose waters are held to be healing despite the fact that logically they should be brimming with bacteria. It makes me wonder about the power of faith over our immune systems. How much do our beliefs play a part as to whether or not we are healthy?

I am actually finding some peace on the boat, far removed from the hassles of souvenir salesmen, when all of a sudden I cringe, hearing that familiar sound.

"Hey meester!"

Oh, no.

"You want to look, maybe buy?"

Wait a minute! How is this possible? I am nowhere near shore. In a panic, I turn to discover another rowboat nudged against mine, crammed with every sort of trinket imaginable. Oh Shiva, is there no escape, even on your holy river?

"Change money? Good price."

Talk about being a captive audience. If the water were any cleaner, I'd be tempted to jump overboard.

The boat ride proceeds, my guide now straining with each glide of the oars, sweat dribbling down the wrinkles of his forehead, bright red frothing from his lips. At first, I think he's bleeding, but then realize it's only the disgusting residue of "betel nut paan," the local, legal narcotic of choice. Basically, paan is a concoction of lime paste, powder, spices, the highly addictive betel nut, and opium in the more expensive variations, wrapped in a green, leafy substance. Though paan can be found any-where in India, Varanassi is definitely paan-central. Everyone seems to be preoccupied with its consumption. Vendors abound on every street corner, selling it to children and adults alike. Paan is a lot like chewing tobacco, stuffed between one's cheek and tongue. The upside is you get a mild buzz. The downside is it rots your teeth, staining your gums and lips a clownish shade of red. It's also not the prettiest of sights to witness everyone horking crimson gobs of goop onto the street, not to mention how hard it is for me to understand the locals' broken English when their mouths are stuffed with a mush of saliva-soaked paan. Ladies and gentlemen, number one thousand and one on the list of Indian dialects, distant cousin to Pig-Latin... Varanassi's own, "Paan-Hindi."

My tour of the Ganges continues past a large pink water tower painted with a massive mural of Shiva; past a section of ghats decorated with hundreds of patio umbrellas; past two ancient palaces built by the Maharajas of Jaipur and Nepal; past a domed Hindu temple half-sunken into the river. Finally, the boat glides in view of Varanassi's cryptic "Burning Ghats" - an outdoor large-scale crematorium where bodies are burned publicly on the edge of the sacred Ganges. From my boat, the Burning Ghats present a startling juxtaposition of gigantic stacks of bleak, brown wood set against mounds of blazing, red fire. Later, back on shore, I find myself drawn there, hoping for a closer look.

The first thing to hit me as I approach on foot is the pungent stench. There is nothing savoury in the smell of burning human flesh. Worn-out woodcutters catch my eye next, swinging huge hammers, breaking apart tree trunks with impressive brute strength. In torn, gray rags, they remind me of a chain gang condemned to a lifetime of hard labour; their slow, grunting movements in themselves a dance of death.

Corpses wrapped in brightly coloured silks - incongruously festive considering the occasion - are strewn upon funeral pyres. Their faces are all covered, but the shapes are unmistakably human - the rounded slopes of skulls, pointed chins, jutting noses. An emotionless man then feeds a torch to straw, wood catches fire, silk ignites and then flesh begins to smoulder. Skin crackles, bones pop, sparks fly. Flesh disintegrates right before my eyes, yet everyone around me seems to be taking things in stride. I'm not so easily detached. The sight of death starts me shuddering. A twist of fear turns my stomach. There is no escaping the cruelty of reality: all that remains at the end of our days are ashes tossed to the river, embers fading into memory.

I sit until evening, cadaver after cadaver paraded before me. Passion and regret, so immediate in life, are purged of their importance in the ravages of fire. Elation and frustration in the end are reduced to nothing more than dust. Existence that so fleetingly flares hot, quickly grows cold in a spent funeral pyre.

I imagine myself, not some stranger on that fire. What void will I create, if any, when I'm no longer here? And what of those things I value so possessively? Do they really carry meaning? It's funny but there have been so many times in my life that I have wanted to die. Life seemed overwhelming. It would close in upon me like a choking, musty odour. It would frighten me into hiding. At times it seemed like it would be more preferable to disappear than endure any more suffering. But now, in the presence of these Burning Ghats, with death so immediate, life strikes me as being urgently precious. Every worry, every stress, in perspective seems too serious.

Sitting by the Ganges, I admire her dexterity, so vibrant with activity yet so receptive of mortality. She is truly the Mother of all India, sustaining her children in life and welcoming them in death, all in a day on the edge of her sacred flowing waters.

Bathing in the Ganges.
An enjoyable exercise…
except for the occasional
floating dead body.
(Varanassi)

SOMEBODY GET ME
DOWN FROM HERE!!!
(New Delhi)

I highly recommend the nose and ear massage. (Bombay)

Would *you* have your hair done at a place that advertises you'll come out looking like this?
(Bombay)

When it's naptime,
it's naptime.
(Downtown, Agra)

Tone-deaf beggar.
Five rupees to hear him
play. Ten rupees to get
him to stop!
(Anjuna Market, Goa)

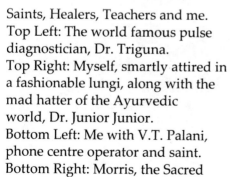

Saints, Healers, Teachers and me.
Top Left: The world famous pulse
diagnostician, Dr. Triguna.
Top Right: Myself, smartly attired in
a fashionable lungi, along with the
mad hatter of the Ayurvedic
world, Dr. Junior Junior.
Bottom Left: Me with V.T. Palani,
phone centre operator and saint.
Bottom Right: Morris, the Sacred
Cow, in the deepest meditative trance I've ever seen. Either that or
she's sleeping.

IV

IS
THAT
A BUDDHA
IN YOUR POCKET
OR
ARE YOU JUST
ENLIGHTENED TO
SEE ME?

Chapter 21

A TRIP TO THE DELHI ALWAYS REPEATS

On the ghats on the shore of the Ganges, I watch in fascination the colourful collection of Sadhus and supposed Indian saints. What is the story with saints in India? Are their legends really true? Do they actually sit in treetops for days or huddle reclusively for decades in caves? Can they really levitate or slow their pulses to the point where they're almost not breathing or stand for years on a single appendage (not necessarily their leg)? I am baffled by the inexplicable occurrences surrounding these miraculous beings.

Here in India, saints are unquestionably holy. If they happen to have a bone in their nose, nobody thinks twice about it. If they happen to be stark naked, it's only a sign of piety. But let's face it, in the West if someone's naked, they're not revered, they're arrested. Someone in seclusion is rarely in meditation, more likely glued to endless reruns on television. But here in India, everything is different. The supernatural is second nature and allows for a certain level of deviant behaviour.

Every Westerner I meet in India is at some level looking for a saint to enlighten them - it's the overriding subconscious reason all Westerners are here. For India is reputedly steeped in the mysteries of spirit. Even I, a self-proclaimed skeptic, become intoxicated imagining that a "saint" may actually be able to reveal the hidden meaning of life, eradicate my problems, erase all my suffering. Even I would willingly surrender better judgment to a guru, simply for some insight into what the heck we're really doing down here.

In Thiruvanamalai, I sought out the ashram of Ramana Maharishi, hoping that *he* might be my guru, only to find, to my disappointment, that he had, in fact, recently passed on. I tried not to take his death too personally. In Bangalore, I inquired into studying with a man widely considered to be a direct incarnation of God - Sai Baba - only to be told he was "presently on tour" (probably opening for Celine Dion). Maharishi Mahesh Yogi, guru to the Beatles, wasn't even in India anymore. He was somewhere in the Netherlands collecting vintage cars. Paramahansa Yogananda, another Indian saint, was available to me only in paperback, and though his book Autobiography Of A Yogi was truly inspirational, I kind of had my heart set on finding a guru who was still alive.

Why are we here? What are we doing? Why do we suffer? How to be happy? All these questions swirl about me after my experience on the Burning Ghats. I am in need of some direction, some guru-like inspiration. I am a lost puppy in the kennel of spirituality, begging for anybody to throw me a philosophical bone. I call my mother long distance. "Ma, Ma, tell me what to do. I'm feeling so confused. I need to find a guru!"

"Guru, shmuru," is my mother's reply. "Why do you need a guru? You've got me."

Hmm… I've got her. Come to think of it, her hair does resemble Sai Baba's Seventies-style afro. That's got to count for something. Besides, who else has exerted so much influence on my life? Who else has taught me how to be in the world? Who else do I call upon in times of need? My mother, that's who - my true guru.

Of course, as far as gurus go, my mother is extremely unconventional, unless you grew up in a Jewish household, in which case my mother would seem completely normal. Traditionally, one would expect a spiritual teacher to lead by example, but my mother always does precisely the opposite of what I think is right. Education through reverse psychology, I suppose. It's a wonder I'm not *more* confused.

"Mom," I plead with her now on the phone. "What is the meaning of life? Is there any point in acquiring possessions?"

"Well, that depends. How much did you pay?"

My mother, like most spiritual sages, has always advocated for being unattached to material things. Unfortunately, my mother is usually referring to *other* people and their possessions. One time at my brother's house, my mother arrived with a suitcase of gifts for her grandchildren. Inside were a stack of children's books, each inscribed sloppily with the name "Mikey" in crayon.

"Who's *Mikey*, Mom?" I asked.

"Nobody."

"How come his name is on all these books?"

"No reason."

"Where did you get these books, Mom?"

"The doctor's office."

"The doctor's office?"

"Yes."

"You took them from the doctor's office?"

"So?"

"You can't just take books from a doctor's office, Mom."

"Why not? No one else was using them."

Two days later, I went to see the eye doctor. In the waiting room, there was an excellent pictorial history of Major League Baseball.

"I didn't want to go in for my appointment," I told my mother later. "I could have stayed there all day reading that book."

"Why didn't you just take it?" my mother replied.

"Well, forget the fact that the receptionist was seated right there, or that the book was a huge encyclopedic volume impossible to conceal, forget even the Ten Commandments! Usually my better instincts simply advise me not to steal."

"Hmm..." my mother pondered. "Did they have any children's books? I should get my eyes checked."

"Mom!"

But somehow, through reverse psychology, my sense of morality became sharpened. The more she made up her own rules, the more I became an activist for an ethical society.

"Mom," again I implore into the phone. "Life is so fleeting. What's the point of even eating?"

"WHAT?" she cries. "Are you not eating?"

I should have known better. The subject of food is sacrosanct for my mother. My mother's answer to any problem growing up was simple: Eat. You're sick? Eat. Worried? Eat. Scared? Eat. Full? Eat. You're fine? Eat. And if that doesn't help? Sleep! Nervous? Go to bed. Restless? Go to bed. Nauseous? Go to bed. And if you're really in tough shape - first eat, then go to bed. Or better yet, eat *in* bed!

You would think from my mother's skewed attitude towards diet, I would have reacted by becoming a health nut. That would have been the correct application of reverse psychology. But as it turned out, all I became was obese. Strangely though, my mother always maintained a slim figure, probably from that most Jewish of all calorie burners - worry. Ever go to a Jewish exercise class? It's twenty women sitting around in chairs fretting. That's low impact. For high impact, add complaining. Nothing sheds pounds faster than a concentrated session of kvetching.

One time when I was fourteen, at my mother's request I actually did agree to go on a diet. "You're only allowed one dessert," my mother said. But that evening, with my mother watching, I remember polishing off a dozen - that's right, *twelve* - chocolate ice cream bars after dinner, which theoretically, still counted as my *one* dessert. One *type* of dessert, according to my mother, apparently fell within the criteria of my diet. You've heard of Fit For Life? Well, this diet was Fat For Life. No wonder I gained thirty pounds in rapid success-ion.

"Now, listen Stewart," my mother imparts her wisdom to me over the phone. "Snap out of it! Don't worry so much about the meaning of life. My philosophy is: drink coffee, smoke cigarettes and eat sugar. Enjoy yourself. What's the point of living *longer* if you're just going to be miserable?"

In other words: Keep it simple.

My mother, as a guru is a little unconventional, but this much I know. She never speaks when angry. She is generous beyond reason and her love is unlimited and unconditional. You don't need reverse psychology to learn from that.

From Varanassi, I consider continuing on to Calcutta but by this time I have had more than my share of big Indian cities. I decide instead to head north to the town of Dharamsala, high in the Indian Himalayas. But ironically, to get to Dharamsala, I have to travel back through a big Indian city, New Delhi, a prospect I loathe to consider. But at least New Delhi is familiar. For once I won't have to fret over where to stay - I'll just go directly to The Anoop Hotel. For once, I won't have to stand uneasily outside a strange restaurant, wondering if it's clean - I know perfectly well Leema's will be filthy.

It is late at night when my train pulls into New Delhi but on this occasion not even darkness can faze me. I am confident, cool. Sauntering up the Main Bazaar, I easily find the Anoop Hotel. The night watchman there instantly remembers me, showing me to the exact same room I stayed in last time, where to the familiar rattle of the air conditioner, I drift into the welcome embrace of sleep.

That is, until I awaken screaming to a dream so stupid it's actually scary. I'm in a park somewhere minding my own business, when all of a sudden, a figure appears rushing towards me wearing a bright, orange flannel body suit joined atop its head in an upright, menacing cone. It looks like a giant carrot, charging directly towards me! I bolt awake, weeping.

Well, I said the dream was stupid. I've heard that in dreams each character represents an aspect of your own personality, but though I lie awake most of the rest of that night, I simply cannot fathom which of my many demented selves could possibly be embodied by something as ridiculous - even to my subconscious - as a psychopathic, man-eating carrot. All I know is that I may never look at a supposedly benign serving of "mixed vegetable curry" in the same way again.

Actually, I do have an idea what may have prompted this sub-liminal interest in carrots. A few months ago, I phoned a friend of mine back in Toronto to find out if his wife had given birth to their first child. He was thrilled to tell me she had, but when I asked him his baby girl's name, the phone line swallowed his voice with a sudden intrusion of static. All I could make out was my friend shouting into the receiver, "Karen with a T. Her name is Karen with a T." Then the connection died completely. Afterwards, I was dumbfounded. "Karen with a T," I kept repeating to myself. "My friend named his daughter, Karet? Like the vegetable?" Oh well, who was I to judge? I just prayed he wouldn't name his future children "Asparagus and Rutabaga." But just recently in Vara-nassi, I spoke with this same friend again.

"How are you?" I asked him.

"I'm fine," he replied. "My wife's fine too and Taren is great."

"Taren? Who's Taren?"

"My daughter, Taren. I told you - Karen with a T."

"Karen with a T? Taren? I thought you named your child Karet."

"Carrot?" my friend laughed. "Why would anyone name a child, Carrot?"

No wonder I'm having bad dreams. I always said the Indian phone system was enough to give someone nightmares.

The next morning in New Delhi, I search out my old haunt, Lee-ma's Restaurant, only to discover that it has been bombed in my absence. *Bombed!* Standing before the rubble, I wonder if the incident was due to an insidious terrorist plot or just someone ticked off at the slow service. I go to another restaurant but am afraid to relax. I tremble as I notice the man next to me leave a briefcase behind as he apparently goes the bath-room. Every day in the Indian newspapers, I read about politically inspired kidnappings, explosions and murders. It's either the militants in the northern state of Kashmir vying for independence, or the militants in the Punjab vying for independence, or the militants in Tamil Nadu vying for independence. Muslims fighting Hindus. Hindus fighting Sikhs. The religious fight the secular and everyone fights the Communists. But nobody seems to be fighting up in Dharamsala.

That evening, I book an overnight train out of New Delhi to the northern town of Phatangkot, from which I am told I can transfer by bus to Dharamsala. My train actually leaves at midnight from the "Old Delhi" station, far from the Main Bazaar. It takes forever to cross the city by rickshaw at night, but I try to remain calm. All the way there, I dread the crush of the station, the hectic, confused searching, the panic of not knowing which platform, which train, which seat, which car. But I try not to worry and sure enough, as soon as I enter the station, a kindly police officer escorts me to Platform #2, where I find the Jammu Mail Express waiting to depart on time. With ease, I find the right car and berth and lo and behold, my seat is even empty. What amazes me is how smoothly things proceed when I decide not to succumb to anxiety. After months of reacting to every situation with confrontation, I am finally learning to remain calm when circumstances become unsettling. Life will unfold according to its destiny, whether or not I waste my time indulging in nervous worry.

I arrive in Phatangkot at five in the morning. The sun has just risen. The weather is hazy and so is my head. I stagger from the platform out to the street, searching for a means to get to the bus station to catch my transfer to Dharamsala. Just at that moment a man pulls up on a cycle rickshaw.

"How much to the -?"

"Bus station?" the driver interjects.

"Uh, yeah. How did you know?"

"Five rupees… and five rupees also for your wife."

"My wife?" I say, turning to see a young, dark-haired woman with light green eyes standing beside me. She is laughing at the assumption of the driver.

"Uh, hi," I say.

"Hello, husband," she giggles.

She tells me that she is indeed heading to Dharamsala. Of course, I think, why else would any tourist in their right mind be in Phatangkot at five in the morning? We decide to share the rickshaw. The driver is delighted since he stands to earn double fare, but after a moment it becomes clear that the logistics of fitting two tourists and their hefty backpacks into one tiny rickshaw doesn't exactly add up to a smooth, easy fit.

"Maybe we should just take a taxi," I wonder aloud, but the driver, eager to secure his ten rupees, frantically begs our patience, attempting to cram a square peg into a round hole.

"No problem," he grunts, pushing and shoving at our bags.

The girl and I move back, watching as the driver struggles to compress our oversized luggage. After forty-five minutes, finally he succeeds, inviting us proudly onto the rickshaw's slightly dislodged backseat. We settle back as comfortably as possible and prepare ourselves for a long, bumpy ride. But not two minutes later, having hardly traveled much farther than just around the corner, to our amazement we arrive at the bus station. I look over at the driver.

"You could have told us it was so close," I say, annoyed at having waited almost an hour for what would have amounted to no more than a five minute walk. Perhaps it's fatigue from the train ride, perhaps it's all the unexpressed frustrations of the past months flooding in upon me at once, I don't know, but I feel the uncontrollable urge to rage at the driver for ripping us off. My jaw tightens. My shoulders stiffen. My heartbeat quickens. But before I completely lose control, I catch myself. Have I learned nothing from all this time in India? I glare at the driver's cowering, apologetic manner and suddenly recognize myself in his frightened face. He looks just as I did so many times as a child - terrified, uncertain. And I am acting precisely like my father, using anger as a weapon to wield power. But the cost is too high. I can no longer live my life this way. At some point I have to make the choice to harness my temper. I must lay my father and my five-year-old self to rest. I open my mouth to speak. The driver cringes as though anticipating a shout, but to both our surprises, I burst out laughing. The driver at first seems dumbfounded, chuckling apprehensively, then after a moment, he visibly relaxes, joining the girl and I in loud guffaws. In the end, I decide to pay the driver not only the full ten rupee fare but slip him an extra twenty as well, for there are things in this world that definitely merit generous tipping. Nothing is as valuable at five in the morning than an unexpected full-belly laugh.

"What's your name?" I finally think to ask the girl.

"Diane."

"I thought I should know, considering the fact that we are married." She laughs. "You know, I can't get over the feeling that I've seen you before. Have you ever been to Canada?"

"Nope. I'm from Melbourne. This is my first trip outside Australia."

"Strange. I could have sworn we had met."

After an hour on the road, the bus to Dharamsala breaks down but somehow this time the delay doesn't upset me. Maybe India is losing her power to infuriate me or perhaps the green-eyed girl's presence is an anesthetic to my nerves. Time passes quickly in the pleasure of her company. The bus is repaired and finally, late in the afternoon, we arrive in Dharamsala.

"Well, see you," Diane says as we exit the bus.

"Aren't you going to a hotel?" I ask.

"Yeah, but not here."

"Isn't this Dharamsala?"

"Well, yes, but I'm going to the village just above, McLeod Ganj."

"What's there?" I ask.

"Well, for one thing, the Dalai Lama."

"What's that?" I ask.

"The Dalai Lama!" Diane exclaims. "He's not a *what*. He's a *who*!"

"Oh, yes, of course… uh, who?"

"You don't know who the Dalai Lama is?'

"Uh, no."

"Come along. You'll find out," she says.

"I usually am reasonably well-informed," I say, following her to a mini bus.

"It's okay. Westerners tend to be a little self-centred," she observes.

The village of McLeod Ganj is an hour's bus-ride directly above Dharamsala up a steep inclining road. All over India at locations of high elevations are remnants of the British occupation, settlements known as "hill stations," built so the British would have somewhere to go to escape the treacherous summer heat of India's low plains. The hill station of McLeod Ganj is like many others, comprised of about four unpaved streets lined with wooden shops, restaurants and an assortment of guesthouses. You would think it was just another Indian hamlet, but from the moment I arrive, I notice something very different. Almost all the people in the village are Tibetan and unlike a lot of places I've been to recently, everyone seems to be smiling.

"Well, see you," Diane says.

"Where are you going now?" I ask.

"I'm going to find a guesthouse in the neighbouring village of Bhagsu. It's quieter there. Want to come?"

"Uh, I think I'll stay here in Mcleod Ganj. I'm intrigued by all the action. But would you like to meet later for dinner?"

"Let's just leave it to the fates," she says, surprising me with a peck on the cheek. I watch her wander away, grappling with whether to change my mind, but by the time I actually decide to chase after her, she is gone. I stand there alone by the bus stand, not wondering if I have ever seen her before, but if I will ever be so lucky as to see her again.

Chapter 22

HE WAS HOLY, I WAS HUNGRY

India abounds with spiritual centres, ashrams offering guidance in Hindu practice, but McLeod Ganj offers the chance to explore an entirely different spiritual bent. This is the place to delve into the teachings of the Buddha. Entering McLeod Ganj is like stepping through a timeless portal into the mysterious civilization of Tibet.

Almost everything in McLeod Ganj reflects Tibetan culture. In the rest of India, Sadhus dominate village streets in their bright orange robes. But in McLeod Ganj, laneways abound with the subdued yellow and maroon attire of Tibetan monks. In the rest of India, hair is often grown long and wild. Some Sadhus in fact wear dreadlocks. But in McLeod Ganj, almost everyone has a shaven head. Hair, any hair, actually stands out as an anomaly. In the rest of India, Indians, as would be expected, operate most of the local shops and guesthouses. But here in McLeod Ganj, it is the Tibetans who own the majority of businesses - except, of course, the taxi stand, which is run by a Sikh - some things are the same wherever you go.

A Tibetan butcher hangs in his window an animal carcass covered in flies - you certainly won't see that in vegetarian South India. The "sidewalk" dentist is also Tibetan (yes, he practices dentistry on the sidewalk), pulling people's teeth in full view of the public, instruments lying unsanitized on a dust-covered blanket at his feet. The roadside barber is

Tibetan as well, so is the customer with his baldhead covered in lather. The vegetable vendors are Tibetan, their produce sprinkled with clippings of hair that have drifted over from the barber's chair. I've never seen heads of lettuce with better hairdos.

Tibetan monasteries and nunneries are on almost every corner. Tibetan "prayer flags" flap from every rooftop; "prayer wheels" whirl in the village centre. There are conical structures known as "stupas" around which Tibetans methodically circle uttering prayers.

Buddhas are visible everywhere. Now, I was under the impression that there was only one Buddha - *the* Buddha - but apparently, I was wrong. Just as I was finally coming to grips with three hundred million Hindu gods, I discover there are at least that many Buddhas! Amitabha, Vajrassatva, Green Tara, White Tara, Avaloketishivara, Padmasambhava, Chenrezig, Manjushri... are Eastern religions meant to be so confusing?

Tibetan tradition is also pervasive in McLeod Ganj's excellent restaurants. I am once again thankful to discover dining establishments serving selections other than Indian food. Now, I know that Indian cuisine is considered to be one of the most succulent in the world, and in some of the more expensive restaurants in New Delhi, I admit, this may be the case. But in the budget traveler diners that I can afford, the Indian food is usually overcooked, greasy, and - to borrow a painfully accurate expression - as fiery coming out as it is going in. In my experience, the best Indian food actually is in "Little India" in Toronto, where produce is fresher, health standards higher, chickens meatier and kitchens staffed by the best Indian chefs, imported from where else - India.

In McLeod Ganj though, the food is mostly Tibetan, consisting of soothing, hearty noodle soups called "Gyathuk" or "Thangtuk" depending on the size of the noodles, and doughy dumplings called "momos." The Tibetans also seem to know how to bake. McLeod Ganj is like Goa, in that after a long, sad period of deprivation, I have once again discovered a veritable gold mine of cake. Not since leaving the sublime beaches of Chapora have I encountered a dessert worth eating. But in McLeod Ganj my prayers have once more been answered. The Green Restaurant & Bakery serves gargantuan portions of the best cake you'll ever taste outside the pearly gates of "Nirvana."

I taste-test almost all of McLeod Ganj's eating establishments. "The Tashi Restaurant" serves excellent soups. "Friend's Corner" cooks a wicked "Eggplant Garlic Sauce." "The Chocolate Log" not only offers a mouth-watering selection of desserts but the name reminds me of what comes out of me after I've eaten too many of their pastries. But my favourite is "The Himalaya Restaurant" on Bhagsu Road, not for its food, which is at best passable, not for its service, which is slow and unpredictable, but for its staff. The Himalaya Restaurant is completely run by children. The cooks are both under ten, the cashier can't be older than five and my waiter is a girl barely out of diapers. In all the times I go there, I never see an adult.

These kids at The Himalaya Restaurant, I find out, are from the destitute Indian province of Bihar, sent to McLeod Ganj to be employed as cheap labour. In India, it is alarmingly common for children from impoverished states to be packed off to richer provinces in the hopes of earning wages to support their families back home. The whole concept seems ghastly to me. I expect these children to be bitter, uprooted as they were at incredibly young ages, dispatched to a strange place to work. But to my amazement, they seem happy and playful. I never once see any of them looking even remotely dismayed. They're always laughing, their smiles never failing to brighten my day. I quickly become a regular and soon whenever I enter the restaurant, the staff instantly and excitedly acknowledges me. They invite me every day to hang out with them in the kitchen, but I decline, afraid that I probably would never want to eat there again if I witness how the food is actually prepared. I become a patron of the patio instead, sitting there for hours each day - well, it usually takes that long for my food to arrive anyway.

They say you should never head for The Himalaya Restaurant when you're hungry. Strange advice, true, considering normally that is exactly when you do go to a restaurant. But at The Himalaya Restaurant, the service is so slow that if you go there when you're hungry, you'll be famished by the time your food in fact arrives - usually two hours after you've placed your order. Better to go an hour and a half *before* you'll be hungry, then just as your appetite is starting to stir, you'll only have to wait another half hour to be fed. And don't be too attached to your menu selection. Because more often than not, after suffering two hours of agonizing anticipation, the Himalaya Restaurant then serves you something entirely different from what you originally ordered. What do you do then? You know if you send it back, you'll probably have to wait two *more* hours with no guarantee that the result will be any better in the end.

What's the appeal then? It's simple. I love the gorgeous smiles of those innocent children, reminding me daily to slow right down and accept whatever comes. What's the hurry after all? Where have I got to go that's so important? Shanti, shanti. Slowly, slowly. Enjoy the luxury of time to kill.

One morning around eleven o'clock, I am sitting inside the Himalaya Restaurant, huddled within my warm woolen sweater, sipping from a glass of "hot lemon." The sky outside is dark, it is cold and blustery, and I have been *enjoying* the luxury of time to kill for the past three hours, waiting for my food. I am famished, irritable, wondering what's become of my breakfast, knowing full well that at this point I'll be lucky if it shows up in time for lunch. I enviously watch the man beside me finish an omelette and drink back the last few gulps of his tea. He notices me salivating over his food.

"You should forget about eating," he says, "and come with me."

"Where are you going?" I ask.

"To see the Dalai Lama."

"Oh," I say, but I don't really hear him, my attention suddenly riveted on a waiter emerging from the kitchen.

"He's holding a public audience today," the man continues, but I barely take notice, so distracted am I by the possibility that my meal may actually be coming.

"Who is?" I ask, gawking lasciviously at an approaching platter of pancakes.

"The Dalai Lama."

"Oh yeah." I say. The waiter is almost at my table.

"I don't know if I'll get in but I'm sure going to try."

"That's nice," I reply. My heart is pounding.

"I mean you can't just pass up a chance at seeing the Dalai Lama."

"Noooooo!" I cry as the waiter passes me by, delivering the pancakes to a couple at the next table. "Uh, sorry, what did you say?"

"You should come with me," the man repeats.

"Where?" My stomach is now grumbling impatiently.

"To the Dalai Lama. The audience with him is at twelve o'clock."

"Twelve? But what about breakfast?"

"Forget about breakfast."

"Forget about breakfast? What about lunch?"

"Forget lunch. You can eat after."

"*After?*"

I hear a rumble of thunder.

"Was that my stomach?" I say. "Listen, thanks anyway, but I think

I'm just going to stay here. I'm expecting a very important audience with a plate of pancakes."

The man seems dumbfounded but I don't understand why. He actually has no vested interest in my joining him. I just think he can't believe I would choose food over this Dalai Lama - whoever he is. Obviously, the Dalai Lama is a very important person, but my fellow diner has no idea how important food is to me. When my blood sugar drops, I can get downright cranky.

"You can't receive a blessing from a plate of pancakes," he argues.

"I don't know, I think my mother would disagree," I retort. "Eating has always been a very religious experience in my family."

The man sighs.

"Look, it's already eleven-thirty," I point out. "I don't think we'd make it there by now anyway."

"Eleven-thirty? Why didn't you tell me? I have to go!"

The man quickly bids me farewell, leaving me with a look like I'm a candidate for the looney bin. Hey, I'm not crazy. I'm hungry. Some people are so judgmental.

At one-thirty, he returns.

"Well, did you get in?" I ask, lethargically.

"Oh, yes," he says. His eyes are dreamy.

"And? So? Did you see that Dalai Lama?"

"Oh, yes. He blessed me personally." His face is absolutely beaming. "Hey, how were your pancakes?"

"They haven't arrived yet," I frown.

"Too bad. I'm on such a high!"

"Yeah, I'm feeling a little dizzy myself. Listen, do you mind if I ask you a question?"

"Sure."

"Just who is this Dalai Lama?"

"You don't know?"

"Well... no."

"That explains it," the man laughs. "The Dalai Lama is considered by Tibetans to be a direct manifestation of the Buddha Chenrezig."

"Oh, okay... is that good?"

"Chenrezig is the Buddha of Compassion!"

"Oh, okay... is *that* good?"

"The Dalai Lama is a reincarnated, living Buddha. He is one of the holiest men alive!"

"Oh, I guess that's good. You think I should have skipped break-fast?"

"I'd have starved for *weeks* for the chance to receive the Dalai Lama's blessing," the man says.

"I might starve for weeks just waiting for my pancakes," I groan.

"Look," the man tries to comfort me. "I heard they're showing a movie about the Dalai Lama tomorrow morning. Granted, it's not the same as seeing him in person, but it's better than nothing."

"Thanks," I say.

"And there's a Buddhist retreat for Westerners starting tomorrow afternoon at the Tushita Retreat Centre. You could do both."

"Really? What time do they start?"

"The film, I believe, begins at ten. The retreat starts at two."

Hmm... sounds possible, but I'll have to reorganize my priorities. Let's see, I could have breakfast before the movie... and lunch before the retreat! There's only one problem though - what about my afternoon tea and cake?

The next morning, I am at the Himalaya Restaurant by six A.M. to guarantee that my breakfast will be served in time for me to attend the movie. At ten o'clock, I squeeze into the back room of a shop selling Tibetan crafts, joining about twenty other tourists, seating myself on a rickety wooden chair before a fourteen-inch television. For the next hour, I watch as the predicament of the Tibetan people is illuminated in shock-ing detail for me through the immediacy of video. It's probably better I grabbed breakfast beforehand, because afterwards, I don't feel at all like eating.

Tibet, even at the turn of the twentieth century was still an isolated plateau hidden high in the Himalayas. It was a peaceful, remote, un-tainted haven dedicated to its religion, Tibetan Buddhism. But in the early 1950's, everything drastically changed. Under the direction of Com-munist leader, Chairman Mao, Tibet was brutally invaded by Chinese forces. A tragic chain of events was created that led to a massive flux of refugees seeking sanctuary over the Indian and Nepalese borders. One of those refugees was the Dalai Lama, a self-proclaimed "simple Buddhist monk," revered not only as spiritual but political leader of his people. Thankfully, the Tibetans were welcomed into India by then Prime Min-ister Nehru, who gave them the hilltop village of McLeod Ganj as a base from which to establish a government in exile and focal point for the preservation of Tibetan culture.

In the years since the invasion, Tibetans remaining on the wrong side of the Himalayas have been systematically subjected to cultural and national genocide. Over one million Tibetans have been mercilessly slaughtered by the Chinese. Chinese tanks have leveled ancient, irreplaceable Tibetan monasteries at point blank range. Sacred, invaluable religious relics have been looted and defamed. Buddhist monks and nuns have been imprisoned, tortured, humiliated, then executed. In one particularly disturbing part of the video, reference was made to Chinese soldiers forcing Tibetan monks and nuns to fornicate publicly in violation of their vows of celibacy. Buddhist texts have been vandalized, religious education outlawed and the Tibetan language banned from schools. Tibetans are actually now outnumbered in their native land, treated as second-class citizens. The mere mention of the name, the Dalai Lama, to this day invites a police beating. Owning his photo could land you in jail.

Over the years, tens of thousands of refugees have risked their lives to escape into India over treacherous snowy Himalayas passes, often without shoes or warm clothing. More and more parents, unable to flee themselves, began sending their children off alone in search of a home where their values might still be respected, where freedom was still possible. Countless children perished, unable to survive the arduous journey. Of those who made it over the mountain peaks, many lost fingers and toes to the flesh-eating cold.

Before the Chinese invasion, Tibetan culture remained for the most part an inaccessible mystery. But since then, Tibetan refugees have extended their unique brand of Buddhism to millions around the globe. Some Tibetans see this as the silver lining, the blessing that has resulted from their national tragedy. That's one advantage to embracing the concept of karma - it's easier to look on the bright side when you believe all events happen for a higher reason.

Today, the quest continues for Tibetan dignity, justice and self-rule, with the Dalai Lama heading a public relations campaign attempting to elicit political sympathy. Unfortunately, world leaders, in deference to China's stature, persist in turning a blind eye. And I realize, ashamedly, that I have been no better. I was not even aware of this calamity until I happened to stumble upon McLeod Ganj, a village of survivors so proud of their heritage that even here in India they carry high the proud flag of Tibet.

The video ends and I emerge from the shop into a somber, overcast day. Up the road, I pass the bustling outdoor Tibetan market, so vibrant in its efforts to endure in a strange land, and I wonder, what chance does a small non-violent nation, like these Tibetans, have against China, one of the most powerful countries in the world? Then I think of Mahatma Ghandi and the British Empire - sometimes patience and integrity, sacrifice and perseverance can overcome all.

Chapter 23

RUN AWAY! RUN AWAY!

That afternoon, inspired by the video, I hike up into the dense forest above McLeod Ganj in search of the Tushita Retreat Centre. The mountain air is crisp and most of the way I am immersed in perfect, unadulterated silence. There is not a timbre of reverberation, not a chirp of a bird, not the slightest hiss of wind. No Hindi show-tunes. Nothing. The stillness is so pristine it is almost tangible. The silence, so refined, becomes almost sensual. And I realize how rarely, if ever, I truly allow myself to be quiet. Living in the city, even when it's "quiet," there's always some noise, some hum of traffic, some ticking of a clock, but here in the startling vacuum of the forest, the absence of sound is profound. Time drifts by. Boundaries become blurred. My soul expands, feasting on an experience of serenity that until now I wasn't even aware I was missing.

I arrive at the Tushita Retreat Centre, register, and am asked to pay a very reasonable fee to cover only food and lodging - in Buddhism, I am told, the teachings should always come free. The Tushita Retreat Centre was originally founded by the popular Tibetan teacher, Lama Yeshe, a gregarious and humorous man, who dedicated his life to spreading the message of the Buddha beyond its home in Asia to centres all across the Western world. He actually chose to die in California amongst Western disciples, so committed was he to the proliferation of Buddhism in North America.

I settle into my assigned accommodation - a modest room that I share with one other - and before dinner, join fifty other Westerners outside the "gompa," or meditation hall. Awaiting orientation, I am studying the diverse collection of spiritual seekers milling about me, people of all ages and from every corner of the globe, when suddenly, who do I notice strolling towards me but Diane, my "wife" from the bus station in Phatangkot. Instantly, I'm inflated with great excitement. There's just something about her so puzzlingly familiar - not her hair, not her face, but those eyes. I jump up to hug her, quickly remembering that we're at a Retreat Centre. Physical contact is not permitted between the sexes.

"Uh, how about a mental hug?" I say to her.

"Consider it reciprocated," Diane replies and we both laugh.

It's so good to see someone I know - well, sort of know - I mean I've only spent a few hours with this woman from Australia. But in the time-distorted world of the traveler, a few hours are often more than enough to make a stranger seem like an old friend. Relationships are intensified by the very fact that as soon as you meet someone, you know that in a day or a week, you most likely will never see them again. Every moment together becomes precious, then fades just as quickly into memory. Which reminds me of Shakti. Just six weeks after our parting and it's as though our whirlwind romance, our magical connection, never even happened.

I enter the meditation hall, subdued by sad recollections, find a cushion on the floor on which to sit and try to "relax" into a cross-legged position. A bald, white woman enters the room draped in maroon and yellow robes. She takes a position at the front of the assembly.

"Hello, my name is Clara," she says with a heavy British accent. "I will be your teacher during this retreat. As you may notice, I am not Tibetan, but don't be disappointed. I am trying my very best to be." She indicates her bald head and laughs. "I am a fully ordained Tibetan Buddhist nun and it is my privilege and good fortune to welcome you to the wonderful world of Buddhism, a deeply philosophical understanding of existence that has completely changed my life, and hairstyle." She laughs again. "What attracted me, a staunchly raised English protestant, to Buddhism, you might be asking yourselves? Well, two things, really. Firstly, that I would no longer need to bother with brushes and unruly curls, and secondly that Buddhists don't believe in God. Yes, you heard me correctly. No God. No white-bearded male dominant figure in the sky inspiring fear. The original Buddha, 'Shakyamuni,' - whose name, I'm embarrassed to say, always starts me humming that song, 'Shake Your Booty' (she chuckles loudly) - was no 'god' according to the Tibetans. He was a man, a human being who through his own great effort, wisdom and compassion, realized true enlightenment and a path to end all suffering. The point is that *any* living being has it within him or herself, through diligent practice, to achieve the same perfection as the Buddha! It's not limited to a god somewhere in the sky, but within all of our grasps to become divine, not dependent upon some outer force to bestow, but contingent on our own willingness to develop qualities already seeded deep inside. This potential we all possess within is our 'Buddha Nature.' It's like a spiritual flower waiting to bloom when nurtured by the teachings of the Buddha, called the 'Dharma.' But don't misunderstand. Buddhism is not passive. It is not enough merely to receive teachings. If enlightenment is to blossom within us, it can do so only through the persistence of our own conscious effort. This implies a lot of responsibility, yes. But it is also the path to freedom."

Boy, I didn't realize Buddhism would involve so much work.

"The first teaching of the 'Lam Rim' or 'Buddhist Path To Enlightenment,' concerns a very active appreciation of our good fortune in being born human. We must passionately realize that this existence of ours is the greatest of all gifts. We are blessed as humans with the faculty of intelligence. We are able as humans to behave morally. We must not waste this precious opportunity. The seed is ripe. The time to apply ourselves is now. The goal is not to become Buddhists. The goal is to become *Buddhas*!

"The second teaching brings our awareness to the truth of impermanence, the third asks us to meditate seriously on death. But Buddhism is not morbid. The point is not to wallow in this knowledge of impermanence and death, but to rejoice in those moments that we are alive. Don't waste a single moment. To quote Ram Das - be here now! And speaking of now, the mess hall will now be serving dinner. Welcome to Tushita."

And so begins my introduction to Buddhist thought.

I realize, somewhat dejectedly, on the way to dinner, how far I actually am from becoming a Buddha. I cannot shake the loneliness I feel, the desperation for the love of a woman. I cannot rise above my feelings of sadness and loss. But I must have good karma that I should wind up in Tushita, in this classroom of life. Clara is right. There is no greater gift than being alive. There is no opportunity like the present to take my first baby steps on that long and winding path to enlightenment. Now is the time to follow the maroon and yellow brick road.

The retreat is scheduled to last eleven days. Eleven days out of my life. Eleven days without cake. It's true - there is no spiritual growth without sacrifice. The first few days, I find myself extremely fatigued. I can hardly stay awake in class. Clara says this is perfectly normal. Not only is my body physically adapting to rising hours earlier than I'm used to, but it's also detoxifying as a natural result of meditation. I think she said that after three or four days I wouldn't feel so tired, but I'm not sure. I was yawning so hard I didn't hear her.

The daily program at Tushita looks something like this (with translation):

5:00 A.M.	Wake Up	(Are they kidding?)
5:30 A.M.	Meditation	(How to sleep sitting up)
6:30 A.M.	Morning Talk	(You can keep your eyes closed, just listen)
7:00 A.M.	Breakfast	(Hope they have strong coffee)
7:30 A.M.	Rest Period	(Back to Bed)
9:00 A.M.	Meditation	(Concentrate on the sound of your own snoring)
9:45 A.M.	Mid-morning Talk	(All this talking is interfering with my sleeping)
11:00 A.M.	Lunch	(We just had breakfast!)
11:30 A.M.	Rest Period	(Afternoon nap)
2:00 P.M.	Visualization	(Try to imagine you're still in bed)
3:00 P.M.	Afternoon Talk	(From a real Tibetan monk, worth waking up for)
4:00 P.M.	Discussion	(Try not to speak while yawning)
5:00 P.M.	Dinner	(I wonder if they'll have cake)
5:30 P.M.	Rest Period	(Watch the sunset while lying down)
7:00 P.M.	Meditation	(Relax before bed)
8:00 P.M.	Evening Talk	(I'm half-asleep now and they expect me to listen?)
9:00 P.M.	Bed	(All this sleeping is exhausting!)

Of course, I'm exaggerating. Indeed, after a few days my body does get used to the schedule and the daily talks are actually very stimulating. I'm rarely bored. The meditations are an interesting mix of focusing on the breath and guided visualization. The discussion periods offer opportunities for questions and answers and sharing of individual experiences. Each day is filled with new concepts intent on challenging me to dissect the unconscious beliefs and assumptions that cause my own suffering.

"Nothing is as it appears," Clara states one morning. "According to the Buddha, we humans exist in a fog of ignorance unable to distinguish between reality and illusion - or *samsara*, as it is called in Sanskrit. We muddle about unwittingly causing our own suffering as if we were negotiating our lives through a thick haze. And the worst part is, we don't even know that our perceptions are clouded. To live an enlightened existence, we must *clearly* understand and abide by the laws of nature. Enlightenment actually means awakening. To become enlightened is to awaken from the deep dream from which we form all of our mistaken assumptions.

"A main cause of human suffering is the fundamental misconception that this physical realm we live in is permanent, comprised of fixed, solid phenomena. We cling to the belief that things are not supposed to change. But through this belief, we develop attachments, wanting things to be and remain in a certain way, when the truth is everything is constantly and rapidly changing. Nothing stays in a certain way. Nothing is solid.

"That chair in the corner is not really a chair. It is not a single, solid object. It is made up of parts: nails and wood on a gross level, molecules, atoms, electrons and quarks, etc. on a microscopic level. Where is the actual chair? There is no *chair*. That is just a label. At its very essence the chair is empty space. And we are no different. We identify with our solid bodies, but really we are no more than molecules and atoms surrounded by empty space. Our cells are constantly dying and being replaced. Our skin exfoliates. We are in every moment changing.

"Have you ever told a lover - 'Don't ever change'? Well, of course they're going to change! Are you the same now as you were when you were five, or twelve, or twenty? Will you be the same if you live to be eighty? Thoughts change, emotions come and go, nothing is guaranteed beyond the present.

"When we become attached to someone or something - thinking we need them to be happy - we inevitably set ourselves up for loss, because at some point that person we depend upon will die or leave us. At some point, that object we cling to for pleasure will break, wear down, or perhaps be stolen. At some point, on the moment of our own death, we will lose everything - our loved ones, our prized possessions, our padded bank accounts, our bodies, our beliefs. It is beyond our choice. Everything is impermanent. Attaching to objects or people and making them conditional for our happiness is to live in constant angst, fearing impending loss as everything we cherish in the material world must crumble and pass away, no matter how hard we try to stop it. When we believe things should stay the same, we are in fact paddling upstream against the ever-changing flow of nature. Enjoy what you have while you have it. Accept when it's time to let go."

There is so much to consider at the retreat. During meditation, we are taught to focus on our breath as a means of bringing ourselves into the present moment. You'd think a task as uncomplicated as that would be easy, but it's amazing and often frustrating, how elusive inhalation and exhalation can be. The problem is not my breathing. The problem is my mind. Trying to bring my attention for more than one second to the sensation of respiration is like trying to corral a tempestuous, ornery beast with a rope the size of a string. My thoughts simply will not comply. They buck to and fro, altering direction with incredible speed from past to future, memory to fantasy.

"It's astonishing, really, when you begin to witness your thoughts, how little time is spent in the present," Clara illuminates. "Your mind is like a little ball, ping-ponging between regrets of days gone by and hopes for years to come. But the past has already passed, the future may never happen. We may die before our plans ever come to fruition."

It's true, I think, but still my mind gets lost in imagination while meditating. I wonder what they'll be serving later for dinner, what other places in India I have yet to explore, what it would be like to kiss the cute Israeli girl sitting in the corner - oops, I'm supposed to have my eyes closed. Well, how do they expect me to meditate anyway, when there are so many distractions? Every fidget, every twitch, every cough in a silent room of fifty people becomes magnified. Every sneeze, every snort, every itch becomes monumental. Now, put fifty people in a silent room after a meal of rice and lentils and KABOOM! The burps are enough to shatter even the deepest of concentrations. The farts? Well, the smell is enough to make you want to focus on anything but the breath below your nostrils.

Still, the worst (or best) diversion is neither auditory nor olfactory; it's optical. It's the women. I find it nearly impossible to consolidate my focus when I could be sneaking a peak at all the beautiful women. I now know why some religions segregate men from women during prayer. Who can meditate on God, when there are flesh and blood goddesses directly in one's view?

I'm learning on this retreat how we all crave things outside ourselves that we think will bring us happiness. This is basic illusion number two: grasping. According to the Buddha, grasping is the endless need to be satiated by outside things, a state of mind that actually brings little pleasure and immense internal suffering. Nothing in the material world is able to really bring us satisfaction. Not even women, contrary to the driving belief that fuels my female obsession.

And yet, though fortified with this compelling rationale, I still find it almost impossible to meditate with all these gorgeous women around me on the retreat. I'm having lascivious fantasies about Diane. I hunger after that cute Israeli girl. I'm drooling over that buxom, sexy Swede. It gives me no rest. I'm always feeling empty. I'm supposed to be meditating, but in truth, I'm in agony.

"The *object* of your desire is not your addiction," Clara says. "Your addiction is desire itself. It's the thrill of craving. You must want nothing to live a life of peace."

Sounds easy. No desire. But suddenly the smell of cooking wafts into the meditation hall, instigating within me an intense and immediate yearning: hunger.

"Remember patience," Clara says.

Patience? I've been sitting cross-legged for hours without moving. The ache in my back is excruciating. Talk about craving - I don't think I've ever wanted anything in my entire life more than just to stretch out my legs - if indeed, that's even still possible.

"Pain is impermanent."

I don't know, this cramp in my buttock feels like it will *never* go away.

"Transcend your desire to run from that which is uncomfortable."

Transcend the uncomfortable? What about running towards the pleasurable? Like those girls! Why do meditating women have to look so darned sexy?

"If you want to be free of suffering, you must eliminate from your mind *all* craving," Clara says. "Examine the object of your desire. Say you are attracted to someone's body. What is that body actually? Blood. Puss. Trillions of dying cells. Is that what you're attracted to? Is that what you crave?"

Hmm... when she puts it that way, maybe she's right. Sounds rather disgusting. Is that really what I want?

So, I'm sitting in meditation, trying to hone in on my breath, taking inventory of passing, impermanent thoughts. There goes a memory... let it go, back to the breath. Future fantasy... let it go, back to the breath. Bird singing... let it go. Sneeze... let it go. Girl... let her go, I mean, let it go. Girl... let it go. Girl... let it go. Hmm, this isn't working. I can't let that girl go. I can't get her face out of my mind. Okay, concentrate. Mustn't be distracted. Breathe. In, out. In, out... suddenly, I'm no longer in the meditation hall. I'm daydreaming I'm on a beach with that Israeli girl, staring into her deep, black eyes, running my fingers through her dark, Mediteranean hair, nibbling on her full, pouting lips, removing her bikini... DISTRACTION! Okay, where was I? Right, I was meditating, breathing. Breathing? I'm panting! Settle down. Focus. Concentrate. In, out. In, out... her bikini top is slipping from her body - DISTRACTION! Okay, okay, remember, she's impermanent, she cannot bring me happiness, there's more to life than sex, pleasure is really suffering, she's now completely naked - DISTRACTION! Alright, she's not her body, she's a trillion unattractive parts, she is blood, she is urine, she is breasts, no, not breasts, blood, puss, yeah puss, that's a good one, I hate puss, legs, no, not legs, lips, no, no lips, blood, urine - yeah - spit, dung - that's right! What did I ever find so attractive about that blood, puss, urine, spit and dung in the first place? I don't know, when I really examine it, the contents may be revolting, but the packaging is still quite alluring! Okay, concentrate. Forget what she's made of and remember - she's impermanent. She won't always look like that. But, what about living in the present? She looks pretty darn good right now! Don't be so superficial. Where's that breath? In, out. In, out. It's not working! Okay, what about death? Remember, she's going to die. I'm going to die. Eventually, she's bound to bring me suffering, so why even bother? What's the point of even initiating attachment? Yeah, that makes sense. Now, I'm feeling better. Now, she's not so engaging. Now, I'm not so obsessed with her skin. I'm hardly thinking of caressing her silky thighs, feeling her nipples harden, stroking her pubic hairs - good God, where's that breath? In, out. In, out - oh, what's the use? I can't stand it any longer! Yes, yes! I want to lick every naked inch of her body! Yes, I want to make it with that big bag of blood, puss, dung and urine that's going to die more than anything I've ever wanted! I don't care if it's temporary! I don't care if I suffer! I don't care if she ties me up and whips me! I want! I want!! I WANT!!!!!!!!!

Ding.

"Meditation period is now over," Clara says. "There, do you all feel somewhat calmer?"

Oh yeah, I think, dripping with perspiration. I'm a veritable pool of serenity.

As much as the girls on the retreat divert me from my meditation, I also find my thoughts wandering repeatedly to images of desserts I have known and loved. Death By Chocolate, Sex In A Pan, Black Forest Cake, apple cake, banana cake, cheesecake, carrot cake - I love cake! I love the sound of the word cake. I love the smell of cake. I love seeing cake first thing when I roll over in the morning. I think I'm happiest eating cake, but...

"What we think makes us most happy actually brings us the most suffering," Clara says. "Take food, for example. Take cake."

"No!" I gasp.

"If inherent in cake was the ability to bring us happiness, then we should be able to eat as much cake as we like, growing increasingly happier in the process. But as we all know, if we eat too much cake, we're not happy at all. We suffer, we feel sick. We can, in fact, have *too much* cake."

No, Clara, I weep. Not cake!

"Cake itself cannot make us happy. No wonder *desserts* spelled backwards is *stressed*. Ha, ha!"

Clara, this is no laughing matter! I begin to shudder contemplating the transience of cake. All cakes must pass. Freshness is fleeting. Nothing is sadder than a good cake gone stale. Can Clara be right? Can satisfaction only be found through non-attachment? Can I really be just as happy with or without cake? I try to convince myself: inner peace does not depend upon frosting. But if it's true I can't have my cake and eat it too... can I at least have ice cream?

The Buddha in his teachings said that there are two things at the very root of all suffering - ignorance and desire. That is, suffering from our inability to clearly see reality, and suffering from our constant, insatiable craving. He stated in his first Noble Truth, "There is suffering." What he meant was not the obvious. We all know there's suffering. We suffer every day. What the Buddha was talking about was accepting the reality of suffering. No one escapes death. No person is immune from sickness or old age. Not even the Buddha. But if we embrace suffering, understand it to be an inevitable part of our growth and stop fighting it, then we'd be amazed at how quickly suffering can be transcended.

The problem is nobody likes to face up to pain. I personally have spent the majority of my life trying to run away from it, distracting myself with emotional dramas, possessions, intoxicants, women. I've complained and kvetched about pain, but have never actually changed my attitudes or actions to lessen it. I realize since being at Tushita that I am riddled with attachments, that I fight tooth and nail against change, that I'm always blaming others or the fates for my misfortune and that I can't bear for more than five seconds anything even remotely unpleasant. I am always running, even here at this retreat. But Buddhism won't let me get away. It's forcing me to face myself, to really look clearly, to take responsibility. I may run, but as Bob Marley and the Buddha both once said, "You can't run away from yourself."

Chapter 24

SILENCE IS GOLDEN

Tushita weather report: another foggy day expected in the world of illusion.

At the beginning of the retreat, I was asked along with all the other students to take a vow, committing myself to five precepts of moral behaviour.

1. Do not kill (sounds easy enough) - even mosquitoes (okay, maybe this won't be so easy).

2. Do not steal (I can do that) - even a glance at the girls during meditation (boy, they don't miss a trick).

3. Do not lie (challenging, but I'm sure I can handle it) - including exaggeration (jeez! I'll have to censor half of what comes out of my mouth) and idle gossip (there goes the other half).

4. Do not consume intoxicants of any nature (I guess that explains

why there were no Buddhist retreats in Goa).

5. Do not engage in improper sexual conduct (that's okay, I can limit myself to proper sexual conduct). No hurtful sexual actions (that's alright, I can be gentle). No lustful thoughts (hmm... this is getting more difficult). No self-gratification (WHAT?).

"Following precepts is one thing," Clara says, expanding on the topic of morality, "but it's not enough just to avoid non-virtuous actions. We must make sure to *do* virtuous actions as well. We may not steal, but does that mean we are generous? We may not lie, but does that mean we tell the truth? As for sexual impropriety, well, as a nun, I feel the best way to avoid hurting others sexually is to abstain completely. It's not that bad, really. It frees up a lot of time for other, uh, more beneficial endeavours."

Like what? Fingernail biting? Nervous twitching? It's one thing not to kill, but no sex? It's a hard sell.

Before the retreat, I was looking forward to the opportunity of extended silence. In fact, I was so eager for the tranquility that comes from not speaking that I was tempted to forgo Tushita entirely in favour of a two-week solitary trek in the mountains. Imagine my disdain then when by day two of the course, I realize the retreat is only half-silent and half-assed at that in its enforcement. The mornings are supposed to be quiet until lunch, but it seems most people on the retreat think whispering is mute enough. I find myself increasingly prone to irritation, as my roommate insists on chattering incessantly. Voices infiltrate the sanctity of the meditation hall. The more the rules are broken, the more incensed I feel, until finally, I am compelled to seek out Clara's advice.

"Perhaps you should look at your own expectations," she says. "Do you see that you have an attachment to things being a certain way? Must there be silence for you to be happy? Can you not find peace amongst noise and chaos? Be like the Buddha, always calm and balanced, no matter what arises, no matter the circumstance, silent or otherwise."

I try this, but the next day I find the noise even more abrasive. I'm so aggravated, I nearly resort to pulling out my hair - and believe me, I don't have much to spare.

"Try to see this as an opportunity," Clara suggests. "A chance to examine your anger. You should be thankful for the occasion. How else can we understand ourselves, how else can we transcend habitual behaviour, unless we are challenged to witness and overcome our darker tendencies? Look into your rage, stare into its eyes, confront your anger. Do you get mad often?"

"I guess so," I say.

"Let me tell you," she says. "It is the angry person who truly suffers with his anger. *He* is the one without peace. You must be gentler with yourself and others. Practice patience as an antidote. Soften your heart."

Next morning though, I wake up on the wrong side of my "Buddha Nature." No matter how hard I try, by lunchtime, I am fuming.

"Try evoking compassion for yourself and for all others," Clara recommends. "Silence can feel frightening to those who are unaccustomed to it. It can bring up uncomfortable feelings in those unfamiliar with its benefits. Mindless chatter is often the way we protect ourselves from the truth. Feel compassion for these vulnerable souls who are unable to keep the silence, for they know not what they are doing."

"That's not Buddhist," I point out. "It's Christian."

"All religions in their essence share the same teachings. Now go, take a long walk and find yourself somewhere to be alone. Why fight so hard to change something beyond your control?"

"I thought everything changes," I say.

"It does, but sometimes, acceptance and surrender are the necessary ingredients for change to occur. Have you heard that old expression, 'the more you resist, the more things stay the same?' I'm not sure the Buddha said it, but I'm sure he would have agreed. The more you attach your happiness to things changing, the more suffering in the present is prolonged. You can't always make others do what you want. Sometimes the change you seek outside is really needed within."

She's right, but I still find it strange that I have to leave the retreat to find silence.

"By the way," Clara says as I reach the door. "Just to put your own suffering in perspective. Twenty-eight thousand people died yesterday in an earthquake outside of Bombay. Meditate on that."

There's a guy on the course from the Netherlands, named Marcel - the perfect addition to any retreat, a man whose voice reverberates like a cannon. In fact, his whole personality is far too highly charged for something as serene as meditation. One night, when everyone is already in a deep trance, Marcel abruptly yells out - though I'm sure in his mind, he thinks he's whispering.

"Clara! Tonight, can't we please *get up* and chant? Hold hands in a circle? Can't we just move for once?"

Clara tries to subdue him with the explanation that this is not the place for holding hands. Better to sit cross-legged and separate, as the Buddha intended. About thirty seconds later, Marcel leaps to his feet.

"What's wrong with holding hands?" he asks.

"After the retreat, you can hold all the hands you like, Marcel."

Another day, Marcel is so restless he bolts from the meditation hall without warning. Five minutes later, he appears outside my window, singing at the top of his lungs, completely unaware that not only is he disturbing me, the teacher and forty-eight other students, but probably all the birds in the area as well. Another morning, I am returning from my post-breakfast walk, when who do I come across outside the retreat centre but Marcel, bare-chested, sweating, jumping up and down, gyrating his pelvis and heaving his fists against his half-naked body.

"Marcel, *what* are you doing?" I ask.

"I'm shaking out my sexual organs," he says. "I learned this at the Osho Ashram. You Buddhists are too sedate, too peaceful. All you do is sit. When do you air out your genitals?"

I'm not sure even the Buddha would have an answer to that.

Osho, or Rajneesh, is a controversial figure amongst Indian gurus. Known in the sixties and seventies as the sex, drugs and rock 'n' roll guru, he was famous for encouraging the indulgence of one's physical desires as a path to enlightenment. His ashram in Puna is still a favourite stop for travelers in spite of the fact he himself died - allegedly poisoned by the American FBI - in 1990. The ashram, known on the traveler's circuit as "the spiritual supermarket," is well equipped to cater to the needs of any spiritual seeker. There's a swimming pool, sauna, tennis court, basketball court, massage parlour, beauty parlour, bistro, book-shop, dancehall and giant Zen garden. Oh yes, there's also meditation. One can partake of any number of workshops (for a costly fee) including: yoga, art, drama, music and dance. It is also rumoured that visitors can partake freely of each other. Once you've passed the obligatory HIV test at the door, sex, I am told, is considered safe and is openly encouraged, even in the form of spiritual orgies. Sounds barbaric compared to the refined Buddhist methods I've been learning, but come to think of it, I have been sitting around cross-legged a very long time, maybe a little barbarism wouldn't be so bad after all. What's so terrible about airing out one's genitals anyway - whatever that means? I'm with Marcel. What this Buddhist retreat really needs is not holding hands, but a full blown, all-out orgy - only in the interest of spiritual advancement, of course.

Now, I know I've been rather fixated on silence since starting this retreat, but I finally garner the courage to speak to that cute Israeli girl, and now... I don't want to shut up. I just want to talk to her. Mindless chatter? Bring it on. What do you mean silence until lunch? I can't wait that long. My mind races through meditation. When's this period over already? I'm impatient to initiate debate, drum up discussion. Who wants peace? I want to postulate, pontificate, expound. I want to - hey, where did everybody go? Boy, you know you're craving bad when you don't hear an entire roomful of people exiting. Well, maybe it's for the best. Maybe I need to be alone. Maybe I need solitude... naah, I'd probably just end up talking to myself, and then even though I might be suffering less from desire, I'd be borderline schizophrenic. Which is worse?

I leave the meditation hall in search of Shira, that cute Israeli girl, whose name means poetry and whose face is a song. I am determined to flirt with her at the expense of inner peace - oh, the suffering of desire! I come across her in the garden, having her portrait sketched by Marcel, who fancies himself an artist. I sit next to them and subtly begin to fawn over Shira, staring into her eyes like a forlorn puppy. Strategically, I slip in a question as to how long she's going to be in McLeod Ganj after the retreat, hoping she will say forever.

"Two days," she says. "I have to be back in Israel in two weeks and I want to visit the town of Manali before then."

ACK!!! Shattered again! Another potential love affair doomed before it could ever be kindled. Oh, the harsh reality of impermanence, attachment and desire. Why, Buddha, why do you have to be so right? Why do I see my suffering coming and just stand there, letting it hit me like a freight train? Why don't I get out of the way? Oh well, if I really get desperate, I can always check myself in for an orgy at "Osho Land."

Sadly, I excuse myself from the company of Shira and Marcel. No sense wasting good flirting energy on a girl who's not only at her very essence empty space, but who is also leaving in a few short days.

Clara tells us that the Dalai Lama believes world peace begins with each individual. "How can anyone hope for *world* peace," she asks, "unless they have created peace in their own immediate circle? How can I hope for world peace unless I am peaceful myself? An angry person is a poor advocate to stop war."

The Dalai Lama teaches that it is every person's responsibility to train his or her mind in the proficiency of peace, to transform the emotion of anger to love, and to profoundly realize the effect of our words and actions on the lives of those around us. Personal enlightenment in Buddhism is not a selfish endeavour. It is pursued for one reason only: to help all other sentient, conscious beings (not just people) reach their own spiritual awakening. Each thought, each word, each action, each prayer, each meditation in Buddhism is dedicated to the cessation of suffering for all beings, not just for ourselves. It is this very wish that is the underlying motivation required for becoming a "Boddhisatva" or Great Compassionate One.

During the lunch break one afternoon I overhear a German woman conversing with another student. "You know," she says. "I come from Germany, but I do not feel German. When I go within myself, when I go inside, I do not find anything there that is German. Yes, it is the country where I grew up, but I feel just as much at home here in India. I felt just as much at home during my travels in China. Because I feel at home inside myself. And so, I feel that if more people will go inside themselves, more people will realize that they are not limited to their country, to their nationality, their beliefs. Perhaps then, we will not have countries making war on each other. Perhaps then, we will not have people hating each other because on the surface we appear different. Perhaps then, we will have peace, because inside we are all beautiful beings. Inside, we are all the same."

Wouldn't it be great if everyone thought that way?

Another day, the same German woman asks to borrow my sweater; she's feeling chilly. Gladly, I agree, but later, before dinner, when I'm cold myself, I'm unable to find her. In the dining room, I discover her happily eating, warm and toasty in *my* sweater. Now, before the retreat, I might have reacted with bitterness and anger. I might have resented her insensitivity for walking off with my only piece of warm clothing. But suddenly, I catch myself and to my surprise, all those Buddhist teachings at once sink in.

I look at her, not with envy, but with compassion, overwhelmed with satisfaction for having played even a small part in her comfort, grateful to be of service. I can't bring myself to ask her for my sweater in return, no matter how cold I am, knowing that she's only wearing a thin t-shirt underneath. I decide rather to meditate on my own intolerance of cold. What I find, if not earth-shattering, is still revealing. My physical discomfort seems intimately related to my state of mind. The more I tense up, the colder I feel. The more I relax, the less relevant the temperature becomes. The implications are profound - I can be peaceful *inside* even when outside my body's turning into a giant icicle.

When I return to the meditation hall, the German woman rushes towards me, apologizing profusely.

"I'm so sorry to have your sweater so long. Can you forgive me? I just forgot I had it on -"

"Wait," I say. I place my palms together gently in front of my heart. "Were *you* warm?"

"Yes," she answers softly.

"Then you wear the sweater tonight."

"But won't you be cold?"

"No. I have a feeling your smile will be enough to keep me comfortable a very long time."

Chapter 25

IMPERMANENCE IS FOREVER

With Buddhism becoming so popular in the West, it occurs to me that it's just a matter of time before "Barbie and Ken" begin to seek a spiritual master, one who can relate to their particular plight as icons of the material world. I can just see them now, searching for divine inspiration in the crowded aisles of toy departments all across America, finally begging an audience with the one stuffed animal whom they hope can help them in their quest for enlightenment - The "Dolly" Lama.

After all, hadn't the Dolly Lama already convinced "G. I. Joe" to abandon his war-like ways in exchange for a doctrine of non-violence? Who better then to steer Barbie and Ken from the shallow beaches of Malibu to a more rewarding existence on the shelves of some Tibetan shop in McLeod Ganj? Who else but a Dolly Lama could entice Barbie to give up her tan for a more radiant expression of inner beauty?

Now on sale: Monastic Malibu Barbie - complete with shaven head, maroon and yellow robes, flip-flops and matching accessories.

Each afternoon at Tushita, a Tibetan "geshe," or expert on Buddhist philosophy, teaches us in place of Clara. The geshe is a man in his fifties with closely cropped white hair and an angelic smile so infectious I feel uplifted just sitting in his presence. That's good, because I don't understand a word he says. The real problem isn't actually with the geshe, it's with the translator, a young Tibetan monk whose English is so disjointed, I can barely decipher where his sentences finish and new thoughts begin. But Clara says that it doesn't really matter whether or not I understand; at some level, she assures me, I am absorbing the teachings simply by being present in a room with a Tibetan master.

So, every afternoon, I bide my time while the geshe teaches, trying to concentrate on passively absorbing, but instead, I all too often find my awareness actively wandering to everyone else in the meditation hall. It's amazing, really, how interesting *others* become as soon as I'm directed to turn my attention inwards. Soon, I find myself mentally criticizing everyone in the room, judging others based on their looks, their clothes, their weird names. Like that tall strapping Australian student who on the first day introduced himself as "Jungle." *Jungle*? Really now, let's be serious. Although, I must admit, the name does rather suit him. With a shaggy mane of hair and stubbly whiskers, he has resembled a human version of "Simba, The Lion King." Today, though, he seems to be impersonating a different member of the animal kingdom. The sides of his head have been clean-shaven, while the top is still a tall bush of matted curls. He looks more like a hyena now than the king of beasts - a noticeable reduction in rank, if not in fashion.

Shaving one's head seems to be the stylish thing to do on this retreat. Every day, two or three more guys show up looking like Yul Brynner, two or three more girls like Sinead O'Connor. Perhaps it's a statement of panache, perhaps it's a sign of renunciation, perhaps it's lice prevention, I don't know. And I'm not sure I want to get close enough to find out.

Finally one evening, Clara thankfully brings up the topic of judgmental thinking - thankfully, because I'm mired in this particular form of anguish. Aren't the worst types of sufferings the ones you really enjoy?

"Judging others," she begins, "becomes an awful habit in most humans. But it merely serves to separate us. It reinforces the duality of the world of illusion, making it impossible for us to experience true oneness. This brings suffering. And judging others is really only a reflection of how much we judge ourselves. If we like or dislike someone *else's* clothing, hair, bodies, personalities, it merely reveals a superficial attachment to our *own* appearances. In fact, we mistakenly identify with our opinions so strongly that we defend them at all cost - even to the point of war. But we are not only shallow opinions. We are not expressions of fashion. We are much subtler bodies of energy, deeper even than thought."

Suddenly, a dog runs into the hall, interrupting the teachings. Clara laughs heartily as the pooch is escorted outside. "Since there are no accidents," she continues, "this dog must have come to us for a reason. Who thinks the dog might really be a Buddha?"

Maybe a beagle, I think, but *a Buddha*?

"I like to think all beings we encounter are Buddhas sent here to teach us," Clara says. "Try considering every obnoxious rickshaw driver, every relentless puja-pusher as a profound teacher, testing our patience, challenging our resources for compassion over hate. Regarding everyone as our teachers, or Buddhas in disguise, helps us view *all* others with equal respect and gratitude.

"So let's examine what we can learn from this dog. It came in the gompa. This is what happened. This was the reality. Now I'm sure some of you may have felt annoyed, some of you might have found it funny and others would have remained neutral - same occurrence, same reality, different experience. The point is that everything in your life is filtered through a process of subjective interpretation. It is your judgments alone that colour events as good or bad, pleasant or unpleasant, beautiful or ugly. The Buddha teaches us that to transcend suffering, we must experience everything and everyone with equanimity, that is, with a balanced, neutral mind, without like or dislike, craving or aversion. This impartiality infers an attitude of acceptance, and acceptance is an invaluable ally on our path to inner peace. Try to love everyone equally. Try to show regard for strangers and even, if you can, for enemies. The Dalai Lama teaches that it is specifically our enemies who should receive our deepest gratitude, for it is they who offer us the greatest opportunity to develop compassion."

Wow, when I think of enemies, or people who have hurt me in the past, the last thing I want to feel is compassion.

"Let's look at it another way," Clara says. "Imagine this situation: a stranger at your hotel is presented to you as a thief, accused of stealing some object. What do you think of her? Later, you learn that the alleged object was actually lost, not stolen. The stranger is not a thief. What do you think of her now? Later still, at a restaurant, the only empty seat is next to this stranger. You find you have a lot in common. You make plans to meet her later. What do you think of her now? Still later, when you are asleep, she steals your wallet! Now what do you think of her?"

Hmm... was she cute?

"Perceptions are not permanent. A stranger can just as easily become a friend as a friend can become an enemy or an enemy your best friend. Try to treat everyone - friend, stranger or enemy - with equal compassion, with equanimity. Remember, other people are just mirrors. If you are judging them, then who is judging you?"

And so, inspired by Clara's words, for the rest of the retreat, I decide to challenge my habit of judging. To start with, I make a personal pact not to look in the mirror. Not that I don't like looking in the mirror. I think I like it too much. It's an experiment to see how much I judge based on appearance. And it's amazing, really, after only a few days, I can barely remember what I look like, relating to myself solely based on my inner state, rather than on outer, facial features. It's suddenly not as important if I *look* good as if I *am* good. Have I done any good deeds, have I had good thoughts? Have I spoken kindly? Soon, I don't care if my hair is a mess as long as I am emanating peace. It no longer concerns me if I've a booger hanging from my nose, as long as I am grounded in love. And I find that I am relating in the same way to others, focusing on their inner qualities, rather than on the giant wart they may happen to have on their face.

Often, in the past, I've been detrimentally insecure around others, worried about whether I will be physically accepted. But here, I find that the less I judge myself on looks, since I have no idea what I look like, the less I am troubled by how others may view me. Judge me on what is inside. See *me*, not my body. Appearances are not only deceiving, but they inevitably fade.

And how many of our judgments are actually based, not on what is true, but rather on what we've learned? Take the concept of personal space. In the meditation hall one day, everyone is asked to line up before the geshe to receive his blessing - Westerners first, Tibetan monks to follow. The Westerner's line, as you might expect, is orderly, spacious, with ample room between individuals, reflecting the Western tendency to cringe at even the thought of being touched in public. The Tibetan's line, however, is a single, amorphous mass of maroon. The monks cram into one another, lean on one another, completely comfortable with physical contact. How much then of our behaviour do we take for granted as proper, when in fact it's merely what we're used to due to the influences of culture? I personally am surprised to find upon investigation that the majority of what forms the foundation of my personality originates in things I have heard or read or been told, not in what is necessarily true. The only measure for truth, the Buddha says, is from first-hand, personal experience. So I shouldn't be so possessive of all my opinions. In the end, like everything else, they're impermanent.

And, opinions go both ways. They can be judgmentally negative or excessively and unrealistically positive. Take for example my newest infatuation with a stunning German girl. At every opportunity I find myself sneaking glances at her green, tiger-eyes, her shimmering, golden hair. Helplessly, I stare at her, projecting angelic qualities on her. Without knowing anything about her, I have formed very solid opinions of her, most of which are exceedingly idealistic. She bewitches me, especially when she parades about in see-through rayon trousers. Powerlessly, my eyes pursue the taut, rounded curves of her buttocks, the long, dark shadows of her legs - when suddenly, all my attention telescopes to a rip in her pants, illuminating a milky patch of thigh. I start to salivate at the sight of bare skin. She is the perfect woman, embodying both femininity and dessert. She is like the scoop of vanilla in which I long to dip the cookie of my desire. Wow, now that's suffering!

For eight days, I discreetly gaze at the gorgeous German goddess, too afraid to approach a woman of her utopian stature. But on day nine, my euphoric opinion of her begins to shatter. In meditation, I notice her becoming increasingly agitated, fidgety, until finally she loses all sense of decorum and begins screeching.

"I cannot hear zis word zuffering any longer!" she shouts in class. "Clara! All you talk of iz zuffering. Zuffering. Zo much zuffering! Well, I don't know, I don't zink I zuffer zo much. I zink I'm happy or when I'm not happy, I go to ze garden and zen I feel better. Why must we talk and talk zo much about zuffering?"

Poor girl. Suffering from talking about suffering. What would the Buddha have said about that? And then one evening, when we are about to be led in chanting, the German goddess again just can't contain herself.

"Ze last chanting, everyone chanted zo loud! Why can't we chant zoftly? I zink it zounds much better to hear it zoft!"

For someone who doesn't want to talk about suffering, she seems to suffer quite a lot. Of course, to me, being Jewish, suffering is second nature. At times I wonder if the Buddha himself was Jewish since so many of his teachings revolve around suffering.

One morning, Clara teaches us a famous Tibetan mantra apparently able to invoke the mystical energy of Chenrezig, the Buddha Of Compassion. Clara stands at the front of the meditation hall, thumbing a Tibetan rosary or "mala," leading us in an hour's repetition of: "Om Mani Padme Hum." Within moments, I sink into a deep relaxation. The drone of the mantra is soothing, the very sound of it said to be charged with primordial vibration. Chanting mantras is not only supposed to hone the mind in concentration, but also keep it from idle thought which could lead to unbeneficial action.

Now, there is a Jewish saying that carries with it a certain primordial reverberation as well: "Oy Vey." Said over and over and over again, with intermittent sighs, this Jewish mantra has the power of invoking the energy of the biblical character, Job. Job could have been a Buddhist. He was definitely someone who spent a lot of time contemplating suffering. As the story goes, God tested Job's faith with every form of torture and misfortune, but no torment was enough to make him waver from his dedication to God. That doesn't mean he didn't complain. Since then, following the example of Job, the Jewish people have combined both spiritual surrender and sacred complaining into one catch phrase - "Oy Vey!" My whole life I grew up to the sound of various relatives exclaiming, "Oy Vey, my head hurts! What kind of God would give me such a pain? Oh well, who am I to question the will of the Almighty?" Or, "Oy Vey, have I got a hemorrhoid! What kind of God would give me such a pain in the - oh well, who am I to question the Almighty?"

So what do I do? Being Jewish, I have years of cultural indoctrination in repeating the mantra of Job, "Oy Vey." But here at Tushita, I find myself reaping the benefits of the vibration of Chenrezig, "Om Mani Padme Hum." Finally, I decide in the spirit of compromise to merge the two, creating my very own, Jewish-Buddhist mantra: "Oy Vey Padme Hum." Not only does it help me with compassion for all my aches and pains, but at the same time it also allows me to complain. It's perfect! The only problem being: is my suffering the result of my own negative karma or is it part of God's almighty plan? Hmm... I might have to consult the "Dalai Rabbi" for an answer.

"The Buddha teaches us that all beings have at one time been our mother," Clara says in one of her lectures.

What exactly does that mean?

"Let me explain. If you take into consideration reincarnation, each of us has been reborn on this planet millions of times. So, conceivably, each of us has been the mother of everyone else and everyone else has likewise been our mother."

This sounds a little far-fetched, even for an Eastern religion.

"The point is that if everyone has at one time been our mother, then *everyone* deserves the same love, respect and gratitude that we show the actual mother who gave us life in this incarnation. Adopting this perspective makes us look at everyone just a little bit differently. It gives us one more reason to extend our compassion beyond our tight circle of relations to include each and every being."

Hmm... I'm not sure what my actual mother in Montreal would think about this one. But let's say it's true, let's say everyone has indeed been my mother, then shouldn't I refer to everyone, including, say, Sylvester Stallone, as "Mommy?" I don't know. It makes me feel a little uncomfortable. But Julia Roberts? Now, that's another story. I would gladly get down on my hands and knees for the chance to call *her* "Mommy."

That afternoon, in order to reinforce the Buddhist view on rebirth, Clara arranges a field trip to visit a real, live, reincarnation. Of course, we're all reincarnated according to Eastern thought, but Tibetan masters are actually supposedly able to direct from *the beyond* when and where they will rematerialize after death. A living Tibetan master then is regarded as a continuation of a consciousness spanning down through the centuries, returning life after life to this plane of existence for the sole purpose of guiding others to enlightenment. In this way, the present Dalai Lama is revered as a reincarnation of the previous Dalai Lama, who was a manifestation of the Dalai Lama before him, and so on, all the way back to the Buddha Chenrezig.

After a master dies, the search begins to find his reincarnation, a child born with an innate awareness of the master's lineage. Once a child is suspected of being a reincarnation, he is scrutinized for the accuracy of his memories relating to his former life. He is asked to recognize people he knew before as the master but is meeting now for the first time as a child. He is expected to pick out from amongst identical replicas, precise objects that belonged to the master before he died - for example, a favourite rosary, prayer bell or cane. Sometimes, these children are even able to recite scriptures that they have apparently never heard before, but which were important to the master in a past life.

These reincarnations of Tibetan masters are called "tulkus," one of the most famous being a young boy named Lama Osel, considered to be the reincarnation of Lama Yeshe, the inspirational founder of Tushita.

What makes Lama Osel so special is that he is the first Western boy to be regarded as a Tibetan reincarnation. Since Lama Yeshe dedicated his entire life to bringing Buddhism to the West, perhaps it's no coincidence that he would choose to reappear as a blonde-haired boy from Spain.

The tulku we are invited to see on this day is the revered Ling Rinpoche, the reincarnation of the Dalai Lama's former senior tutor. Led by Clara, about a half hour's walk from Tushita we come upon a little cottage in the hills. Inside, we are introduced to a boy of about eight, seated on a miniature throne, dressed in golden silk robes. He has olive skin, a shiny bald head and an air of royalty that belies his young age. A man old enough to be his grandfather caters to the boy's every whim. Everyone appears to be walking on eggshells around him.

One by one, we are asked to kneel before the boy to receive his blessing. He seems dreadfully indisposed, tapping each of us indifferently upon the head, much like that elephant in Thiruvanamalai, only the elephant acted with more sincerity. I must admit, I feel a little weird, bowing before a child, even if everyone does treat him like "The Little Prince."

"Jungle," from my retreat, asks the Rinpoche if he would allow for some entertainment. The young boy waves his hand lethargically. Taking that to mean yes, Jungle proceeds to serenade us on his didgeridoo - an Australian aboriginal instrument - delighting the Rinpoche with sounds resembling the low chanting of Tibetan monks, the high yelp of dingoes and the pattering of hopping kangaroos. Next, Andrew from England puts on a show juggling three yellow balls. The Rinpoche grows tired of this quickly. He interrupts, motioning for Andrew to hand him two of the balls. Andrew complies respectfully. The Rinpoche then passes one of the balls to Clara, the second to a Swedish girl, named Ingie. He points to Clara, indicating he would like her to throw him the ball. She does so a little too enthusiastically.

"Not so hard," he warns, returning the ball.

Ingie gets set to throw but the Rinpoche holds up his hand.

"Not your turn," he commands.

Clara gets another try, throwing softer this time, then it's back to Ingie. She winds up and whips the ball dead centre off the little prince's head! There is a hushed silence as everybody waits for the Rinpoche's reaction. He turns to Ingie with a clearly threatening look, raising his tiny index finger in menacing reproach. I fully expect him to blurt out, "Off with her head!" Instead, he bursts the tension with hysterical laughing.

"Not so good," he says, with a grin.

Then, the fun really starts, as someone brings out three farm fresh eggs, which Rinpoche asks Andrew to juggle. He does pretty well, for about five seconds, until one of the eggs splatters messily on the ground. Rinpoche then takes the remaining two eggs and stares mischievously at Ingie.

"Oh no, Rinpoche, no, don't," she pleads, but sure enough, he rears back and pitches the egg on a beeline, straight for Ingie's head. Unfortunately, she ducks and who is standing right behind her? Yup. Me. That's me with egg all over my face, literally. Oh well, there must be some blessing involved in being pelted by a Rinpoche. Ingie is doubled over with glee, but no sooner does she straighten up than Rinpoche tags her with the other egg. Now it's the boy's turn to fall down laughing.

All the while, I'm thinking, wow! This Rinpoche has a wicked arm and he's a southpaw at that. He should forget Buddhism and start training for Major League Baseball. I can just see him now, running the bases, sliding into second wearing spiked flip-flops. Imagine the headlines: FIRST RINPOCHE TO PITCH FOR THE YANKEES - PRACTICALLY UN-HITTABLE.

Well, sure he's un-hittable, I think. How many other pitchers can de-materialize the baseball before it ever reaches the bat and rematerialize it after in the catcher's mit? When questioned about his won-lost record, the Rinpoche, always compassionate with members of the media, gently replies, "In Buddhism, everything in the physical world is illusion. Nothing really exists. I don't exist. You don't exist. The ball doesn't exist. The other team doesn't exist. Surely it follows that my losses also don't exist! Losses are strictly the suffering of samsara."

Then my whole fantasy comes crashing down as I realize the Rinpoche would never accept "Yankee Pinstripes" in place of those yellow and maroon robes.

That night, back at the retreat center, I am unable to sleep and wander from my room down to the garden outside the meditation hall. The full moon is high, the sky phosphorescent. Dark outlines of mountains span the horizon. Treetops are aglow. All is silent. All is peace. No one is awake but me - or so I think. Suddenly, I hear a twig snap and turning, recognize Diane strolling towards me on the path.

"What are you doing up?" I ask.

"I couldn't sleep. I was thinking about you."

"About me?"

"Do you believe in reincarnation?" she asks.

"Uh, I guess so. Why?"

"Ever since the first time I saw you, I felt strangely like I had met you before."

"You did?"

"Yeah. I wasn't going to tell you this, but before I left Melbourne, a psychic told me that while I was in India, I would meet my husband from a past life. He would appear to me as a Canadian, from Montreal."

"You mean *me*?" I ask, dumbfounded.

"When I first saw you," Diane says, "I recognized your eyes."

"This is kind of spooky. I felt the same thing about your eyes."

"According to the psychic, in this particular past life, we were both Native Americans. I was called Fair Weather because I had the power to conjure rain. You were my husband."

"You mean that rickshaw driver in Phatangkot was actually right when he assumed we were married?"

"I guess so."

"A clairvoyant rickshaw driver. How do you like that? I'm glad I gave him those extra rupees."

"Stew, I feel as if I've been searching for that 'special someone' all my life," Diane says. "And now here you are."

"Well, this is great, Diane. We could hang out after the retreat and get to know each other, uh, again."

"No. I have to head back to Australia straight away." Tears begin trickling down her face. "Look, I know I'm not allowed to do this on the retreat, but --"

Without warning, Diane leans over and kisses me passionately on the lips. The kiss is long and sorrowful and I feel her pain and ache for her with a strange combination of compassion and lust. I wrap my arms about her tightly, never wanting our connection to end, but abruptly she breaks away.

"I guess I'll just see you next lifetime," she smiles sadly, wiping her eyes. "Please, let's not speak of this again."

Before I can protest, she disappears along the path into a thicket of trees, leaving me to linger in moonlit solitude. Must *everything* be a lesson in impermanence?

Chapter 26

PRACTICE MAKES PERFECT

Retreats end, like everything else, arising and passing away. In her final talk, before sending us off to the "real" world, Clara shares with us her deepest wishes for our continued practice.

"Don't give in to laziness," she says. "It is the single major obstacle preventing us from transforming our minds. Keep your intentions clear. Develop your compassionate heart. Practice equanimity. Overcome habit. Bring awareness into every moment. Meditation is not just for sitting - it is for life! Make your world a sacred place. Find a "sangha," a community to support your spirituality. Shine a light on all around you. Be a beacon of love."

She leaves us with this prayer: "Should anyone see us, think of us, touch us, talk to us, remember us, may they be freed from all suffering in that instant, and may they abide in perfect happiness forever."

It's back to the front lines. The retreat is over. But the retreat is not the only thing coming to an end. If I have learned anything, it is to face reality in every moment, and the unavoidable reality of my present situation, disconcerting as it may be, is that I am down to my last few precious hundred dollars (not including money put aside for airplane fare). I figure if I am frugal, I *might* be able to stretch out my resources for another two weeks before I am forced to return to Canada.

With a heavy heart, I leave Tushita and make my way back down the steep forested hillside to McLeod Ganj, when suddenly, I encounter a belligerent mob of monkeys brawling on the path. Upon seeing me, they startle and scatter angrily, resuming their conflict high up in the trees. But one old monkey, with scowling chops and beet-red buttocks, refuses to budge. Normally, monkeys get out of my way, not necessarily out of fear, but resigned to the fact that humans, somewhat to the monkeys' dismay, are here to stay. But this old monkey has decided to challenge the status quo, baring his teeth as if daring me to pass.

Immediately, I jump back. I'm not stupid. I know I'm no match for any monkey. I try to send the animal subliminal vibes of peace, but the old baboon roars, sending a surge of adrenaline shooting through my veins, washing away any possible thought of compassion. Right Action? Forget it! I reach in defense for a rock. But before I can volley, the monkey grumbles, snarls, and leaps to a branch, freeing the path. I seize the opportunity and bolt past, running the rest of the way to McLeod Ganj. Once there, I rent myself a room at the Paljor Gakyil Guest House and breathlessly lock myself safely behind a hefty wooden door. Well, eleven days of teachings on patience and loving kindness and it doesn't take much more than a monkey to coax panic and anger into rearing their ugly heads. Fear makes one act in very un-Buddha-like ways. It certainly makes me appreciate just how fraught with hazards this road to enlightenment is - even the monkeys here in India serve as my teachers. But I don't know, Buddha, are you sure they were also all at one time my mother? And does that mean my mother in Montreal was also at one time a *monkey*? I really don't know what she's going to think about that.

That night, I am exhausted and long to drift into slumber. By eleven o'clock, I am tucked cozily in bed when out of nowhere a thunderous noise awakens me. I jolt upright. What could it be? A bomb? An earthquake? An avalanche? Then I hear it again. Wait... I can't believe it - it's laughter! I venture into the hallway. Twenty tourists are partying on the terrace just outside my door! So much for my beauty sleep.

I return to my room and crawl into bed, planting my head beneath the pillow, but it's no use. Every time I'm about to doze off, another wave of hilarity abruptly interrupts my snoring. Now, before the retreat, I probably would have laid awake, fuming, cursing, churning myself into a progressively volatile state of rage. Tonight though, I consciously try to take the Buddha's middle way, remaining calm, choosing patience over irritation, truly attempting to feel happy for those who are so obviously and vociferously, if not perhaps a little inconsiderately, themselves having such a good time. And it works. I manage to remain relatively unruffled, even until three in the morning when those dear, delightful party-mongers FINALLY SHUT UP!

Well... I did say *relatively* unruffled.

Once outside the retreat, everything I do seems to become an exercise in Buddhist training. Especially bathing. Now, understand, that to the budget traveler, hot showers become a luxury so rare, I often find myself pining for the good old days in North America, when I could linger under the spray of warm water, daydreaming as the heat penetrated my shoulders. But here, at the Paljor Gakyil Guesthouse, there are no hot and cold switches. There is only one tap and one temperature: freezing. The water is piped in directly from Himalayan mountain streams, making it so cold, that plunging under the showerhead after many moments of naked procrastination is enough to shock my system immediately into the Buddhist experience of "being in the moment." No time for daydreaming. BE in that shower! SEE stars explode like icicles before your eyes! HEAR that rat-a-tat chattering of teeth! FEEL goose-bumps pop like icebergs along the length of your arms! SHUDDER as frigid water deadens your fingertips and lips! No worries, no past, no future, no distractions, just one thought thrusting me forcefully into the present, blaring in my mind like a mantra gone mad - QUICKLY! Soap, sud, rinse, breathe. This isn't just cold - it's cold of a higher realm. It's so cold I'm about to transcend mundane reality - or black out. It's so cold that I have achieved equanimity with all sensation, because I *have* no sensation at all! I'm completely numb! I know it's an opportunity to practice detachment, but I'd just as soon detach myself to a beach in the tropics. No wonder so many kids in Dharamsala are dirty - you won't catch me taking too many more showers after this.

The rest of the day, I hide in my room wrapped in every piece of clothing, shawl and blanket I can find. But it was worth it. I think I'm definitely getting nearer to enlightenment. Not only am I more awake after my shower, but my skin is also closer to that same shade of arctic blue belonging to Shiva, Krishna and some of those Buddhas.

I am experiencing a difficult transition returning to civilization. If I thought the whispering at the retreat was annoying, McLeod Ganj is positively deafening. After being removed from external stimulation for over a week, I find the racket from trucks, buses, taxis and people exaggerated to the point of being unbearable. I feel as if I've been suddenly squeezed out of a silent, comfortable womb into a world of cacophony and chaos, forced from cozy introspection into a state of overwhelming distraction.

I'm trying to apply Buddhism to all aspects of my life, but what would the Buddha have possibly said about this? It seems I'm a tad constipated after the retreat and I find that it's causing me suffering on many levels. Forget the physical discomfort, what's worse is I have *desire* for my bowels to move. I am also tormented by the illusory belief that this condition may be *permanent*! I try to remind myself that all sensations are transient, but I must have some pretty deep underlying attachments to be grasping so possessively to this much excrement. Well, they say the best thing to do in these situations is pray, so... "Dear Buddha. Help my feces pass as gracefully as a cloud. Help me surrender my poop to the squatter. May I become regular in my daily practice without cause for flatulence or thunder."

Hmm... maybe I should forget praying and go buy a laxative.

The Buddha said that we should never accept what we're told as fact without evaluating it ourselves. And so, my second day in McLeod Ganj, I decide to test out Clara's theory and see if indeed cake can bring me suffering. I swagger over to the Green Restaurant, plant myself at a table, and order five pieces of cake. Well, I never thought it would be possible, but I must admit that after the fourth piece, I am beginning to feel a little sick. After the fifth slice, I am definitely suffering. Hmm...this could entirely change the way I look at things.

I leave the Green Restaurant, battling nausea and reflecting on the Buddha's words about releasing all desire, when all of a sudden, I notice a Western girl carrying an attractive Nepalese handbag. The first thought that pops into my head is - "I SHOULD GET ONE!" - meaning, of course, the handbag, not the girl, though on second glance, I wonder if they come as a package. Good God! I am so conditioned by desire, my mind snaps into craving like a reflex, attaching to outside things, thinking they will make me happy. Becoming a Buddha is going to take a lot more effort than I had originally calculated. I had hoped to just kind of *slip* into enlightenment, but the material world is a treasure chest of temptation. I don't think it's going to be that easy.

I wander through town, attempting not to be drawn into the stores. They're just feeding on my suffering, I think, but everything looks so darn appealing. I try to pass by. I try to turn my cheek. But Buddha, there are shops on either side! I know possessions won't bring me happiness. I know that objects are impermanent. But can't I just buy one thing, one small thing without becoming attached to it?

I stop in front of a petite shop called "Mementos." I'm only going to browse, I tell myself. I'm only going to escape the midday heat. I open the door and somewhat guiltily step inside, just then catching four other people from my retreat sensuously sampling fabrics and caressing sta-tues. They immediately stop in their tracks, cheeks flushing. Apparently,

I'm not the only one who couldn't wait to leave Tushita to do some shopping.

The proprietor of the store, Amit Sood, is a warm, amiable man born in the Punjabi town of Amritsar. Instantly upon entering his shop, he makes me feel at home. He offers me a cold drink and a chair to sit on. He shares with me the lunch his wife has prepared; delicious homemade chapati, rice, bean curry and savoury, salted pieces of pink ginger. He presents himself as a contented man, forty-years-old, loyal to his family, grateful for his good fortune. After every sale, I watch as he performs an elaborate ritual of appreciation, waving his newly acquired money before several images of Hindu gods, past a photo of the Dalai Lama, over smoking incense, around a lit candle, to his forehead, to his lips, and down into an aluminum cash box which he quickly locks.

He loves McLeod Ganj, a place where there is never any trouble, a quiet place with good people. I don't ask, but I imagine he is somewhat familiar with trouble, coming from the war-torn state of Punjab. He remarks gleefully how he is never bored. He receives great pleasure simply from conversing with the customers who grace his small shop. He proudly presents me with a tall stack of letters from people all over the world thanking him for his kind service and excellent quality of goods.

"I am even mentioned in a German guidebook!" he exclaims.

I have to agree with the assessment of his stock. I have been to shops all over India, from Kanyakumari to Varanassi, having seen more than my share of statues and shawls, but the collection in Amit Sood's tiny store impresses me beyond any other for its authenticity, artistry and originality. Four hours later and two hundred and fifty U.S. dollars lighter, I emerge from Mementos with some very costly and heavy souvenirs: an antique woolen shawl weaved in the northern town of Kulu; a stunning Punjabi tapestry; two sandalwood statues - one of Ganesha, one of the Buddha; three bronzed statues of Tara, Shiva and a sexy, buxom Lakshmi that I must have picked up a dozen times before deciding *not* to buy it. Amit gave it to me for free. But definitely, most treasured is a sublime antique "thangka" or Tibetan religious painting, depicting my personal favourite, Chenrezig, the Buddha of Compassion. Standing in the sun outside on the street, I feel almost dizzy, disoriented after such an intensive bout of spending. I went a little crazy. But I feel as if I've actually come out of Amit Sood's shop so much richer, not for having accumulated a bag full of possessions, not for being laden down with a sack full of new attachments, but for having made a new friend. Of course, I now will have to fly back to Canada earlier than expected. Hmm... friendships can be costly.

That evening, I am out for a leisurely stroll, when an old Tibetan woman passes me on the street. "OY!" she groans loudly as she walks by.

Funny, she didn't look Jewish.

All these weeks spent amongst Buddhists reminds me of one of the first Buddhists I ever knew, a fellow back in Toronto. His religious preference actually came to light one day at the office while he was talking with one of my co-workers on the phone. All through the conversation, as my co-worker tells it, she heard a bell clanging repeatedly in the background, making it difficult for her to concentrate. Finally, she could stand it no longer, shouting out with her usual, lovable, and questionable tact, "Hey! What's going on? What do you have, a cow in your living room?"

There was a long, uncomfortable pause.

"That's my wife," the fellow finally said. "She's meditating. We're Buddhists."

My co-worker turned quite a dazzling shade of scarlet. It took several seconds for her to remove the proverbial shoe - or high heel in this case - from her mouth, but at last, she managed to whisper, "Uh, I'm sure your cow - I mean, wife - is lovely. I think I'll hang up now."

Fortunately, Buddhists tend to have highly developed senses of humour.

After a while I begin to feel hungry, so I head over to the Himalaya Restaurant. When I arrive there, it is even more than usually packed with customers. I end up sharing a table with a girl from New York City who has recently been traveling in Tibet. She describes to me the oppressive nature of the situation there, with Tibetans routinely arrested if caught possessing an image of the Dalai Lama. Though personally sympathetic to the Tibetan cause, she tells me that while in Tibet she made a point of staying out of trouble, having heard so much about the unpredictable brutality of the Chinese police, even towards tourists.

One day though, innocently meandering through a market in the Tibetan capital of Lhasa, she was suddenly, unexpectedly, and roughly brought into custody. At the police station, waiting to be interrogated, she still had no idea what transgression she was accused of having committed. Finally, a policeman shed light on her alleged crime.

"You dare walk through Lhasa with a photo of the Dalai Lama on your clothes!"

"What?" she protested. "No, I didn't. I don't even own a picture of the Dalai Lama."

"Your shirt!" the policeman shouted, pointing at her chest. The girl looked down naively, then gasped, noticing for the first time how much the image on her shirt of American comedian Phil Silvers resembled the Dalai Lama. With bald heads and dark-framed glasses, the two were almost identical!

"There's been a mistake. Haven't you ever seen the TV show Sgt. Bilko?" she pleaded, realizing that the chances of a Chinese policeman in a place as remote as Tibet having seen a 1950's American sitcom were slim indeed. After several hours though, she was released, but not her shirt. She was returned to her hotel with full police escort in a borrowed police button-down. Shaken up, she decided to escape Lhasa on the next available flight, but not before burning her other Hollywood t-shirt - the one displaying the bald head of comedian Don Rickles.

The whole time she is talking, I watch as the New York girl eats a scrumptious banana pancake. I, of course, am waiting the obligatory two and a half hours for my own dinner. All of a sudden, the girl excuses herself, gets up and pays, leaving half her pancake behind - right in front of me. For months now, I've been eyeing the food that others leave unfinished on their plates. "What a waste!" I have muttered countless times under my breath. And now, I can't stand the thought of that pancake ending up in the garbage. I mean, it is perfectly good food and people in the world are starving. So, as inconspicuously as I can, I slide her plate in front of me, lest anyone think I'm eating someone else's food - which, of course, is exactly what I'm doing - and begin gobbling down the abandoned pancake. But about two chews in, it strikes me that this girl is a stranger and might have some sort of communicable disease. Oh well, I reason, it's not like I'm using her fork, and continue feeding.

Later, after I've finished not only the girl's pancake but a bowl of noodle soup, plate of chowmein and banana pancake of my own, needless to say, I'm feeling quite over-satiated. Suddenly though, I notice the people at the next table rising, leaving behind them more than half a plate of uneaten momos. I love momos! Okay, I know I'm so bloated another bite might make me barf, and I know there's a fine line between just being a glutton and being a glutton for punishment, but it upsets me too much to see all those helpless momos heading for the trash. I'm about to snatch them from the next table, when a waiter swoops in out of nowhere, clearing all the dishes and whisking away those poor, defenseless dumplings before I can save them from a rubbish worse than death.

Sadly, I slouch out of the restaurant. But turning the corner, I happen upon one of the cooks in a white apron at the back door. To my surprise, he is feeding leftover momos to a dog and pancake scraps to a cow. Suddenly, I feel very guilty at having eaten that girl's pancake, for in gorging myself beyond the boundaries of decency, I may have denied some poor hungry critter its dinner and only ended up fattening another animal of sorts - of course, I mean me, the rare, white, two-legged, Canadian piggy.

Oink, oink.

Chapter 27

SUCK ON THIS

In the West, we are taught to believe only what we see, but in India, I am constantly seeing things I can't believe.

One fine, sunny morning, I take a mini-bus down the mountain from McLeod Ganj to the town of Dharamsala on the hopes of locating a Tibetan faith healer - or "oracle" - that this traveler I met told me resides there. On the bus are fifteen rowdy tourists, loaded down with expensive photographic equipment.

"Where are you going?" I ask them.

"We're going to see an oracle!" they cheer.

In Dharamsala, the chatty tourists descend the bus happily, lugging their equipment single file up a nearby road. I decide not to follow their procession. I'm looking for an authentic experience after all, not a performance staged for a roomful of Westerners. I loiter by the bus stop awaiting the next shuttle back to McLeod Ganj and stare at a sign advertising the services of: DR. SANJEEV OF JAMMU. SPECIALIST IN SEX, V.D., WEAKNESS AND PILES. I can just imagine his radio ad campaign: "Syphilis got you down? Hemorrhoids keeping you up? Too tired to get out of bed? Too weak to have sex while you're there? Call Dr. Sanjeev of Jammu - India's own Dr. Ruth. (Lessons in technique available)."

At the bus stop another loiterer, a local, strikes up a conversation. I tell him I was hoping to see an oracle. He tells me there are actually *two* in Dharamsala, one whom all the tourists go to see, the other, considerably more low-key. He offers to escort me to the second for free and I agree.

He leads me through a dusty neighbourhood of modest dwellings until we reach a small home packed with Tibetans, Indians and Sikhs, all seated on the floor. Not a tourist in the crowd. A man immediately offers me a chair as guest of honour.

"I'm really okay on the floor," I say, actually preferring to remain inconspicuous, but he insists. The room is charged with anxiety, fearful expressions tensely gripping the faces of every man, woman and child present. "What have I gotten myself into?" I think, when suddenly, I hear a shriek from behind and quickly turning, see a young Tibetan woman barge into the room screaming hysterically. Frantically, she pushes her way to the front, crashing to her knees before an altar of candles, hands held tightly about her temples. For twenty minutes, she howls as if subjected to great pain, screeching, chanting, bowing, convulsing, all the while dressing herself in a blue, silken robe, a crown of many Buddhas, and a kerchief of red across her face, making her look like a Tibetan "Jesse James." Intermittently, she slaps a scalding dagger on her tongue, which has been resting on fiery, hot coals, the sizzle of which has everyone in the room cringing. Finally, she stops wailing and swirls around abruptly, seeming like a different person entirely. She holds her body tautly. She speaks in a shrill, wrathful, impatient manner, eyes peering intensely over her camouflage of red cloth.

Then, she turns on *me*, nearly knocking me over in my chair just with her stare. She growls something in my direction, growing noticeably more irritated the longer she is made to wait for a response - but I don't know what she's talking about. Fortunately, a shy Tibetan woman comes forward to translate.

"She would like to know if you have come here for healing," the woman says.

"Me? Oh no, no, definitely not."

"You have no sickness?" the woman asks.

"Me? No, no, I'm fine. Thanks for asking. Couldn't be better."

The oracle flips some grains of rice into the air. She watches them land on a small hand drum, inspects the pattern they form, then squeals sharply, pointing directly at me.

"She says you have some problem in your kidney," the translator informs me.

"Well, that's true, I suppose," I say, not wanting to admit weakness, but also not wanting to lie. Ever since those kidney stone attacks, I have had a chronic ache in my left side.

Suddenly the oracle shrieks - startling me so unexpectedly, I nearly have a heart attack!

"She says you are to have treatment."

Yeah? But for what - my kidney stone or the *coronary* she's just caused me? Then out of the blue a hand grabs my shoulder, sending me leaping from my seat. "Stop scaring me!" I cry.

A man motions for me to kneel on the floor. I'm perspiring heavily. The room is spinning, frightened faces leaning in closely all around me. I have no idea what this oracle might do to me. I keep thinking of that hot dagger - maybe she's going to cut me, maybe she's going to remove my kidney and sell it on the black market, maybe she's going to slice me, dice me and fry me up for dinner. Lord, how I wish there was another Westerner here with me. I wanted authenticity? Well, now I'm going to get it!

The oracle hovers over me, studying me with intense, bulging eyes. Two men hold me down, lifting my shirt to my chest, exposing my trembling belly. The oracle bends, bares her teeth and edges in close to my side - oh my God, I think she's going to bite me! But to my surprise, I feel no fangs sink into my flesh, just a suckling of the skin below my ribcage, directly on the spot where I've been suffering all my pain. Every few moments, the oracle stops to spit out mouthfuls of blood or a black, sticky substance reminiscent of tar. That's coming out of me? Tentatively, I look down at the reddish-purple circle on my side. The skin is definitely not broken. So, how exactly is all that goop passing from my body to the oracle's mouth? Surely, she can't be producing it within herself. I have no time to ponder further though, because suddenly, the oracle rises from her sucking to reveal a small, gray stone, like a pebble from the road, perched like a pearl on the oyster of her tongue.

"This from your kidney," the Tibetan translator whispers.

I am handed the stone. The two men, previously holding me down, now help me up. I almost swoon into blackness as I'm aided to my chair. My knees are so wobbly, my thoughts so delirious, I consider a visit on my way back to McLeod Ganj to Dr. Sanjeev of Jammu to see if he can cure me of this weakness. Slowly though, I am able to steady myself with deep, controlled breathing. The oracle speaks again, still squeaky, but not nearly as harsh.

"This old sickness," the Tibetan translator explains. "You must return tomorrow and also Friday for more treatment. Oh yes, bathe before, please."

Oops! Now, I'm embarrassed. I guess it has been awhile since I've braved that refrigerator of a shower at the Paljor Gakyil Guest House.

For the next two hours, I watch in wonder as the oracle sucks out an assortment of items from the physiques of some of her other patients. A huge wad of chewing gum entangled in a hairball is pulled from a crying baby's chest. Blood and tar are siphoned from the temple of a young man complaining of headaches, as well as from an old woman's leg. All the while, the oracle holds her wrists firmly clasped behind her back, so even though my Western mind is searching desperately for reasonable doubt, my eyes can find no evidence of sleight of hand, no opportunity for trickery.

Still, upon my return to the oracle twice more that week, I am determined to scrutinize her treatment more scientifically. It's that old Western upbringing: seeing may be believing, but *trusting* is another thing entirely. This time, as she sucks my lower abdomen, I consciously concentrate on the feelings in my body, startled to find myself becoming aware of a sensation as if *something* is moving deep inside me. The more she suckles, the more I feel a vague but discernible slipping of something outwards from within me in the area of my kidney, following quite intently the feeling until it occurs to me it is nearing precisely where her mouth is kneading at my skin. Then, at the very moment when the thought flashes in my mind, "She's got it!" - at that exact instant, the oracle suddenly bolts upright with another stone rested on her outstretched tongue.

How it got from inside my torso to her tongue without an actual opening in my skin, I don't think I'll ever really be able to explain. I know the proof may not be empirical and the data may easily invite skepticism, but in my mind at least - or should I say, in my body - intuition is still the most reliable measure of faith.

Feeling is believing.

I often think of the oracle, wondering if she was real or merely the clever manipulator of theatrical illusion, but the test of time still does tell: I have never since had another incident of pain related to my kidneys.

Unfortunately, neither have I ever received a hickey of such enduring, psychedelic proportion as the one the oracle bestowed upon me... no matter how many women I've pleaded with to try.

Chapter 28

ANGELS AMONG US

There's a sidewalk musician in McLeod Ganj busking for rupees on the road to the monastery, Namgyal Gompa. He amazes me. All at once, he is able to strum on a mandolin, keep a beat on a hand-drum, operate puppets with his feet, play brass chimes, and sing. I think he's a genius. I always give him money when I pass, just as I give the lepers here in Mc-Leod Ganj rupees every day.

Clara once said, "Generosity is such a strong positive karmic action, that anyone who allows you to give to them, is actually doing *you* a great, good deed." And so, strangely, I find myself thanking the lepers every time I give them money. After all, not only are they helping me increase my good karma by receiving my rupees, but also, through the act of giving, I get that much closer to becoming a Buddha.

Further on the road towards Namgyal Gompa, I notice two ragged men slaving in the heat, stuffing mounds of rotting garbage into enormous, black bags. A little off to the side of them, a woman sits by a makeshift tent, breastfeeding her baby in the shadow of a mountain of trash. My heart sinks as I realize their home isn't just a dump, it *is* the dump! I can't help but feel guilty, thinking of the money I so liberally spent on luxuries at Amit Sood's shop. I am so fortunate, but what of this family? What of this child being suckled amidst refuse? Where will *he* play? What of *his* future? What hope is there for him to realize his own Buddha Nature? There may have been a time when I could have just walked by, but today, I can't ignore the misery. Their suffering has become mine.

At Namgyal Gompa, I walk somberly around the grounds of the monastery, the hills of Dharangkot and Triund rising behind me, the Kanga Valley swept in fog below. I spin a long series of prayer wheels, stroll by boulders painted brightly with the Tibetan characters, Om Mani Padme Hum. I stop at a stupa, whose doorway is marked by images of black, grinning skulls; reminders of death, impermanence and the folly of attachment. Encased in glass in the middle of the stupa is a small, golden Buddha, smiling kindly down upon me as if with great empathy. I close my eyes and pray. Pray to the Buddha, pray to the Universe, to the Creator, pray to Shiva, pray to God, pray until my heart throbs and tears burn the corners of my eyes: "Thank you for the blessings of my life, for my health, for this day, for each precious moment I'm alive. Thank you for all the love in my life. May I give as much or more in return. May each breath bring me closer to enlightenment, so I may end for all time all suffering, loneliness and pain. Show me how to be of service. I want to help. Show me the way to help."

After several moments, I lift my reddened eyes and am met by the warm regard of the golden Buddha. Above, prayer flags sweep softly in the wind. Monks are chanting low in the distance. The orange sun is setting on another day gone by. Who knows what tomorrow may bring? But at least, suddenly, I am confident that I am on the path of my own destiny, no longer needing assurance as to where the road of life is leading, just that what is, is meant to be. For once, I find satisfaction with my present situation, not lacking for anything intangible to make me complete, yet secure enough within myself to know that even happiness passes, and when it does, to allow for its gentle fading. All I have is this present moment. "Don't sweat the small stuff," Clara said. "Relish in it. For it is exactly the small stuff which gives life its flavour, sometimes savoury and sometimes sweet."

These days in McLeod Ganj are the most peaceful of my life. One of my daily activities is morning yoga in the forest just outside of Bhagsu, a half hour walk from my guesthouse. Classes begin at six-thirty A.M. To arrive on time I have to wake up at five-thirty. Before the retreat, I would have considered this a disagreeable, if not ungodly, hour to rise, but now I find myself enjoying being up so early. The hush of the early morn and soft glow of the lavender sky soothe me into a deep state of calm well before I even reach the secluded grove where classes are conducted. An American named Michael is the yoga instructor. He introduces himself as being forty-seven years old. I thought he was barely thirty. Besides being an example of youth and vitality, Michael models for me a man grounded in inner strength and tranquility. And did I mention generosity? His classes are actually free - his small gift to humanity, he humbly tells me.

Michael's method of instruction is gentle but firm, pushing his students to excel, but forever forgiving of individual limitations.

"Don't hurt yourselves," he says. "Just do your best."

His focus in yoga always returns to the breath.

"Relax your breath and your mind will follow" is his motto. "Loosen the muscles in your face and watch all tightness in your body disappear. Let your mind go free. Become pure awareness, as expansive as the sky."

This is the first time I've ever tried yoga with any regularity and I must say, I find myself leaving class each day feeling electric, flexible, energetic yet calm. As far as becoming "as expansive as the sky," I figure I'll achieve that soon enough, flying in an airplane back to Canada.

It must be time for me to go home. I enter a telephone centre in McLeod Ganj to make a call and to my surprise the owner is watching "Fashion TV" on a satellite channel, a television show shot in downtown Toronto. The next day, I return and he is viewing a movie called, "Breaking All The Rules," once again filmed in Toronto. Coincidence? With a mix of dread and longing, I gaze upon images of Queen Street, The CN Tower and Lake Ontario. But later, outside, I stare with serenity at the snowy outline of the Himalayas and wonder, where is my place in this world? Here in India where my spirit is being nurtured or back in Toronto with family and friends? Where is home to the wandering soul?

Dwindling funds may be the answer to that question. I dejectedly decide that in three short days I absolutely must return to New Delhi to catch a flight to Canada. The next morning, I awaken, determined to make the most of my remaining time in the mountains by trekking to the Himalayan lookout of Triund, high above McLeod Ganj. My hike begins upwards through hillside villages, farms and wheat-coloured fields, then moves higher into thick green forests, and higher still into a sparse landscape of boulders and shrubs, reminding me of the barren highlands of Scotland. Several hours later, I arrive at Triund, ten thousand feet above sea level. Triund, it turns out, is nothing but a small abandoned lodge, closed for the season. Beyond the lodge though is a massive wall of mountain rising into a colossal snow-capped peak. Now I know why people make the considerable effort to climb here.

I stand there gawking before the breathtaking mountain, the bitter cold biting at my cheeks, when low flying clouds suddenly sweep in completely obscuring the scene. Within seconds, there is absolutely no sign that at anytime anything stood before me, let alone something as imposing as a Himalayan giant. Had I arrived just ten minutes later to Triund, I would have never known the glacier was even there. Again, everything reminds me of impermanence.

I meander away from the lodge, through the thickening fog,

attempting to appreciate the bliss of the near vacuous silence, but the ceaseless chatter of my thoughts persistently frustrates my efforts. It strikes me that even here, miles removed from the clamour of civilization, I still am unable to escape the noise of my mind... except, according to the Buddha, through meditation. So, I sit and close my eyes, try to clear the stream of clutter from my brain, but my mind is like a rampant locomotive, distracted by the rapidly dipping temperature and the wind picking up speed. I rise and press on. The fog is now heavy, the landscape unfamiliar. I feel as if I'm moving through a dream. I pass by the eerie remnants of a stone Hindu shrine. Three rusted tridents lean lifelessly by its crumpled façade. I pass by a roofless, decimated structure. A brown ratty blanket blocks the entrance, covering something resembling a dead body. Suddenly, a ghostly gust of wind startles me from behind. I start to walk faster, faster and before I know it, I'm running through a dense veil of mist, down past unfamiliar boulders into an indistinct forest. Finally I stop to gasp for air and looking around, realize - I'm lost.

One moment so certain of the path, the next, confounded, disoriented, perplexed - does everything have to be a metaphor for spiritual life? I glance at the horizon. The sun is beginning to set. I consider climbing back up towards Triund to search out the proper route, but decide that would take far too long. Instead, I forge downward through the maze of trees, figuring, I may have no idea where I'm heading, but one thing's for sure - I've definitely got to go down.

And down I go, racing through the forest in a panic, when all of a sudden, the ground itself crumbles beneath me and I begin sliding uncontrollably past thorns and sharp branches that rip at my skin, slice at my face. Down and down I fall, helplessly, until miraculously, I manage to break my momentum and abruptly stop my wild descent. And it's a good thing, because another two inches and I would have flown off the edge of a cliff!

Catching my breath, I check the ground for stability and lean over the brink. It doesn't look good. Beyond the cliff's edge is a sheer drop into a wide, open valley, comprised almost entirely of loose rock. The sun is now sinking rapidly. I realize I had better come up with a brilliant idea, fast. Sleeping in the forest is definitely not an option. Even if I survived being eaten by tigers, which is unlikely, I'd probably die from the freezing temperatures! With little time for deliberation, I choose what seems to me the most rational course of action.

I jump.

I leap off the cliff into mid-air and for a suspended moment sail through the ether without an attachment in the world. Then, I happen to glance down and realize that if I don't think of something quick I'm going to be *attached* to a wall of rock in the next ten seconds. Somehow, I've got to break my impending impact! Fortunately, at the last moment, I spy a dangling vine and grab hold for dear life, swinging there feebly like a poor imitation of Tarzan, desperately groping for a toe-hold to access the steep slope. But no matter how hard I stretch, I can't reach. I'm simply not tall enough. Why didn't I grow up eating Wheaties? Then, unable to just hang around forever, I... let go.

"Aaaaaaaaaaaaaaaaaaahhhhhhhhhhhhhhhh!"

Talk about completely surrendering! Next thing I know, I'm rolling, crashing, propelling downwards, loose rocks flying, knocking me in the head. I'm screaming profanities, picking up speed, tumbling like a cannonball, when all of a sudden, I blur past something that undeniably resembles a path. Mustering all my strength, I dig my nails excruciatingly into the ground, until finally I am able, bleeding, to stop my downward progress. When the dust clears, I notice that indeed, above me, is a path! I don't know where it leads, but it's got to go someplace better than where I'm heading, which about now appears to be to my death. I try to scurry up the slope, but the shale is so unstable that for each movement upwards, I slide back down twice as far. It is now well into twilight, the sky a deepening blue, my chances at survival growing dimmer. As the song goes - "It's now or never!"

With a rush of adrenaline, I *will* myself up the sheer rock wall, throwing myself heroically onto the flattened surface of the narrow path. Next, without even taking a moment to recuperate, I rise and quickly scuttle along the trail, wary not to plummet once more off the edge. Then, the worst thing happens - yes, even worse than having just jumped off a cliff - I come to a fork in the road. Now what do I do? Neither path looks any different, yet one may lead to McLeod Ganj, the other to certain disaster. How can I possibly choose?

"There are no obstacles, only challenges," I hear Clara's voice in my head.

"Not now, Clara! I'm busy!" I shout then realize, what am I doing? She's not even here. I haven't seen another soul for hours!

I stand at the impasse, tears streaming from my frostbitten eyes, unable to decide, when suddenly, the thickened mist subsides, revealing an Indian man standing at my side.

Where did he come from?

He is sixty years old, with pearl-white hair, a pale-yellow turban and a red dot of ash on his third eye. His very presence seems dubious. First of all, we're in the middle of a wilderness. There are no homes nearby. Secondly, he is strangely wearing a chocolate-brown suit, an incongruous choice of clothing considering the temperature and elevation. Thirdly, his clothes appear too neatly pressed for the mountains - I doubt there's a drycleaner's in the vicinity. How did he get here? He doesn't seem to be sweating from hiking, nor does he appear in the slightest to be bothered by the cold. He doesn't speak. He doesn't smile. He does only one thing, after awhile. He gently raises his arm and indicates with his finger the path on the left.

"That way?" I say. But he doesn't respond. He just keeps pointing. "Is McLeod Ganj that way?" I ask, but still he remains silent. I find his company unnerving. Abruptly, I race past him down the path on the left, not even thanking him - I don't know what to think of him! A few yards down though, I turn back apprehensively, in time to see the man literally being swallowed by clouds. In a moment, he is completely gone.

An hour later, on my last legs, desperate as darkness has descended and my flashlight's batteries are running low, I astoundingly happen upon McLeod Ganj, falling to my knees in gratitude and relief. But who am I thanking? I have never been one to truly believe in angels. I'm just glad that one believed in me.

Chapter 29

TWO TIMES LUCKY

The day before I am to leave Mcleod Ganj, I am thrilled to find out that that very afternoon the Dalai Lama will once again be offering a public audience. The Buddhas must be smiling upon me. Sometimes you do get a second chance.

I rush to a shop to buy a "kha-dag," a white ceremonial scarf used in Tibetan pujas, and hurry over to line up before the Dalai Lama's residence. At precisely one o'clock, the gates are opened and I am directed to an outdoor courtyard where Westerners are asked to line up on one side of a long, red carpet, Tibetans on the other. To my left, about a hundred yards away is the Dalai Lama's home. To my right is a podium decorated with prayer flags and flowers. For about twenty minutes, I stand along with two hundred and fifty other people waiting in anticipation of an appearance by the Dalai Lama. Suddenly, far to our left, a door is opened and a long procession of monks in maroon robes appears.

"Which one is the Dalai Lama?" I think aloud, but don't really need an answer. Soon enough, it becomes perfectly clear. Though the monks are all smiling, there is one in the middle who is absolutely radiant, waving, laughing. He is a small man with glasses - really, I expected him to be bigger - but there's an aura of grace, humility and elegance about him. I think he might even be blushing.

Many of the Tibetans drop immediately to their knees and even I feel a rush of excitement, a pure unexpected joy as he passes. It's amazing that at this distance, with so many people around, this physically unimpressive man is still able to exude genuine concern for each individual. He has the presence of royalty, yet at once he seems as modest and unassuming as any common man.

I watch, fixated, as the Dalai Lama proceeds to the podium, where one by one, he greets each member of the audience on stage, blessing each man and woman personally with an abundance of patience and love, making it seem as though *he* were the one enjoying the privilege of meeting *us*, and not, as one would expect, the other way around. When finally my turn comes, I'm so nervous, I am barely aware that my feet are carrying me to the stage and am almost surprised when I find myself situated before the Dalai Lama. I bow in deep respect, offering him my silky, white kha-dag, as is the Tibetan custom. The Dalai Lama then takes the scarf from my hands and with great warmth, places it gently over my shoulders, signifying the bestowing upon me of his blessing. A shudder electrifies my spine. I am afraid to look him in the eyes for fear of overstepping my standing, but something inside impels me to raise my head slightly, not enough to seem irreverent, but enough to absorb the full impact of the Dalai Lama's face. He is absolutely glorious, resplendent, bursting with light and joy.

I want to laugh but find instead I'm crying, sobbing uncontrollably as unexpectedly the Dalai Lama reaches forth and takes my hand, holding me tenderly for what seems like an eternity, meeting my eyes with a quality of compassion you would only expect a mother to render unto her child.

And then, as quickly as it comes, the moment is gone.

As I'm led from the podium, I am dizzy, no longer weeping, but giggling quite hysterically. I have never felt so happy. I have never felt so loved. It's as if my whole body has been filled with hope and possibility. I feel so airy, I wonder if I might be levitating. My face is stained with tears, but my cheeks are sore from smiling. Standing before the Dalai Lama, I felt that at some level I was like him, that I could be like him, that I wanted to be like him, that I have those qualities, however undeveloped, somewhere within me. In the presence of such unrestrained kindness, it felt as though all my pretensions were being melted, all my defenses burned away. And in that state of vulnerability, I was able to recognize in the Dalai Lama's face not only my humanity, but also my own potential for divinity.

I want to be that loving. I want to touch people's hearts with that kind of energy. I want to heal the world with an end to all suffering. I want to be gentle and wise. I want to be generous and kind. And here is a man, the Dalai Lama, a living Buddha, proving to me that it is possible, modeling for me that it is not merely the whimsy of dreams. If only I could become even a fraction as loving as he, what meaning my life would have, just from simply being.

Exclusive club, for babies
only. Anyone over five
must present valid I.D.
(Mcleod Ganj.)

Hey, did you hear the
one about the priest, the
rabbi and the Dalai
Lama?
(McLeod Ganj)

Excuse me, sir. You seem
to have lost a part of your
buffalo.
(The hills above McLeod
Ganj)

Tina Turner hairdos.
Very popular in the
Himalayas.
(McLeod Ganj)

"Look, Mom, I'm tall!" That's me with the thirty-year-old "Room Boy" at the Paljor Gakyil Guest House in McLeod Ganj. Never before going to India had I experienced the euphoria of actually towering over crowds.

Amit Sood, humble shop owner and overly enthusiastic hugger. I'm smiling for the camera but wondering... what's his knee doing in my crotch?! (McLeod Ganj)

V

RETURN
TO
SENDER,
ADDRESS
UNKNOWN

Chapter 30

DEFEATING EVILS

On the eve before becoming the Buddha, Prince Siddhartha sat beneath the sheltering leaves of the Bodhi Tree, contemplating the truths of
the universe. He saw the vast effects of karma, the treadmill of reincarnation, the suffering of desire, the agony of attachment and loss. He
had tried all the known methods of the times for reaching enlightenment
and had found each and every one lacking. He had starved himself,
tortured his body, renounced all form of pleasure, but still he found
elusive the ultimate treasure - liberation. Finally, he decided not to move,
not to rise, not to open his eyes, until he had awakened within himself
the compassion and wisdom needed to transcend the trappings of human
suffering.

It is said that on this evening, all the evils of the universe conspired
against Siddhartha, tempting him to stray from his noble quest. He was
visited by seductresses, women bent on taunting him with lusty desire
and pleasures of the flesh. He was attacked by strong emotion - anger,
jealousy, fear and hate. He was even, I am told, teased by a particularly
luscious slice of Devil's Food Cake. But Siddhartha did not succumb, nor
did he resist. He merely remained calm, in a balanced, sedate state,
allowing every feeling to rise and ebb, every craving to swell and subside, every temptation to appear and pass away. Nothing could sway
Siddhartha from his goal of inner peace. And in the morning, when he
opened his eyes, lo and behold, he had become the Buddha. No longer
attached to the folly of worldly drama. No longer seeking gratification
from experience that was clearly impermanent. No longer limited to the
vain pursuits of ego. He realized profoundly his connection to all beings
through a Higher Mind. His vision had transcended the limitations of the
physical world. He had found the middle way, the path to enlightenment, driven by a motivation of love. He was ready to begin teaching.

This is the image I now take home with me, better than any souvenir, any photo, any trinket reminding me of India. This image of the Buddha, defeating evils, remaining perfectly balanced no matter what circumstance, what thought, what emotion, what temptation may arise - this image is the model for how I want to live my life.

The choice is mine - suffering or peace. Nothing can hurt me if I remain calm.

Still, as I am packing up my belongings, preparing for my return to New Delhi and then Canada, I feel as though a million butterflies have taken up residence in my intestines. My stomach is not as enlightened as my intentions. I am filled with remorse at the thought of returning to Toronto. Canada seems like a dream to me now. It is India that has captured my heart. What will I do back in the West? Where will I live? What new career awaits me? Canada feels full of uncertainty now, just as India did at the beginning of my trip.

At a travel agency in McLeod Ganj, I buy a bus ticket back to New Delhi and reserve a flight to Toronto three days hence. I can't believe it, my last Indian bus ride - well, there may be some positive aspects to going home. The journey to New Delhi is another overnighter and I am once again the only Westerner on board - all the others by this time probably know better.

At four in the morning, the bus pulls over on a deserted street of a dark town. The only soul around is an old chai salesman with bloodshot eyes, obviously straining to remain awake in order to sell tea to buses such as ours. I stumble out of the bus, half-delirious and desperate to pee. Now, it's not always obvious at these pit-stops where to relieve oneself and usually I just follow the other passengers, but on this night, I'm so bleary and slow, that by the time I get outside, I can't find where everyone went. I see a dark alley but it seems to me too perfect a setting for a mugging. I check around the corner, but I don't want to get too far from the bus, lest it leave me behind without warning.

My bladder is now throbbing, but what's worse, the driver of my bus has begun to rev the engine impatiently. With little time and apparently no other option, I settle upon a reasonably secluded corner and anxiously allow my urine to drain, when all of a sudden, I feel a cold droplet on my neck - strange, because there's been no sign of rain - then, WHOOOOSH! A flood of freezing water showers unexpectedly down upon me, effectively stopping me in mid-pee. I spin around to discover the old chai salesman standing there with a now empty pitcher, yelling ferociously at *me*! What is he shouting at me for? I should be wailing at him. It's four in the morning, bloody cold out and now I've got fourteen more hours on a bus to spend SOAKING WET! He keeps pointing at the wall onto which I was peeing, but as far as I can tell the building is abandoned. "What's your problem, man?" I want to scream. I'm furious. I want to pick him up and throttle him. I want to walk over and destroy his tea stand. But in the end, I do nothing.

I do nothing because I'm in unknown territory, the only white person for miles around. The last thing I need, three days before going home, is to end up being beaten, killed or even worse, thrown in jail. But on a deeper level, I do nothing because since Tushita, I've decided I no longer want to be a Jeckyl and Hyde, switching from someone mild-mannered into one who vents his frustrations by kicking over tea stands. I've been trying to transcend my angry tendencies.

A Tibetan lama once said that the East may endure *physical* poverty, but the West still suffers more from self-hatred and low self-esteem. In Tushita, the teachings really spoke to me with regard to my anger, preaching patience and compassion in even the most frustrating situations. The Buddha stressed control over one's reactions as a method to achieving peace. He advocated the mindful examination in every moment of every thought, word and deed to see if they will be of benefit. For each angry outburst creates an inevitable ripple of karma, suffering not just for others, but also for me.

I am told the Dalai Lama once reduced the entire essence of Buddhism into a single catchphrase: "Don't hurt anything," he said, "and if you can, help." I no longer want to hurt others with my anger. Buddhism has taught me to look at those who offend me in terms of *their* suffering. A person angry with me deserves not a return of aggression but an attitude of compassion, for their anger reveals the suffering of an agitated mind. They should be treated with love, because it's obvious from their actions that they themselves are tormented by a lack of inner peace. We are all of us just blindly walking this Earth, wanting to be loved, while unknowingly hurting others and causing ourselves pain.

There is no eye for an eye in Buddhism, not even a turning of the cheek, just a calm, balanced acceptance, forgiveness, tenderness and love. Someone strong in compassion has no need to be defensive. A lion that knows his heart has no need to roar.

The chai salesman yells at me for several more minutes, then returns to selling tea. I just stand there, dripping, consciously restraining my impulse to rage. Anger flushes through me in waves, but I don't allow myself to be swept away. I detach. I watch the anger, let each surge pass and resist the urge to add inflammatory thoughts to the emotional fire. I focus on my breath, relax, until calmness descends upon me despite my physical discomfort. I won't give in this time to anger.

I am determined to live my life peacefully. I am committed to overcoming destructive habitual behaviour. A few months ago, I probably would have thought myself crazy to sit on a bus drenched and shivering, practicing affirmations of serenity. But that is exactly what I do. And guess what? It really works. It is almost that simple: an exercise of will.

Moment by moment, I accept the reality that I am soaked and surrender the desire to change what I cannot change. And somehow in the absence of resistance, in the midst of circumstances far less than ideal, though logic would defy it, I actually feel happy. Suffering is in the mind, not in a wet body.

Chapter 31

LEAVING ON A JET PLANE

International airport, New Delhi.

It's hard to believe I'm actually here. Waiting for my flight, I find it hard to shake a pervasive sense of mourning from my body. I don't feel like I'm going home, more like home is where I'm leaving. I have come full circle, once again flying into a future I cannot possibly predict, only this time my destination is Toronto.

The airport this morning is filled with frustrated passengers, waging their last battles against Indian bureaucracy. I overhear an exasperated Swede ask a turbaned Sikh official if he knows the way to British Airways. The Sikh responds with the usual vague wave of the hand, indicating somewhere, *over there* - that's about as definite an answer as you'll ever get in New Delhi.

Everyone seems to be acting out their anxiety in strange ways. Two frayed Frenchmen, sorting through their tickets, light cigarette after cigarette; not exactly croissants, but breakfast nonetheless. A Muslim man in a flowing white robe and starched white cap pulls an unexpected wheelie in front of me with his luggage cart. A Japanese traveler dressed in round, wire rim glasses and psychedelic Sixties attire, reminding me of "John Lennon-san," sits two seats down from me, scratching his body incessantly. Another soul tripped up in the hippie time warp of Goa.

But it's an American in the distance who really catches my eye, stiffly approaching the Passport Control counter. He is at least six-foot-four and is wearing a cowboy hat, but that's not what holds my attention. He is limping... with both legs. I imagine that he is braced at both knees, or perhaps he is an overzealous John Wayne fan with psychosomatic saddle sores, ambling with an exaggerated B-movie, Wild West gait. Legs spread, hands by his side, high noon. DRAW! This here's my passport, podner. Stamp it. I dare you.

I move up to take a closer look, having to behold for myself why he's walking like a rusty robot, but when I see the reason, I'm not sure I believe it. He's wearing ski boots! Downhill, winter, ski boots. In New Delhi. In heat-struck, ninety-five degree New Delhi. Was there not a soul to suggest to him that a more practical choice of footwear might be flip-flops? Was there not a Sadhu, a holy man, to enlighten him to the reality that he had not, in fact, landed in Switzerland, no matter what the travel agent might have told him? Was it simply a fashion statement?

I guess I'll never know, because before I can garner the courage to ask him, he retrieves his passport and clunks across the airport floor, lumbering off into the sunset of Personal Security Check.

Suddenly, there's a commotion at the Aeroflot counter, Russia's pride of the airways. I am not at all surprised to find Aeroflot in disarray. Aeroflot is generally the cheapest airline to fly, and, as with most inexpensive items, there's often a price other than money to pay. On my last Aeroflot flight, besides the delays, the inconvenient stopover in Moscow and the horrible food, the floor of the plane was occupied by a dozen hyperactive puppies, one of which, I'm certain, "wee-wee-ed" on my shoe.

The ruckus is actually due to Aeroflot's opening for business - not only an hour late, but at a different counter entirely from where its sign was displayed and passengers were lined up neatly. Panic and stampede ensues as hundreds of Aeroflot customers hurry to secure a position in the new queue.

Anarchy, chaos and disorder: my last glimpse of India. You don't know what you've got 'til it's gone.

Korean Air. Flight 636 from Bangkok to Seoul.

I am experiencing turbulence.

In order to book a flight so soon out of New Delhi, I had to compromise on direction. Normally, I would be flying to the West by going west through the Middle East, over Europe, a stop in London, and transAtlantic straight into Toronto. Instead, I am flying to the West by going *east* through Bangkok, Korea, over Japan, trans-Pacific to Vancouver and then to Toronto. Since thirteen months ago, I boarded a plane in Toronto and flew east to India, I feel now, by continuing east, I have avoided retracing old steps. Even though I am "returning," I am forging new pathways. I am going east to the West, stopping in the West of Canada before advancing to my final destination, Toronto, in the East.

Confused?

All I know is that either way, the future lies forward, my destiny unknown, and all I can hope for is that when I do arrive in the eastern part of the West, I can incorporate into my new Western life these thirteen months in the East.

I wonder if the stewardess has a Tylenol.

In the airport in Korea during a stopover, I phone my mother to tell her I'm on my way back to Canada.

"Oh my God, you're coming home?" she exclaims. "Where are you now?"

"Seoul."

"Sole? Isn't that the stuff you bread and fry?"

"No, that's fish, Mom. I'm in Seoul, Korea. You know, the city in the sitcom, M*A*S*H*."

"Oh yeah." Now she remembers. Actually, it's the first destination in Asia that I have visited whose name my mother has recognized.

"You're there?" she says, after thinking about it a moment. "Isn't it dangerous?"

"Uh, I'll only be in the airport, Mom," I say. "And besides, the war here has been over for nearly forty years."

"I know the war is over," she says. "It's in reruns."

Which raises the question - if a war is in reruns, does it still threaten airport security?

Vancouver airport. Transit Lounge.

The clock on the wall indicates *13:13* P.M., Vancouver time - a bad omen?

My watch reads 6:18 A.M., Korea time.

My body is still back on 3:00 A.M., India time.

My watch says November 26th.

The airport calendar says November 25th.

Last I remember on November 25th, I was in New Delhi - according to the calendar, I should still be in India.

I am scheduled to arrive in Toronto at 9:20 P.M., November 25th.

I left Korea at 8:30 P.M., November 25th.

I will have just sat on a plane fifteen hours to travel less than sixty
minutes. I will have gained a day, lost a day, spent a day, then somehow,
gotten it back. I will have two shots at November 26th.

What will I do with this extra time? Solve world hunger? Check out
tomorrow's stock prices today? Bet on yesterday's horses? Or will this
simply afford me the additional hours necessary to puzzle over just what
time it is, or what day?

As past and future become ill-defined, the only thing that truly
maintains its dependability is the present. No matter what day or time it
is, one can rest reasonably assured, that at any given moment, it is now. If
it is not now, by the time you come to that realization, now has become
then anyway - so don't worry about it.

The point is that, for now... caught somewhere between November
25th and 26th, it's enough for me to take comfort in a sentimental vision
of my future epitaph. On my gravestone, may I be remembered as someone who exuded such passion for life, such joie de vivre, you might think
to say, "He lived that extra day."

Chapter 32

SCORPIO RISING

How can I be somewhere I have lived for eleven years and still feel
so lost?

Standing in my sister's apartment, staring out at the Toronto sky-
line from her penthouse view, all I see is concrete, miles and miles of
cement. Whatever happened to nature? Where are all the cows?

It's hard to believe that just two days ago, I was in India. The heat, the crowds, the bus rides - all were so real such a short time ago. I feel like I've died, but I haven't gone to heaven. I've been reborn here in Toronto and am floundering like an infant fresh from the womb, helpless to make sense of my surroundings.

My adventure in India already feels remote to me. I can see myself in a few months having to go for some past life regression therapy just to remember what happened to me there. Everything that was vivid has drifted into the foggy realm of memory. But I need to keep these recollections alive. I need to integrate my experience in order to proceed. I need to learn from what has happened to grow into the man I want to be. I need to write it all down, perhaps for others, but even more, for me.

I am reminded of the wise words of an Israeli I befriended in McLeod Ganj, who looked up at me from a steaming bowl of noodle soup, squinted through his slightly crooked, mist-condensed glasses and said, "Perhaps in the end all of life is just a dream."

My second day in Toronto, I awaken to the worst snowstorm in over fifty years. People are cross-country skiing down the main roads. All public transit has been suspended. Snow in the mountains is beautiful. Snow in the city quickly turns to brownish slush. I feel trapped. I am used to days filled with constant new experiences. Here in Toronto, life seems stagnant, old.

I call up my best friends. They are happy to have me home, but when I actually do see them, I wonder if we have anything remaining in common. They flip quickly through my photos then return to discussing baseball statistics, completely excluding me. When I bring up Buddhism, one of my friends warns me against joining "that cult." Another friend's interest in my travels is limited to my bowel movements, satisfied to learn only whether or not I followed his sage advice to "always wipe that one extra time, just to be safe." It seems that nothing here has changed, except me.

The next day, my mother, sister and I go to The Promenade, a Toronto shopping mall. Once there, I find myself almost paralyzed, in awe of all the people aggressively engaged in pre-Christmas purchasing. A frenzied woman almost tackles me as she hurries by clutching parcels possessively to her chest. A teenage girl with black hair, black shirt, black pants, black boots, black make-up and white cigarette impatiently pushes me from her path - obviously late for her *Anarchists Anonymous* meeting. Everyone is scurrying about with faces strained, foreheads clenched and

veins protruding. It's as bizarre as anything I saw in India. It is material-
ism personified. All these people in search of objects to make them happy
but none of them look happy at all. They seem to be suffering from their
own craving - just as the Buddha said.

At a supermarket, I am stunned by the abundance of food. So many
kinds of fruits, vegetables, meats, cheeses, seafood, baked goods, bottled
goods, canned goods. More food than can possibly be consumed - and
this is only one store! And then I think of the starvation I witnessed in
India, the thousands of beggars with sallow eyes, the desperate lack of
supplies and I can't help it - in the middle of aisle number five, I break
down and cry.

Throughout my time in India, I was warned by other travelers to
expect "reverse culture shock" upon returning to the West. They said it
would be much more difficult to adapt to Canada after being in India
than it was the other way around. Considering how challenging my first
few weeks were in India, I'd be crazy not to be terrified now that I'm
"home."

Standing by the penthouse window, snow falls on the concrete below. The never-ending traffic sounds like monks chanting the "Holy
Om" - spirituality in the city. I try to tell myself I am still traveling, only
now in Toronto. Destiny has brought me here. To find true peace, I must
be happy anywhere. And what will it matter anyway where I've been, as
long as I've tried, wherever I was, to make others happy? India or Canada, I want to see people smiling. New Delhi or Toronto, I want to hear
people laughing. But most of all, I want to dedicate myself tirelessly to
inspiring peace, wherever this journey of life may or may not in the end
take me.

Chapter 33

EPILOGUE

Life has a way of bringing you to moments of choice and transition
when all that has previously occurred suddenly accumulates in your
awareness to make you who you are and will be. Consciousness, brought
into the moment, is empowered to ignite endless creative choices, endless

opportunities for change, growth, love, divinity. Bringing consciousness into the moment with any regularity is the difference between a spiritual life and one of escape, the difference between love and fear. In the moment, one can expand, one can open, one can overcome. In ignorance of the moment, one can only suffer. The endless struggle to rise from the ashes, to rear one's head from the muck, to gaze upon the radiant possibility of each moment and soar like the phoenix to embody our highest ideals, these are the teachings of the Buddha. Life begins and ends with each moment.

Never has that been as clear, profound or tangible as when life tossed my unsuspecting Western butt into the maelstrom of Mother India. At first it was hard to imagine rising from any ashes, when everything surrounding me appeared caked with dust. But in time, India's relentless demands to question and alter my most basic beliefs, changed at a deep level the way I interact with a world that is ever-changing. Perhaps my greatest lesson came from the knowing eyes of begging children, rising with such magnificence from faces layered with filth and snot. Perhaps it was in the attitude of cows, in the cities, on the beaches, whose detachment reached regal, even saintly proportions, as they ploughed through mounds of garbage with single-minded concentration. Perhaps it was in the mountains, the breathtaking Himalayas, whose silent dominance and majestic calm made me feel part of a greater landscape, part of the winds that swept to the valley, part of the rocks that formed sheer cliffs. Perhaps my lesson was hidden in all these and more; in every person I met, every setting or circumstance in which I found myself struggling. India, the patient teacher, set obstacle after obstacle at my feet, smiling serenely as I grappled to retain balance and flexibility. Until finally I surrendered, nestling myself in the pores of her skin. Finally, I came to breath with her rhythm and she, to share in my dreams.

This work was undertaken from the humble desire to encourage us all to follow our dreams, to remind us that there is a whole world out there that operates contrary to the values that drive our Western civilization, where spirit is respected, magic is commonplace and the dollar is not the end to which mankind strives, but inner peace.

It strikes me now, that the most profound lesson of my entire travels occurred even before I ever first entered Toronto's Pearson Airport that overcast day in October 1991. I had a secure job in the big city, a comfortable life, loving friends, yet I chose to risk losing all for the promise of something even greater - spiritual awakening and the adventure of the unknown. It was in the letting go of everything I held to be secure that true miracles were allowed to occur, and I was rewarded with a sense of freedom and empowerment beyond my imagination.

I was to be changed forever.

I found that the more I opened to myself, the more I was able to open to others, and the more I was able to open to others, the more I opened to myself. And the longer I walked the ancient, holy lands of India, the more India pried open in me a wonder-struck appreciation for each precious moment.

And for that, I am forever grateful.

ABOUT THE AUTHOR

Actor/writer/comedian Stewart Katz was born and raised in Montreal, a city renowned for its great philosophers and better bagels, where he earned a degree in Literature and Theatre, graduating with distinction from McGill University. Soon after he moved to Toronto in search of the Canadian Dream, only to find himself ten years later in a nightmare of traffic and smog. In 1996, fate landed him in the most beautiful place in the world, Salt Spring Island, British Columbia. A self-proclaimed cross between Woody Allen and a Tibetan monk, Stewart has toiled as a theatrical agent, a massage therapist, a teacher and as a professional actor. He has been a student of Buddhist meditation for over ten years, having completed extended retreats at the Tushita Retreat Centre in India, Kopan Monastery in Nepal, and at Wat Kow Tham in Thailand. But most of all, he is an insatiable traveler and animated storyteller. He's got tales to tell from Europe, Asia, the Middle East, Canada and America - from Jerusalem to Paris, Bombay to Kathmandu - and let's not forget all those family vacations in Florida.

Stewart is presently hard at work on his second book, *Yak Attack! Hilarious Mis-Adventures In Nepal.*

ACKNOWLEDGEMENTS

Heartfelt thanks to my wife Julie and son Nathan for their patient support and considerable skill in editing. To my sister Ann-Karen, her husband Brahm, and to Bev and Richard Howard, for housing and feeding me while I was hashing out that enigmatic first draft. To my brother, Mark, and his family for photocopies and encouragement. To my aunt Tenda, for giving me the idea that my mother was my guru. To my friends on Salt Spring Island for providing me with a sense of community that makes everything seem possible. To Shari Geller, without whom I would have never even thought to go to India. To those who so generously donated funds, especially Nancy Franz, Jerry Alkoff, Sheri Israels and Geoff Butcher. A special thank you to Karen Hood-Caddy and Aylwin Catchpole for their perceptive editorial suggestions, and to Mark Hand for his artistic inspiration in designing the cover. And finally, to my mother, Elaine, whose love is unimaginably huge... and her sense of humour ain't bad either. I couldn't have done it without you, Mom.

HOLY COW!

can also be seen
"live"
as a
trilogy of one-man plays
written by and
starring
STEWART KATZ.

• •

TO ORDER
ADDITIONAL COPIES
OF

HOLY COW!
HILARIOUS
MIS-ADVENTURES
IN
INDIA

Please send a cheque or money order in the amount of
$22.95 Cdn. ($20.00 U.S.) plus $5.95 shipping and handling,
payable to **Stewart Katz** at the following address:

105 Ontario Place
Salt Spring Island
British Columbia, Canada
V8K 2L5
* Please allow approximately four weeks for delivery.

For more information, **Stewart Katz** may be contacted at:
holycow@saltspring.com

WHAT THE CRITICS SAY ABOUT
HOLY COW!

"Compelling, engrossing and fun."
- The Gulf Islands Driftwood

"As thoughtful as it is hilarious."
- The Salt Spring Village Views

WHAT SOME READERS HAVE SAID:

"A great read!!! Loved every bit of it. Stewart is an important Canadian author/performer."
- Rick Kunelius, Banff, Alberta

"Holy Cow is a thoroughly enjoyable read, difficult to put down."
- Marv Goble, London, England

"Your book with all its unabashed reality and earthy humour was a terrific shot in the arm."
- Jill Louise Campbell, Salt Spring, B.C.

"I loved your book. I wanted more. It was so much fun and at the same time full of so many truths."
- Elly McKeague, Salt Spring Island, B.C.

"Thank you for sharing yourself with the world - your laughter and your pain - and telling it beautifully both on stage and the page."
- Cheryl Wiebe, Salt Spring Island, B.C.

"I loved the characters you encountered on your trip, but especially loved your vulnerability in showing us who you are."
- Fran Willgress, Ladysmith, B.C.

HOLY OM!

ISBN 141202603-2

9 781412 026031